ÆSCHYLEAN
DRAMA

Michael Gagarin

ÆSCHYLEAN
DRAMA

University of California Press
Berkeley · *Los Angeles* · *London*

University of California Press
Berkeley and Los Angeles, California
University of California Press, Ltd.
London, England
Copyright © 1976, by
The Regents of the University of California
ISBN 0–520–02943–7
Library of Congress Catalog Card Number: 74–30520
Printed in the United States of America

For Charlie and Ted

Contents

Preface

This book is written primarily from the point of view of and for classical scholars, but it is my hope that nonclassicists will read it as well. To this end, I have tried to avoid professional jargon, at least in the body of the text, and have translated almost all the Greek in the text and notes. Moreover, in order to keep the cost of the book down I have transliterated most of the Greek citations. I trust this will not unduly trouble classicists.

I have been selective in my references to the views of other scholars, mentioning only those works that have helped me formulate specific points, from either agreement or disagreement. Those whom I cite often in disagreement are, of course, also among those I have found most helpful.

It is impossible to mention all who have aided me in writing this book. Two were especially influential in the formation of my views on Aeschylean drama: Eric Havelock, who as teacher, colleague, and friend first led me to think about the meaning of Greek literature to the Greeks themselves, and Kenneth Cavander, playwright and sometime classicist, with whom I spent many hours discussing the impact of Greek drama on Athenian society.

Most of the research and writing was done at the Center

for Hellenic Studies in Washington, D.C., where I spent an extremely enjoyable year as a junior fellow (1972–73). Its director, Bernard Knox, and the other fellows provided an ideal climate of friendship and scholarship. Particularly helpful was Suzanne Roy-Saïd, whose work on causation and responsibility in Aeschylus led to many stimulating discussions.

An early version of the book was read in its entirety by Tom Cole, Tom Gould, Eric Havelock, and Bernard Knox, all of whom contributed important criticisms and suggestions. Various parts of the work have been read at various stages by William Calder, David Claus, Peter Rose, Suzanne Roy-Saïd, Bernd Seidensticker, and the late Douglas Young; I am especially grateful to the last of these for his enthusiastic encouragement of my work. It is a pleasure to thank all of the above for their friendship as well as for their helpful criticisms. The faults that remain in the book are, needless to say, my own.

I would like further to express my gratitude to the University of California Press, especially to the director, August Frugé, to two anonymous readers who offered valuable suggestions for improvement, to the editorial supervisor, Susan Peters, and to my copyeditor, Zipporah Collins, whose painstaking care has helped make the book as readable as it is.

Finally I dedicate the book to my first two teachers of Greek at Stanford, whose stimulating teaching and warm friendship induced me to turn from theoretical mathematics to the broader and more satisfying pleasures of classical culture.

Bibliographical Note

References in the notes are generally brief and sometimes abbreviated (*e.g.*, Lesky, *Tragische Dichtung*). Full bibliographical information is given in the Bibliography.

References to Aeschylus are to Page's Oxford text (1972), whose readings I follow unless otherwise indicated. References to fragments of Aeschylus are to Mette's edition, with an indication of the fragment's number in the Loeb edition (Smyth and Lloyd-Jones).

References to early Greek poetry are to Page, *Poetae Melici Graeci* (*PMG*), Lobel and Page, *Poetarum Lesbiorum Fragmenta* (LP), and West, *Iambi et Elegi Graeci*, although, for Archilochus and Solon, I include references to Diehl's numbering (D) where it differs from West's.

I

The Early Greek World View

EFORE we can examine the ethical, social, and political content of Aeschylean tragedy, we must reach a general understanding of how the Greeks before Aeschylus viewed human conduct. The evidence for this is only literary, but I believe we can draw a coherent picture of what I call the early Greek world view. Contemporary scholars have taken a great interest in this matter, and Snell, Dodds, Adkins, Lesky, Havelock, and Lloyd-Jones,[1] to mention just a few, have contributed significant studies to the intellectual history of early Greece. But consensus is still not apparent, and I must therefore present my own views on the matter before proceeding. Except for the discussion of moral responsibility, the following survey is not a new analysis of the problem but rather an eclectic overview, elements of which are borrowed from all the above-named scholars. My reason for beginning a book on Aeschylus with such a survey is that, like Lloyd-Jones, I believe there was a fundamental continuity of thought from Homer through the tragedians, although my understanding of the elements of this continuity differs from his in certain important respects.

I base my remarks primarily on evidence from the Homeric poems. These are by far the largest single source for the period, and their influence on all later Greek authors was considerable. However, I also consider more briefly the evidence in Hesiod and some of the lyric and elegiac poets. To clarify the major issues in my understanding of the early Greek world view, I preface this survey with a few remarks on certain aspects of Aristotle's views of tragedy as presented in the *Poetics*. I begin in this fashion because a discussion of Aristotle's view helps us to see the problem more clearly and to understand how the early Greek world view differed from both that view and our own.

The first point to consider is that, in his discussion of tragedy, Aristotle gives "plot" (*mythos*) the position of highest importance and allows "character" (*ta ēthē*) only secondary importance (1450a38–39). This view of the priority of plot over character in Greek tragedy is generally accepted by scholars. Indeed even those who find character portrayal important in Greek tragedy rarely go so far as to give it primary importance.[2] Later in his analysis of the tragic plot, however, Aristotle implicitly qualifies this relative ranking of plot and character by in effect making plot depend on character. This can be seen in his discussion of the different possible kinds of tragic plots: he begins by saying (1452b34–36), "first of all it is clear that it [the plot of the best tragedies] should not show good [*epieikeis*] men passing from good fortune to bad fortune, for this is neither fearful nor pitiable, but an outrage [*miaron*, literally 'a pollution']."

We should recognize that the plot Aristotle has just rejected has two basic elements: first, the action represents a downfall from prosperity to adversity; secondly, the "hero"[3] whose downfall is depicted is good. Furthermore, this goodness must be a moral quality, first of all because it is likely that these *epieikeis* are equivalent to those later (1453a8) described as "outstanding in *aretē* and *dikaiosynē*," [4] and more decisively because *miaron* clearly indicates a moral outrage. The fall of a morally good man is undeserved and outrages our sense of moral justice; thus Aristotle rejects this type of plot for the best tragedies.

This rejection has surprised some critics, [5] who understand the expression "it is clear that" (*dēlon hoti*) to mean "it is obvious from an examination of existing tragedies," rather than "it is obvious in view of our assumption that the best tragedy should be morally acceptable." The former statement would indeed be surprising, but the latter is certainly more likely to be Aristotle's meaning. Aristotle has already maintained that poetry is philosophical, since it presents a general truth (1451b5–7); he is surely influenced by Plato's argument that poetry should not represent good (just) men as unhappy (cf. *Republic* 392b). [6] On this assumption, it is indeed obvious that the plot in which a good man is ruined violates moral standards and should therefore be disallowed.

It is also clear that the fall of a thoroughly bad man from good fortune to bad would be morally acceptable. This plot is thus called *philanthrōpon*, [7] but it does not arouse pity and fear and so is unacceptable as tragedy (1453a1–7). [8] The elimination of this plot seems to leave no possible solution, since Aristotle has excluded plots involving the passage from bad fortune to good as untragic, as well as those involving a fall from good fortune to bad, whether of a good man or of a bad man. These last two plots, which differ only in the moral character of the hero, are both unacceptable: the fall of a good man is morally unsatisfactory, the fall of a bad man emotionally unsatisfactory. Thus Aristotle is led into a dilemma by his systematic analysis of the tragic plot in terms of the moral character of the hero.

The solution he offers to this dilemma has undoubtedly prompted more discussion than any other statement in the history of literary criticism: "There remains the mean [*metaxy*] between these two, and this is the sort of man who neither stands out for his virtue [*aretē*] and justice [*dikaiosynē*] nor falls to misfortune because of his evil [*kakia*] and wickedness [*mochthēria*], but [rather falls] because of some *hamartia*, one of those men of high repute and good fortune, such as Oedipus and Thyestes and famous men from such families" (1453a7–12). In the continuing debate over the meaning of this famous statement, opinion has shifted, among classical scholars at least, away from the view that *hamartia* is a moral "flaw" in the hero's character and toward the view that it is a nonmoral error, usually ignorance or some failure of recognition.[9] But the difficulty still remains: if *hamartia* is a nonmoral error, the hero is not morally flawed at all, and the situation is essentially the same from a moral point of view as the possibility that Aristotle rejected as *miaron*. It thus seems that Aristotle must have intended this *hamartia* to have some moral effect.[10] On the other hand, if *hamartia* is a moral flaw, the hero is evil and deserves his fall, and this would make the plot no longer tragic. In short, as long as the question is posed in moral terms, the dilemma remains.[11]

We have seen that behind Aristotle's dilemma lies the assumption that the best tragedy should be morally acceptable. Modern scholars often reject this requirement and accept the fact that tragedy is indeed immoral,[12] but deny that this is any reason to reject it. On the contrary, some argue the immorality of tragedy is essential to its effect, either because watching the injustice of innocent suffering is in itself a moving and pleasurable experience for people, or because the greatness of man is best revealed through his ability to struggle against the injustice of the universe.[13] Scholars who thus attempt to replace the morality of tragedy with the immorality of tragedy have certainly had a beneficial effect on our understanding of Greek tragedy, but they still err in two related respects, both inherited from Aristotle: first they continue to view the action in terms of systematic moral categories,[14] and secondly they continue to direct primary attention to the character of the hero.[15]

Such criticism is, in my opinion, misdirected, since the systematic moral view of human behavior that it assumes was unknown to the early Greeks. Rather, as I shall argue, the presentation and evaluation of behavior in early Greek poetry and in much of Greek tragedy lacks certain elements that are essential to traditional moral judgments, most notably the concept of a morally responsible agent. The concept of moral responsibility is so thoroughly a part of our moral thinking that it is tempting to call the early Greek world view "nonmoral" in order to distinguish it from ours; but, since this expression may suggest, for example, that the Greeks never judged people's actions, I will not use it.[16] I do wish to emphasize, however, the difference between our own moral judgments and early Greek judgments about human behavior. I am referring primarily to several factors that I discuss below in some detail—for instance, the fact that the early Greeks show relatively little concern for portraying or evaluating a person's character or the intentions or motives leading to an action but rather are primarily interested in the actions themselves and their consequences. Such actions may be presented as basically right[17] (*e.g.*, Pelasgus' protection of the Danaids)[18] or basically wrong (*e.g.*, Xerxes' attack on Greece) or as both right and wrong (*e.g.*, Agamemnon's sacrifice of his daughter); in none of these cases, however, is the agent judged in strictly moral terms—that is, as morally good or bad, guilty or innocent—although in each case he must suffer the consequences of his action. Nor is the overall operation of the universe and its gods portrayed as either morally just or morally unjust, but rather as subject to many separate and sometimes conflicting rules and divine forces. Wrongdoing is regularly punished in this universe but without regard to a person's moral responsibility. It may, of course, be objected that Greek tragedy portrays precisely those actions (murder, impiety, etc.) that we evaluate in moral terms and about which we make moral judgments. This is true, but the early Greeks perceived and judged such events in a significantly different way. Not until the growth of the sophistic movement in the late fifth century (whose influence is clearly present in some late plays of Sophocles and Euripides) did the Greeks begin to evaluate people and their actions primarily in moral terms.

Before considering this early Greek world view in greater detail, however, we need to examine a basic assumption of traditional Western moral thinking, namely the concept of a morally responsible agent. The fundamental question of what distinguishes a moral judgment from other value judgments is generally ignored by contemporary moral philosophers, who are more concerned with such issues as whether *good* is an evaluative or descriptive word, or how moral judgments are related to imperative constructions. Those concerns are not much help when it comes to understanding why certain kinds of value judgments (*e.g.*, "a good man") may be moral judgments, whereas others (*e.g.*, "a good classical scholar") are not.[19] I think such distinctions can best be understood if we approach the question by looking at our concept of moral error. Briefly, we believe that human beings may make many different kinds of mistakes or errors, only some of which we consider moral errors. One difference between these moral wrongs and other errors is the kind of activity involved; *i.e.*, wrongs that harm other people or society in general may be moral wrongs. A more significant criterion, however, is that a moral wrong must in some sense be intentional. In any moral system or moral evaluation, an essential distinction is made between voluntary and involuntary acts.[20] Thus voluntary homicide (murder) is a moral wrong, whereas a truly accidental or involuntary homicide is not. Another way of saying this is that, to be judged morally for an act, one must be morally responsible, and no system of morality or moral evaluation can exist without a concept of moral responsibility.[21]

The concept of moral responsibility also has a significant place in all modern legal systems, but, whereas responsibility seems to be a necessary element of any moral system, it is not absolutely necessary in a legal system. It is possible to argue in fact that responsibility should not be considered in a legal system; for instance, there might be fewer hunting accidents if such accidents were treated legally as intentional shootings. In fact, even our own legal system recognizes certain "statutory" crimes, in which the question of intent is irrelevant for legal purposes; primitive legal systems exist, moreover, in which this seems to be generally the case. Such a system is said to have the principle of "strict liability," that is, every violation is punished, regardless of the intent of the violator.[22] A system of strict liability, however, is considerably at variance with our traditional moral views, and we would undoubtedly consider such a legal system unjust (in a moral sense).[23] In Homer, however, as well as in much of Greek tragedy, men are generally punished or rewarded for actions according to the principle of strict liability. We can only conclude that the early Greeks lacked our concept of moral responsibility and that their view of human behavior was thus significantly different from ours. This can be illustrated most easily by looking at Homer.

That the society portrayed in the Homeric poems treats human behavior to a large extent in terms of strict liability is revealed in many places, but nowhere does this view of human behavior seem more foreign to our own way of thinking than in the treatment of homicide. In Homer, homicide is clearly a wrong, and the killer must submit to punishment, just as in our own society. This punishment is generally either execution or a fine or exile, and it is exacted by the injured party, in this case the dead man's family acting on his behalf. In Homer, however, there is no consideration of intent; no differentiation is made between accidental and deliberate homicides.[24] Moreover, any homicide requires only this compensatory punishment; no further moral stigma is attached to the deed, and the killer is not considered to be an evil person in any way. He has only committed a wrong against the victim and the victim's family.[25]

A striking illustration of this is the treatment of a minor figure in the *Odyssey*, a man called Theoclymenus, who meets Telemachus on his way home and travels with him to Ithaca. His later role in the poem is limited to prophesying Odysseus' return and the destruction of the suitors, and he is clearly one of the "good" people in the poem, in the sense that he is on Odysseus' side. When Theoclymenus first arrives at the ship, he asks Telemachus who he is, and the latter answers that he is from Ithaca and is looking for news of his father.

Then godlike Theoclymenus said to him in answer:
"So I too am out of my country, because I have killed
a man of my tribe, but he had many brothers and relatives
in horse-pasturing Argos, with great power among the Achaians.
Avoiding death at the hands of these men and black doom, I am
a fugitive, since it is my fate to be a wanderer
among men. Give me a place in your ship, since I have come to you
as a suppliant, lest they kill me; for now I think they are after me."
    Then the thoughtful Telemachus said to him in answer:
"I will not willingly thrust you away from my balanced ship.
                                                Come, then,
with me. There you will be entertained, from what we have left."
                        [15.271–81 (trans. Lattimore)]

To the modern reader this seems an extraordinary way for Telemachus to behave: he shows no interest whatsoever in the circumstances of the homicide, but welcomes Theoclymenus as a friend without hesitation. Apparently the act of killing another man, even a relative, does not in itself affect how others estimate one's character and does not lower one's general worth, although it does require compensation, in this case Theoclymenus' exile from the society of the dead man's relatives. But there is no suggestion here of moral judgment.[26]

Homicide is no isolated exception; any wrong committed accidentally, such as a forgotten sacrifice (cf. *Il.* 9.532–37), is punished. And acts that we would consider justifiable on other grounds incur equally heavy punishments. For instance, Odysseus' blinding of the Cyclops is, in our eyes, a clear case of justifiable self-defense, but he nonetheless incurs Poseidon's wrath and suffers grievously for the deed. In all cases it is the act itself that is punished (or rewarded), and none of the extenuating circumstances that we would consider valid, such as ignorance or delusion, affect the punishment received. There are occasional examples of people pleading external compulsion, such as Phemius the bard, who is spared by Odysseus, but this seems to be a special case.[27] And delusion (*atē*) is pleaded by Agamemnon in a famous passage in the *Iliad*, not to absolve himself from the necessity of paying a full penalty, but to lessen his public shame at the failure of his leadership. It is not he who is *aitios* ("blameworthy"),[28] he says, for being such a failure, but "Zeus and Moira and the Erinys" (19.86–87). Such a plea is necessary to soften the impact of his failure, but it in no way lessens his liability for the consequences of his actions.[29] Every action creates a consequent liability, even if the action is somehow attributable to Zeus or *atē* or any other external power.

Similarly the Greeks never believed in completely unmotivated punishment. No one is destroyed by the gods, for instance, without some wrong having been done, however disproportionate the penalty might seem to us. And a complementary aspect of this belief is the conviction that no misfortune is without cause: a plague, say, must be the result of

some (often unknowing) error, and other disasters are all
somehow the result of error on someone's part. The companions of Odysseus, for example, are doomed from the moment Poseidon hears and acknowledges the Cyclops' prayer
that he punish Odysseus by depriving him of his companions
(9.536). They are not destroyed immediately, however.
Rather they are put in a situation where, in order to avoid
imminent death by starvation, they are forced to eat the sacred
cattle of the sun. Essentially they are presented with a choice
between death by starvation and death by shipwreck, and they
understandably choose the latter. They choose, but they choose
under a definite compulsion, and we would, I think, have to
consider them morally innocent. For the Greeks, however, the
question of the companions' moral responsibility is irrelevant;
what matters is that they have committed an offense, and
thus in terms of strict liability they are punishable.

Even more striking is the case of the Phaeacians, who also
are punished on account of Odysseus. These people, who represent in many ways a perfect society, have traditionally fulfilled
the helpful task of conveying wayfarers to their homes. After
granting Odysseus every hospitality he could desire, they bring
him home to Ithaca laden with gifts. In the eyes of Poseidon,
however, this noble act is a wrong (an injury to him), and he
complains to Zeus:

"Father Zeus, no longer among the gods immortal
shall I be honored, when there are mortals who do me no honor,
the Phaeacians, and yet these are of my own blood. See now,
I had said to myself Odysseus would come home only after
much suffering. I had not indeed taken his homecoming
altogether away, since first you nodded your head and assented
to it. But they carried him, asleep in the fast ship, over
the sea, and set him down in Ithaca, and gave him numberless
gifts, as bronze, and gold abundant, and woven clothing."
                              [13.128–36 (trans. Lattimore)]

The two gods then agree that Poseidon should turn the Phaeacians' ship to stone when it returns and bury their city under a mountain.[30] Again, the question of the Phaeacians' intentions is never raised. If it were, and if we were to judge them in moral terms, they would certainly be found innocent; but in the Homeric view they have simply committed an offense against Poseidon and are punished for it.

In the Homeric world, then, the basic pattern is one of reciprocity. Any wrong against another person or god is punished according to strict liability,[31] and conversely any disaster is traceable to some previous wrong, generally an offense against a god. Given this system of strict reciprocity, it is not surprising that we can easily find examples of acts followed by punishments that from our moral point of view are justified (such as Odysseus' punishing the Cyclops), and we may be tempted to consider these as evidence for a Homeric sense of moral justice.[32] But, if these are found along with other examples of punishments that from our moral point of view are unjust, then we have no right to ascribe a belief in moral justice (or injustice) to the Homeric Greeks, for any author who portrays human behavior from a point of view of strict liability will describe some events that another observer could understand in terms of moral justice. But this does not mean that the author has a moral view of such actions.

Consider, furthermore, the killing of the suitors in the *Odyssey*: they are for the most part unpleasant people who are clearly injuring Odysseus' household, and one of them at least (Antinous) is an utter villain. But it is also true that the suitors have some justification for their position and some legitimate grievances with Penelope (cf. 24.121–90). Moreover, some of them, such as Amphinomus, are decent men who are nonetheless killed with the rest.[33] The issue as Homer presents it, is not the moral character of the suitors, but the fact that they are seeking possession of Odysseus' wife and property, which would have been their customary right in the event of his death. Their ignorance and shortsightedness together with their weakness in battle lead to their ruin. This is perfectly proper in the Homeric system, where every bit of foresight and strength is needed for success. But the lesson of the story is not that crime does not pay; rather it is that strength and intelligence together with the help of the gods (obtainable partly by frequent large sacrifices) are necessary for success.

The nature of this "success ethic" has been examined at length by Adkins (in *Merit and Responsibility*), who shows that the most important terms of value in Homer, such as *aretē* ("excellence") and *agathos* ("good"), denote competitive qualities, and are therefore quite different from our terms of moral evaluation. Judgments about people or their actions are based primarily on their success or failure and the criteria for success or failure are external and material: wealth, military strength, political power, etc. It is not surprising that in such a society, where success is the highest value, intentions should be of little concern, for it can generally be assumed that everyone intends to succeed. Different criteria for success were, of course, applied to different groups of people (kings, servants, women, etc.), but everyone tried his or her best to succeed. This is true not only for such obviously competitive endeavors as fighting in battle, but also for what Adkins calls "cooperative virtues," which in fact are also judged by results rather than intentions and should not therefore be considered the equivalents of our moral virtues.[34]

That these so-called cooperative virtues in Homer are not moral virtues in our sense can be seen by looking at the Greek word *dikē*, which is often translated by the English "justice" without any further examination of what either word means. Justice has many meanings, ranging from moral right (the

Platonic and Aristotelian *dikaiosynē*) to administration of the law, which is not necessarily in accord with a moral system.[35] *Dikē* also has a variety of meanings, most of them legal: *e.g.,* settlement, plea, trial, legal process.[36] It is true, of course, that *dikē* as legal process is nearly equivalent to justice in the sense of administration of the law, but not in other senses, and, since the moral aspect of justice is the most prominent one in common English usage, it is misleading, at the very least, to translate *dikē* as justice.

Dikē in its largest sense is the society's system for settling disputes peacefully.[37] This system among the early Greeks differed in a fundamental way from our own legal system. The legal process in early Greece was essentially a system of peaceful arbitration, whereby a settlement (*dikē*) is made between two conflicting claims, each claim being itself a *dikē*. The fairness (straightness) of the settlement is determined by its acceptability to both sides and to the public, and the disputants can appeal to traditional norms of behavior, which were gradually written down as law codes during the seventh and sixth centuries. These provided some sanction for legal decisions, but the whole system does not appear to be sanctioned by any higher moral sense of justice. Furthermore, one *dikē* can be and often is directly challenged by an opposed *dikē*, and in such cases there is no necessity for only one of them to be a true (or "just") *dikē*; similarly, the command of one god may conflict directly with the command of another, in which case obedience to one often results in punishment from the other. This rather illogical (to our way of thinking) coexistence of valid and opposed *dikai* within an overall process of *dikē* should not be identified with our moral concept of justice (though it is certainly the forerunner of the later moral concept of *dikaiosynē*). If we equate *dikē* and moral justice, we will undoubtedly be led to make the former more systematic than it really is and thereby distort an important element of early Greek thought. We will also expect to find a moral element in Greek *dikē*, which it never possessed.

The adjective *dikaios*, moreover, does not have the moral sense of "just" (which is how even Adkins translates it) before the late fifth century, though there are many passages where the precise meaning of the word is difficult to determine. It means rather "peaceful," "law-abiding" (in a strict sense), or "properly behaved," and a good example of this last meaning can be seen at the beginning of Book Three of the *Odyssey*. Telemachus and Athena (who is disguised as Mentor) reach the palace at Pylos, where they are greeted by Peisistratus, one of Nestor's sons. Peisistratus fills a golden cup with wine and hands it to Athena first, since, as he says, she is the elder of the two guests. "So he spoke, and put in her hand the cup of sweet wine, and Athena was happy at the thoughtfulness of a just [!] man, because it was to her he first gave the golden goblet" (3.51–53). The translation is by Lattimore, who gives the traditional rendering of *dikaios*. Yet clearly there is no question of a moral judgment here, and we must translate *dikaios* not as "just," but as "well-mannered" or "properly behaved."

The standard of behavior referred to here by *dikaios* is not a moral one in the strict sense, since it contains no reference to a sense of moral responsibility; rather it is a standard of propriety, which operates in some ways like our own rules of etiquette, and in which intention is no more a factor than it is in competitive situations, such as fighting in battle. To behave improperly in proper society is not excusable on grounds of ignorance or accident. If one uses the wrong fork for the fish, for example, a plea of ignorance does not alter one's failure to meet the standards of proper behavior. In such cases it is the behavior itself that matters, or, as Long puts it in referring to Homeric society, "in every case it is the external aspect of the situation which receives evaluation. If it looks right, or sounds right, then it is right. And the criterion for what looks right or sounds right is common opinion or social precedent."[38]

In fact it should not surprise us that the standard of behavior in Homer is one of propriety, if we consider the great emphasis that is placed throughout the poems on conformity to the traditional and accepted rules of proper behavior. Eating, dressing, sacrificing, speaking in council, fighting, and many other activities all have their traditionally proper and to some extent ritualistic forms, and the traditional elements of Homer's style, the formulas and repeated themes, add to this feeling of traditional norms of behavior.[39] One theme of the *Odyssey*, in fact, is the education of Telemachus, who learns to behave himself properly in several different situations—as the guest of others or the prospective head of his own home, for example. And the poems continued for centuries to teach Greeks everywhere the proper standards of behavior.[40] Thus, it seems quite in keeping with the traditional nature of Homeric society that the behavior of people in that society should be evaluated in terms of how well it conforms to traditional standards of propriety, without any reference to inner motivation.

Several points have emerged in our discussion of the Homeric standards of propriety and success that suggest a related aspect of the Homeric view of human behavior. We have observed the lack of concern with moral responsibility in punishing or rewarding behavior, the absence of moral stigma attached to a person committing a punishable homicide, and the external and material nature of the criteria by which people and their actions are evaluated. All these factors may lead us to suspect that there is something lacking (from our point of view, of course) in the Homeric view of the human personality. Others have already investigated this question of

Homer's concept of the human self, most notably Snell, who has shown that words like *thymos* ("spirit"), *noos* ("mind") and *psychē* ("life-breath") describe both physical organs and physiological functions associated with those organs, but that there is no integration of these organs into a unity that could be called a "soul" (there is also no word for the "body" as a unified whole in Homer).[41] Thus there is no language in Homer to designate a person's "self" or "character" or "personality" as an integrated whole, and this suggests that Homeric man had no concept of an internal integrated human personality corresponding to the Platonic (Socratic?) *psychē* or "soul."[42]

To say that Homer lacked the concept of an integrated human soul or personality is an important statement, but it is also a limited one. It does not mean that Homer had no concept at all of a person's "character," in the sense of a consistent pattern of behavior (though he was much less concerned with this character than we generally are). Rather a person's characteristic ways of behavior were not seen by Homer as forming an inner unity that could be judged morally. This does not mean that Homeric man was unable to make a decision or that Homer does not describe men making decisions, as Snell tried to maintain,[43] but rather that the Homeric description of the decision-making process is different from our description of it, and his understanding of the effect of a decision is also different. When a decision is described in Homer, it is often in terms of a conflict of separate forces, a hero and his *thymos*, for example (*e.g.,* Odysseus in *Il.* 11.401–10), or between a hero and a god (*e.g.,* Achilles in *Il.* 1.188–222). Even decisions that are described in other ways, such as by the phrase "it seemed best to him," are made on the basis of the probable results of an action and not its effects on the person's inner self. This suggests that there is no single organ or "soul" that is affected by a decision in the way that the

Platonic soul is harmed by an unjust act.[44] The effect of a particular decision is seen in, and its rightness or wrongness determined by, the success or failure of the resulting action, and not the effect it might have on any psychological entity. Thus Homer is capable of describing the same kinds of human behavior as we are, only in different terms: he sees and values the external, nonmoral aspect, not the internal, moral aspect, of behavior.[45]

This lack of an internal integrated soul or personality in Homer accords well with what we have observed of the absence of morality and moral responsibility in the epics: it follows that without the concept of an inner personality there can be no concept of moral responsibility, because there is no separate entity to which that responsibility can be attached. A person must be valued in terms of external success or failure if there is no internal personality that might be valued in contradistinction to external success or failure. Furthermore, punishment must be external and can include no inner moral stigma or guilt if there is no inner self to which guilt can be attached. Thus a given act makes a person liable (in the strict sense) for a given penalty, but does not stain or injure his character. In short, the criteria for making a decision in Homer and the consequences of that decision are entirely external.[46]

The question of Homeric man's internal self is related (as Lesky has shown) to another unusual feature of the epics, the existence of what is called "double motivation." When Achilles kills Hector, for example, in Book Twenty-two of the *Iliad*, he is assisted by Athena to such an extent that the modern reader may feel Achilles would have been defeated without her help. Yet everyone knows that Achilles himself kills Hector and would always kill him in single combat, for he is the better fighter. Furthermore, Athena's help detracts nothing from Achilles' glory, and there is no hint that Achilles is not to be given full credit for his victory.[47] Likewise, when

Athena restrains Achilles from drawing his sword in Book One, he also restrains himself; and in another case Phemius can claim that he is "self-taught and the gods planted all sorts of song in me" (*Od.* 22.347–48). These are all instances of the convergence of human and divine activity, and in such cases both partners are fully active. The gods are not merely convenient tools for describing impulses behind human action; nor on the other hand is man a mere puppet in the hands of the gods. Gods effect results, and men effect the same results; hence the term *double motivation.*[48]

As Lesky quite rightly insists, moreover, there is an illogical duality in this concept of double motivation that is difficult if not impossible for us to understand analytically,[49] for our own way of thinking generally forces us to choose either divine causation or human causation, but not both. In modern terms, freedom and determinism are usually considered incompatible, and seldom is it maintained that both exist together,[50] though it seems that this is the answer that the Homeric Greeks would have given if they had asked the question. For them the gods (and other cosmic forces such as fate, *moira*) "cause" all human events and men "cause" these events too; neither factor can be ignored.[51]

It should be noted, moreover, that this phenomenon of double motivation accords perfectly with the early Greek lack of a concept of moral responsibility. Agamemnon, for instance, is still liable for the consequences of his actions even though he has blamed *atē* for them. If more than one factor can be the "cause" of an action, then the person himself remains a cause even though one or more other causes are adduced. Thus, naming another cause detracts nothing from a person's own liability, though this liability is, to be sure, not the same as our own sense of moral responsibility.[52]

Another way of describing this Homeric view of human behavior is by the term, *shame-culture* (sometimes also *re-*

sults-culture). This term was first applied to Homeric society by Dodds, and the appellation is now widely accepted.[53] Briefly, in a shame-culture the worst failure a man can suffer is failure in the eyes of others, or loss of reputation. Failure to meet one's own standards or a moral or religious code is in itself unimportant: what is important is the community's approval or disapproval.[54] In the face of evident failure and community disapproval, no Homeric hero can take any comfort from having a "clear conscience" or from knowing in his heart that he "did the right thing." The only meaningful determination of worth is public recognition.

That Homeric society is a shame-culture rather than a guilt-culture should be clear from the description of other aspects of the society that we have already noted, such as the lack of an integrated internal personality, the absence of moral guilt, and the emphasis on success. Certainly with no concept of a separate conscience one cannot take comfort from knowing that one's conscience is clear. Nor do the gods provide the Homeric hero with any values to oppose to those of the community, though they may grant him the power or the wealth that make him valued by the community. In fact, nowhere is this materialistic shame-culture seen more clearly than in the behavior of the gods, whose entire existence seems to be spent maintaining their individual and collective honors, powers, and privileges, as well as those of their protégés. This apparently nonmoral shame-culture of the Homeric gods has often puzzled modern readers, partly because of our association of religion with morality. But it is clear that the values of the gods in Homer are no different from those of men, and, though the gods are more powerful than men in many ways, they have no superior moral worth.[55] If we accept the fact that Homer lacked our own moral concerns, however, this is just what we would expect, for, if the Greeks value power and success most highly in human affairs, then it is natural for them to endow their gods with superhuman amounts of these attributes.

I have thus far described the Homeric world view as a shame-culture that places primary value on success, lacks a concept of the internal integrated human personality, judges behavior according to strict liability rather than moral responsibility, and has an "illogical" sense of double motivation. Before proceeding further, let me make clear that, although I have described this world view in terms that often stress the absence or lack of certain concepts or values, I do not wish to imply that it was deficient or defective in general. The early Greeks did indeed lack certain of our concepts, but in some ways this gave them a clearer and more effective view of behavior than ours. As Lloyd-Jones has put it, "The early Greeks were capable of their unique achievements largely because they could bear . . . very much more reality than most human beings,"[56] and their ability to "bear more reality" certainly stemmed in part from their ability to see that reality more clearly and directly. To impose systematic moral categories on one's view of human behavior is to distort that reality. We have learned this from such recent thinkers as Freud, who have given us a new understanding of human behavior by stepping outside moral categories. Thus in some respects the early Greeks had a clearer vision of man than did Plato and other more "advanced" thinkers.

Before leaving Homer, let us consider one more factor that may have influenced his world view. It has recently been argued by Havelock and others that some aspects of this world view are related to the oral nature of Homeric society, where poetry was composed orally and sung to others, not written and read. A major reason for the difference between the Homeric and the Platonic world views, Havelock contends, is the transition from primarily oral to primarily literate communication, a transition that made its full force felt only toward the end of the fifth century. Many aspects of this theory need further investigation, but the general conclusions reached by Havelock seem to me to shed light on and provide at least a partial explanation for the Homeric world view that I have described, and for the difference between it and the Platonic view.[57]

Briefly, the "oral theory" maintains that oral communication creates a different relation between the poet and his audience from that of literate communication, that the circumstances of the oral recital and of oral composition create a preference for certain kinds of statements (narrative as opposed to analytic), and that the oral poet's position in the community fosters his concern for the traditional, communal, and public as opposed to the private or idiosyncratic. The oral poet preserves the traditional culture of the community, he tells the stories of its traditional heroes, and he sees those heroes primarily as members of the community. Thus he stresses the propriety or impropriety (by traditional standards) of their behavior, the external and public aspects of their success or failure, and the external aspects of their mental activity. As I have mentioned, he will often describe in terms of an external dialogue (*e.g.,* between the hero and his *thymos*) what we would describe as private or internal mental activity.[58] Moreover an oral performance tends to draw the listener into the story and involve him emotionally rather than allow or force him to separate himself from the material and reflect upon it as the reader of a book may do.[59] Our literate education trains us to think analytically, but in an oral society one does not find the same emphasis on analytic thought. This may help explain why the Homeric audience was not so troubled by apparently "illogical" dualities as we are.[60] Oral poetry is essentially an extension of the society, whereas written literature tends to separate the reader from his experience in society and force him to view it analytically.[61]

Thus the oral theory may account, at least in part, for some unusual features of the Homeric view of human behavior—features that I think are undeniably present, even if they have little or no connection with the oral nature of the poems.

Two consequences of this "oral state of mind" deserve special attention. The first is the public nature of oral poetry, not only the fact that it is recited publicly but also that it has an important function in the society. We do not know just how, when, or for whom the Homeric poems were first composed, but they were soon so widely known that they became a central authority in the life of all Greeks, much as the Bible used to be the central authority in the life of many Western societies.[62] Havelock has described the Homeric poems as a "tribal encyclopedia," which rightly calls attention to their function as a repository for the traditions and paradigmatic myths of the society. In this sense the poems were an important part of the life of the society; they preserved its historical traditions and helped give all Greeks the sense of a common cultural background. The heroes portrayed in the poems, moreover, are all public figures, their activities affect the whole society,[63] and the poet's concern is thus to portray not so much the inner character of his heroes as the external effects of their actions on that society. We shall see that Aeschylus too shows a greater concern for the larger social and political forces represented by his dramatic figures than for their inner characters.

This connection between poetry and society continued with the growth of the polis as an autonomous social and political unit in the seventh and sixth centuries and with the development of choral lyric poetry. Scholars since Snell[64] have generally been more interested in the growing concern for the individual among the lyric monodists of this period than with the more meager remains of early choral lyric. But now that the sands of Egypt have begun to produce more fragments of choral poetry, especially of Stesichorus and Ibycus, we see more clearly how these poets combined mythical legend and direct political reference in their works, as one might expect of a choral (and therefore public) poet.[65] And the decline of Doric choral lyric after the middle of the sixth century coincided with the rise of its successor, Attic tragedy,[66] which showed a similar concern for the contemporary polis, as we shall see.

The second point is that oral communication does not force the listener to adopt an analytic attitude toward the poetic material, whereas written communication can and often does force the reader to analyze what is being read. Thus an oral society can preserve certain "illogical" ways of thinking, and indeed early Greek thought often reveals an illogical structure of duality and opposition. I have already mentioned certain manifestations of this tendency to think in terms of a structured opposition: the concept of *dikē*, which denotes both the overall system for settling opposing claims and also each claim itself, and the concept of double motivation. Both of these involve a duality of opposed elements within an overall unity, and such a structure seems to have been taken up by several of the pre-Socratic philosophers (particularly Anaximander and Heraclitus) in their attempts to find an order in the universe. A related concept, moreover, is the notion of balance and strict reciprocity, which, as we have seen, pervades the epics. All these factors contribute to the basic sense of duality that we find in early Greek thought and that plays such a large role in Greek, and especially Aeschylean drama.

I have described this early Greek world view primarily on the basis of evidence from the Homeric poems, and so the question naturally arises to what extent this world view also exists in Greek tragedy. Snell maintained that there was a wide gulf between Homer and Aeschylus, arguing that in the epics men never make real decisions on their own, whereas in

Aeschylus' *Supplices*, then thought to be the earliest extant tragedy, we find "for the first time" a true decision being made by Pelasgus.[67] Other writers since Snell,[68] however, have challenged this view and have denied that the portrayal of decision-making in Homer was much different from what we find in Greek tragedy, or in modern literature. I am in agreement with these scholars about the relative similarity of the Homeric and the Aeschylean portrayals of the decision-making process, but I find Aeschylus' presentation of it as different from our own as I have argued Homer's is.

This thesis can be satisfactorily defended only by looking at the tragedies themselves; for the moment a few brief observations must suffice. First, the portrayal of a man on stage making a decision does not compel us to judge that decision in moral terms, if, as in the case of Pelasgus, the decision is made entirely or at least primarily on the basis of its practical (nor moral), external consequences.[69] Nor does the growth of the belief in pollution imply the simultaneous development of a sense of moral guilt, though the concept of pollution may have helped prepare for the eventual development of the idea of guilt.[70] Rather, decisions like those of Agamemnon (to kill Iphigeneia) and of Orestes (to kill Clytemnestra) in the *Oresteia* are apparently the result of the same double motivation as decisions in Homer; heroes like Ajax and Oedipus (in *Oedipus Tyrannos*) exhibit precisely the behavior of a shame-culture hero faced with a failure for which he is liable in the strict sense though not guilty or innocent in our moral sense.[71] Furthermore, Homer was the most important single influence on almost all Greek culture until the end of the fifth century. We know that the choral and tragic poets drew much of their material, and to a large degree their language, from the epic tradition (dominated by the Homeric poems). Thus it should hardly surprise us to find similarities between the basic world views of epic and tragedy.

On the other hand, Aeschylus is different from Homer in many respects. He has in general a more complex view of the world and of the forces (divine as well as human) influencing human behavior, and he understands more fully the difficulty of finding acceptable solutions to the complex problems facing man.

This difference is in part a result of the influence on Aeschylus of intervening authors, especially Hesiod. In the *Theogony*, Hesiod portrays the establishment of Zeus as permanent ruler of the gods; in the *Works and Days*, he turns to human society and sets forth rules of behavior covering everything from the overall operation of society to the smallest details of planting and harvesting. Unlike Homer's heroic, competitive world, the world of the *Works and Days* is one of small, ordinary men trying to produce enough for their own livelihood. It is a world at peace, where the bad *eris* ("strife") does not belong, though the good *eris* ("striving") is allowed (*WD* 11–26). Such a society can function properly, Hesiod feels, only with a legal process (*dikē*) for settling disputes peacefully, and one of the main purposes of the *Works and Days* is to urge acceptance of such a process (*WD* 213–85). For this purpose, *dikē* is given the highest sanction of Zeus' power. But, as I have argued elsewhere,[72] Hesiod's *dikē* is not given a moral sanction. Thus, although Hesiod's *dikē* is a more highly developed process than Homer's, it must not be understood as equivalent to our moral sense of justice.

Nor does Solon, who further develops Hesiod's views on law and social order, develop any sense of moral justice.[73] His longest and most famous elegy (13 = 1D) about prosperity (*olbos*, 13.3) accepts the traditional Homeric standard of doing good to your friends and harm to your enemies (13.5–6), but qualifies this by affirming, as Hesiod had, that wealth should not be acquired unlawfully (*adikōs*, 13.7). And in his poem on *eunomia* (4 = 3D) Solon also portrays the destructive effect of the absence of *dikē* in society in very Hesiodic terms. Solon's *dikē* is less mythological than Hesiod's, and his economic and social order is more advanced, but the values of both poets are essentially the same: they value prosperity and the legal process (*dikē*) necessary for such prosperity, but neither presents a concept of moral justice. When we examine the *Oresteia* (see chapter III), we will see that Aeschylus' *dikē* is an even more complex force of balance and order, in society and in the universe, but it too is not yet moral justice.

Thus we will see that, although Aeschylus presents a more complex view of human behavior than Homer, he builds this world view on a strong Homeric foundation, and he preserves in large part the elements of the Homeric view that I have described. These elements may be labeled primitive by some, but I think it is precisely this "primitive" element in Aeschylus' world view that enabled him to acquire his insight into human behavior. As I maintained in discussing the Homeric world view, the fact that Aeschylus' world view was not obscured by moral categories allowed him an understanding of human behavior that in some ways was more accurate than our own, which imposes moral categories on behavior.

Finally, it is this absence of moral judgment in Greek tragedy that accounts for much of the difficulty that Plato, Aristotle, and later critics have had in analyzing it. One of Plato's great achievements in the study of human behavior (based on the work of Socrates, the Sophists, and perhaps also the Pythagorians), was the creation of the concept of the human *psychē* as a moral and intellectual entity existing in its own right, independent of a person's physical body. The success and failure of this *psychē*, which is the only important success for a man, indeed its very "life," are divorced from the external, bodily life of the physical person, just as the Forms are separated from the material world. And the success of the *psychē*, its moral and intellectual excellence, lies in its "knowing" the Forms, especially the moral Forms of Justice and Goodness. Thus, in the Platonic view, knowledge or ignorance leads not necessarily to material success or failure but to justice or injustice (*i.e.,* morally right or wrong action), and this is the most important standard in evaluating human behavior. Traditional rules of behavior are no longer of primary value; only by true knowledge of justice can one decide what is right (morally) in a situation. In the ideal world of the just state, moreover, justice is its own reward; the best life is the just life and vice versa. Even in our imperfect world, justice is more beneficial to a person than external success, for justice improves a person's soul.[74]

When Plato imposes categories of moral judgment on the stories of Greek tragedy, he finds examples of the just being punished and the unjust rewarded. Such stories are intolerable in his system and are therefore rejected.[75] Aristotle on the other hand accepts tragedy, but as a follower of Plato he must reject the simple tragic plot (a good man falling to misfortune) as immoral. As we saw he also rejects the simple moral plot (a bad man falling to misfortune) as untragic. In order to resolve this dilemma he deliberately (I suspect) employs an ambiguous word, *hamartia*, which he does not often apply to moral error, but which may sometimes be used in a moral sense. In the *Poetics* Aristotle subtly has it carry both meanings at the same time, a moral meaning so that the hero's fate is just and a nonmoral meaning so that it is tragic.

The use of such an illogical ambiguity has no validity in a strictly analytic system, and later followers and critics of Aristotle have generally insisted on giving *hamartia* either a moral or a nonmoral sense, not both. But it is a tribute to Aristotle's genius that he recognized, as I think he did, the difficulty in his analysis yet did not let this deter him from leaving us what is still one of the most persuasive (if mistaken) discussions of Greek tragedy. Aristotle's synthesis of morality and tragedy is a tour de force whose very brillance should probably make us suspicious of its correctness. Only when we challenge this synthesis at its root and remove the basic moral framework from our discussion of Greek tragedy are we able to see it through the eyes of the fifth-century Greeks themselves: eyes from which the veil of morality has been lifted.

II

Persae

THE ORIGINS of Greek tragedy remain something of a mystery for us, but we know that tragedy was formally established at the Greater Dionysia in Athens in 535 B.C., when Thespis won the prize, and it seems to have thrived, as did Athens itself, during the more than half a century before our earliest surviving play, Aeschylus' *Persae*.[1] During this period most tragedies, like most of the epic and choral poetry that preceded it, dealt with mythological subjects, but we know of at least two plays in addition to *Persae* that depicted recent historical events,[2] *The Capture of Miletus* and *Phoenissae*, both by Phrynichus.[3] The latter of these is especially interesting for us since we are told[4] that Aeschylus modeled his *Persae* on it.

Phrynichus' play (produced between 479 and 473) was set in Persia and had, as the title indicates, a chorus of Phoenician women, probably the widows of the Phoenician sailors in Xerxes' navy. The play must have been a lament of Xerxes' fall, and thus directly or indirectly a celebration of the Greek victory. It presumably emphasized the naval victory at Salamis, which was primarily the work of the Athenians under the leadership of Themistocles. It is quite likely, moreover, that Themistocles was *chorēgos* for *Phoenissae*,[5] and that he was seeking to benefit from the public recollection of his success. Indeed, even if someone else was *chorēgos* for *Phoenissae*, the play would undoubtedly have inspired support for the Athenian policy of naval strength and for Themistocles, who was the leading proponent of that policy in the years just before Salamis.[6]

We do not know how Phrynichus' *Phoenissae* fared in the competition, but it probably was not a complete failure, since soon afterward Aeschylus copied its basic structure in his *Persae*, which similarly presents the Greek victory at Salamis from the perspective of the defeated Persians. *Persae* is set in Persia, all the characters are Persians, and, on the surface at least, the dramatic action of the play is a lament for the Persian defeat rather than a celebration of the Greek victory. This has led to some confusion about the nature of the play and Aeschylus' intention in writing it; the question is often asked whether *Persae* is a "true" tragedy, in the Aristotelian sense of a fall from prosperity to adversity, or merely a patriotic commemoration of the Greek victory.[7] The first view is supported by the internal structure of the play, which in broad outline seems to conform to Aristotle's pattern. The second interpretation is most obviously suggested by external considerations: could a play about the defeat of the Persian forces at Salamis be presented to the Athenian people who had participated in that battle only eight years earlier without it being seen as a victory celebration? Rather than argue the validity of either of these views, I accept both interpretations not only as valid but also as part of Aeschylus' purpose, and it is on this basis that I will examine the play. Indeed I will argue that Aeschylus intentionally presents both the Athenian and the Persian perspectives simultaneously in a way that creates a basic tension or irony throughout the play. In order to under-

stand the total effect of this irony, however, we must examine
Persae from each perspective separately before considering
how the two are combined.[8]

In view of Phrynichus' two historical plays, and from what
we know of the political aspects of the Greater Dionysia,[9] it
seems clear that the celebration of an Athenian victory and
other patriotic themes would be perfectly suitable material
for the tragic competition. There is further support for this
view of *Persae* in a pre-Aristotelian source, Aristophanes.[10] In
the *Frogs* (405 B.C.) Aeschylus recalls his presentation of
Persae, in which "by glorifying a great deed I taught [the
Athenians] to desire always to conquer their enemies" (1026–
27). This is, of course, not necessarily Aristophanes' or
Aeschylus' view of the main purpose or effect of the play, but
it proves that such a view was legitimate and that the fifth-
century Greeks were not necessarily disturbed by the thought
that the primary purpose of a tragedy might be to stimulate
the martial and patriotic spirit of the audience. There is also
abundant internal evidence that this was the intention, or at
least one of the intentions, of *Persae*, and we shall look first
at some passages that clearly were written to stimulate patriotic sentiment.

The most obvious case is the long description of the Greek
victory at Salamis. The battle is described from the perspective
of a Persian defeat, but it is clear that the messenger includes
in his account details intended specifically for the Greek audience. For instance, the Greek fleet coming into view as the
day dawns is described in all its splendor (386–401), and
the messenger caps his description by reciting the Athenian
battle-cry: "Now, sons of Hellas, now! / Set Hellas free, set
free your wives, your homes, / Your gods' high altars and
your fathers' tombs. / Now all is on the stake!" (402–5
[trans. Murray]). To this the Persian response is merely a
"clamor of tongues" (*glōssēs rhothos*, 406), which is how the

Persian war cry must have sounded to Greek ears. No moment of glory, moreover, is granted to any warrior on the Persian side,[11] and no minor Persian success is mentioned, whereas a relatively unimportant Athenian success at Psyttaleia is described in detail (447–71). These and other features of the messenger's report indicate that he is speaking specifically to the Athenians in the audience, not only to the Persians on stage.

Similarly the last strophic pair of the first stasimon concludes a lament for the Persian defeat and a description of the grief in their city with references to specific elements of the newly obtained Greek freedom. The Greek cities are not mentioned by name, but the verses must refer to them, since they were the only ones liberated by the defeat of Xerxes. No longer, sing the chorus, are these cities ruled by Persia (585), nor do they pay tribute compelled by a despot (586–87), nor do they fall to the ground in reverence (588–89), but they now have freedom of speech (591–93).[12] This catalogue of newly acquired Greek freedoms goes beyond the requirements of the Persian lament and would (especially in the last two instances) convey to the audience not so much grief for the Persian loss as joy for the Greek gain.

Later, in the third stasimon, the chorus praise the glorious empire acquired by Darius and by implication contrast it with the present disaster. From a Persian point of view, however, it is a singularly narrow praise of Darius' achievements, for he in fact made conquests all along the borders of Persia as far east as India. None of these is mentioned, except for the Ionian cities in and around the Aegean, and the detail with which these cities are described, including the list of Ionian islands in 880–86, is quite out of proportion to their importance for Persia. From the Athenian perspective, however, there is good reason to mention these Ionian cities, since at the time of the performance they were Athens' political allies. We can conclude from these passages that Aeschylus included at least some material in *Persae* primarily to stimulate patriotic feelings in his audience, and we can now examine more precisely what effect the whole play would have had from this Athenian or external point of view.

Perhaps the most obvious aspect of this external perspective is that it is almost totally Athenian.[13] The terms "Greece" and "Greeks" are often used, to be sure, to refer to Persia's enemies, but, whenever a specific Greek polis is singled out, it is Athens. The only exception is Darius' reference to the forthcoming Persian defeat at Plataea "by the Dorian [*i.e.*, Spartan] spear" (817), but this reference is overshadowed a few lines later by the old king's ringing command, "remember Athens and Greece" (824). Everywhere else the focus is entirely on Athens. When the queen questions the chorus, for example, she begins not by asking where has Xerxes gone or why has he set out for Greece, as one might expect, but "where is Athens?" (231). All the chorus' answers in this stichomythia (232–45) are calculated to stir the Athenians' pride, not just in their superiority over Persia but also in their leadership of the whole Greek world. Note especially 234, where the chorus reply that, if Xerxes could conquer Athens, "all Greece would become a vassal of the king."

Another interchange between the queen and the messenger that must have pleased the Athenians is the mention of the sacking of Athens. The messenger has just observed that a *daimōn* overthrew the Persian force, although it had superior numbers, and he concludes in high tragic style with a grand line, beautifully balanced and alliterative: *theoi polin sōizousi Pallados theas* ("the gods preserve the city of Pallas, the goddess," 347). In fact, the Persian army sacked Athens before the battle of Salamis, when the citizens, following the advice of Themistocles, abandoned the city and took refuge on Salamis and elsewhere; so the queen asks (348), "is Athens indeed not destroyed?" Here one might expect the messenger to describe the sack of the city, one of the few Persian successes,[14] but instead he replies in another memorable line, *andrōn gar ontōn herkos estin asphales* ("as long as there are men, there is a sure defense," 349), a sentiment that was undoubtedly familiar to the audience as a justification for Themistocles' risky policy of leaving the city and taking refuge in the "wooden walls" of their ships. Athenians hearing these lines would recall with pride this daring maneuver in their hour of greatest danger.

The other mentions of Athens in the play confirm the conclusion that Aeschylus intentionally and effectively designed *Persae* to stimulate the Athenians' pride. The name of their city is not mentioned often in comparison with the numerous mentions of Greece, but it is always brought up at an important moment. Immediately after the announcement of the defeat Athens is mentioned twice in the short *amoibaion* between the messenger and the chorus (285, 286); the agent who delivers the false message to Xerxes before the battle is an Athenian (355); the queen laments the blow dealt her son by "glorious Athens" (474, followed by the play's only direct mention of Marathon); she announces to Darius that the whole army was destroyed near Athens (716); and Xerxes refers to "ancient and hated Athens" in his lament (975–76).

Equally important for this stirring of Athenian pride is the emphasis on Salamis, which was considered an Athenian victory just as Plataea was considered primarily a Spartan victory. The battle itself is described at length, and the description includes a full account of the relatively small engagement on Psyttaleia.[15] Moreover Salamis is often singled out during the Persians' laments as the main cause of their defeat,[16] a view that would support the Athenian position on the war and would validate Themistocles' policy of rapidly increasing Athens' naval power to prepare for the invasion.

Similarly, support for the Athenian view of the victory and for Athens' naval policy comes from the emphasis throughout *Persae* on the defeat at sea rather than on land. This emphasis is so frequent and obvious that it is unnecessary to examine specific passages (*e.g.*, 278–79, 554, 560–62, 678–80, 728, 906–7, 1037, 1075–76).[17] At the beginning of the play the chorus talk mostly of their land army and the Persian skill with the bow, but as the play progresses it becomes evident that their traditional strength on land was undermined by the weakness of their navy. Conversely, of course, it becomes clear that the Athenians' policy of maintaining a strong fleet and putting their principal trust in it was the correct one.

This naval policy continued after the Persian defeat (and was still maintained by Pericles[18] at the beginning of the Peloponnesian War). In the winter of 478, immediately after the Persian forces had withdrawn from the Aegean, Athens began to form a military alliance with many Aegean islands and some Ionian cities on the coast of Asia Minor, centered at Delos.[19] The Delian League was originally a defensive alliance against Persia, and each member furnished either ships or tribute. Athens, with by far the largest fleet, was the acknowledged leader of the league, and by the middle of the fifth century if not earlier the league had become de facto the Athenian Empire. By 475, the Persians had been pushed out of the north shores of the Aegean, but it was not until the battle of the Eurymedon, perhaps as late as 466, that the Persian threat to the southwest corner of Asia Minor was finally removed. Thus in 472 Persia was still a potential threat to Greece, and the security provided by the league was probably still viewed as a benefit by its members.[20]

Consequently there would also be political implications in any reference to the Ionian Greeks who had been subjugated by the Persians before their "liberation" by the Athenians (584–94, 771, 880–901).[21] In 880–901 the chorus praise

Darius' earlier conquests and give a list of Aegean islands and
mainland Ionian cities he conquered. The audience would
certainly recognize this as a partial list of the members of the
Delian League, and they would undoubtedly be reminded of
the improved position of these cities as partners in the league
in contrast to their former subjugation. Aeschylus also includes
in *Persae* references to the participation of the Ionians in the
victory at Salamis (563, 950–51, 1011, 1025; cf. 178), without mentioning the fact that some of them had served
in Xerxes' navy. These references would remind the Athenian
audience of the unity of Athenian and Ionian interests and
would thereby strengthen their support for the Delian
League.[22]

In sum *Persae* would have inspired in its audience a sense
of pride at the Athenian victory over the Persians and a feeling of support for Athens' current foreign policy, which was
based on a strong naval federation of predominantly Ionian
states. This aspect of the play could be called propaganda, but
it is propaganda for the whole city, not for any one political
faction or individual. No Athenian is named in the play, and
although the audience would remember the heroes of Salamis,
especially Themistocles and Aristides,[23] its principal feelings
would be of pride in the entire city and of support for a naval
policy that by now most Athenian citizens favored.[24] The victory that is celebrated in *Persae* is Athens', and few if any in
the audience would have disputed Aeschylus' view of that
victory.

The audience must also have been aware, however, that
from the point of view of the figures on stage *Persae* was a
tragedy—a fall from prosperity to adversity. The tragic action
from this perspective is fairly straightforward: the power and
grandeur of the Persian empire are destroyed; the army that
had left in glory returns in ruin; and its leader and king is
brought on stage at the end in rags. Yet there are difficulties

even with this simple view of the play as a fall from prosperity. Is Xerxes the "tragic hero" if he appears only briefly at the end of the play? If he is not, who (if anyone) is? What is the cause of the downfall, and is it justified? And why does the announcement of the defeat come so soon, leaving the last three-quarters of the play for lamenting it? We must look more closely at the "tragedy" in *Persae* and come to a better understanding of the action from the internal Persian perspective before we can come to grips with the play as a whole.

There is no need to demonstrate that, from the Persian point of view, the play presents a fall from prosperity to adversity: the contrast between the grandeur described in the parodos and the wretchedness lamented in the final threnody is obvious and is reinforced by the later mention (958–1001) of many of the same exotic names of Persian warriors who were hailed in the opening anapests. Moreover, the traditional language of the fall from prosperity is prominent in the play, especially when Darius expresses his views about the disaster and about Xerxes' role in it, and the contrast is repeatedly drawn between the prosperity of Persia under Darius and its miserable condition now under Xerxes. But, unlike most other tragedies that exhibit the same general pattern, in *Persae* the condition of prosperity is extremely short-lived. The formal announcement of the disaster is made early in the play (249–55), and, even before the messenger arrives, it is made clear that Persia's prosperity is seriously threatened and that fear and worry dominate its inhabitants. From the very beginning, in fact, there are indications that not all is well in Persia. Even as the chorus describe the grandeur of the departed expedition in the opening anapests (1–60), they conclude this section with a brief description of how the entire land, especially the wives and parents of the soldiers, groan with desire and worry over the long absence of the army (61–64).

The overall structure of these opening anapests, namely the

movement from the chorus' account of the departed expedition
to their description of the impact its departure has had on the
city and those left at home,[25] is repeated in the lyric section of
the parodos (65–139), which begins with a further account
of the expedition and ends with another description of those
at home, especially the women who grieve at the absence of
their husbands. This repeated pattern has the effect of linking
the expedition in all its grandeur with the suffering of those
at home, especially the women; moreover, by describing this
suffering before the defeat is announced, the chorus make
clear that this domestic suffering is not caused solely by the
possibility of the army's defeat but also is a necessary consequence of the foreign expedition regardless of its outcome.[26]

The connection between the military expedition and the
despair of the women at home is forcefully evoked by the last
word of this section, *monozyx* (literally "yoked alone," 139),
which is used to describe the women left at home without their
husbands. This striking image recalls three previous uses of
the metaphor of yoking: once it is said that some warriors are
eager to "throw a yoke over" Greece (50) and twice (72,
131) the chorus refer to the army's "yoking" (*i.e.*, bridging)
of the Hellespont.[27] The image of the women alone in the
yoke reinforces the feeling that the wretchedness of the Persian families at home is directly connected to the departure of
the expedition in its attempt to yoke Greece, for which it
must first yoke the Hellespont.

Thus, even in the parodos the description of Persia's prosperity is undercut by the recognition of domestic misery caused
by the army's absence and by the chorus' own worry about the
army's possible defeat (115–19). The first exchange between
the chorus and the queen only increases this sense of worry
and fear. The queen expresses her anxiety directly (161–69)
and recounts her dream and the omen that appeared after it,
both of which clearly portend the defeat of the expedition.

Nothing in the scene conveys a sense of prosperity: even the queen's assertion that the Persians have enough wealth (168) only increases her fear about the safety of their men.

The first quarter of the play thus brings us slowly away from the confidence of the opening lines to a position of greater and greater anxiety, which the queen accurately summarizes as "dread to think about" (245). This mood has resulted from some initial expressions of confidence in the army followed by expressions of apprehension, so that these two conflicting sentiments seem to be inextricably linked, and we sense that the strength and grandeur of the expedition in themselves create concern for both the army and the city. The stichomythia between the queen and the chorus (232–45), moreover, provides a transition from the general foreboding of the parodos and the portents described by the queen to the specific danger presented by the Athenian forces, thereby preparing the audience for the messenger's description of the disaster. The result is that, when the messenger enters (249) with news of the defeat, the downfall of Persia has been thoroughly anticipated on stage.

We can conclude that even in the first quarter of the play the prosperity of Persia is so seriously undermined that it appears to belong only to the past, to that time when the expedition first set out, as described in the parodos. In contrast to this past prosperity, the Persians are from the beginning of the play in a state of worry and fear. And the lament for the defeat of the army, which dominates the last three-fourths of the play, certainly overshadows the much briefer descriptions of past prosperity. In sum the major emphasis of *Persae* is on the disaster and the consequences of this disaster rather than on the prosperity that preceded it.

One effect of this is that the causes of the disaster, which I examine more fully below, are less important dramatically than they might otherwise be. An equally important effect is

that the description and lament of the defeat are seen not only
as results of a negative condition, absence of prosperity, but
also as means to a positive new condition of survival. This
theme is introduced by the queen immediately after the brief
amoibaion (256–89) that follows the announcement of the
defeat. In her first comment on the disaster she explains that
she has kept silent till now, "stunned by the evils," for the
disaster surpasses telling or asking about. "Nonetheless," she
continues, "it is necessary for mortals to bear the woes that the
gods give them," and she then bids the messenger tell the
whole story of the disaster. These lines (290–95) introduce
a significant aspect of the attitude the Persians will take toward the disaster during the rest of the play: the evil is an
unspeakable catastrophe, yet it must be borne, and thus they
must lament it openly.

There is a general truth in these verses, that it is necessary
to speak about evils in order to "endure the unendurable,"
to survive in the face of catastrophe. There is both comfort
and strength in lamentation and in the retelling of troubles,
and from the Persian point of view the account here of the
disaster, the choral lament that follows, and especially the
long threnody at the end all serve this function: they enable
the survivors to cope with and endure beyond the disaster, and
thus they help the Persians accept their new situation. The
queen herself is a symbol of this endurance, moreover, for she
has outlived her husband and clearly has the strength to survive this disaster. She never wavers, never suggests that all is
lost. The survival of her son, Xerxes, certainly contributes to
her ability to endure, and his continued rule (already predicted in 213–14) is important to her and to Persia. But her
own strength and her presence on stage during most of the
play give the audience the feeling that although Persia's prosperity has been destroyed, its continued survival is not in
danger, at least not by the end of the play.

After the messenger has delivered his full account of the disaster, the queen announces that she will prepare sacrifices to the gods in the hope that the future at least may be better (521–26). It is in this spirit of looking forward that she asks the chorus to welcome Xerxes and lead him into the palace if he returns before she does (529–31). These instructions to the chorus have troubled many critics, since they may lead the audience to expect Xerxes' entrance, which does not come until much later.[28] But the reminder here that Xerxes is coming is in keeping with the queen's effort to look ahead, and both the audience and the chorus are alerted that the past, present, and future king will soon appear, providing the stability necessary for Persia's survival.

A similar effect is achieved just before Darius leaves the stage. He has himself just cast doubt on Persia's future survival by predicting yet another serious defeat, Plataea (817), but he then turns abruptly to the queen and bids her take proper clothing, meet Xerxes on his return, and console him. This request turns the audience's mind away from the predicted defeat and again reminds them that Xerxes will soon return. Furthermore, the concern that Darius and the queen show here for Xerxes' clothing (cf. 199, 468, 1030) is important.[29] Xerxes will enter in rags, which signify his defeat, but at the end of the play he enters the palace, where he is to receive the new royal clothing mentioned by Darius, confirming his survival and rehabilitation.[30]

The exodos, which begins when Xerxes enters (908), also conveys this sense of his survival and rehabilitation. It is divided into two parts,[31] in the first of which (908–1001) the chorus and Xerxes focus on the battle of Salamis, recalling and lamenting various aspects of the defeat. The chorus are not overtly antagonistic to Xerxes, even though they emphasize the ruin he has brought on the land. They do not seek to blame him personally, for instance, so much as the *daimōn* (*e.g.*, 921), they do not challenge his rule (cf. 918, 929), and even when they point out that Xerxes has "stuffed Hades with Persians" (923–24) they seem to be only lamenting the fact and not deriding him on account of it.

There is a change of emphasis in the second part of the exodos (1002–77), when the chorus cease trying to explore new aspects of the disaster and in particular stop cataloguing dead Persian leaders. Their grief now becomes more general, and both Xerxes and the chorus focus on their present grief and on Xerxes' lamentable condition, especially his meager equipment and torn robes, rather than on the past defeat and those who have died. As the play ends and the chorus accompany Xerxes into the palace, we sense that the worst is over, that Xerxes has been supported and comforted, and that a new life as king (and new clothing) await him in the palace. It would be an exaggeration to say that the Persian tragedy closes on an optimistic note, but the play does give us at the end a certain sense that the city and its king have come to an understanding of the disaster, have managed to survive, and will continue to survive in the future.

Persae, then, does present a fall from prosperity to adversity, but almost the entire focus is on the condition of adversity, which becomes a basis for survival and even a starting point for renewed prosperity. I return to this later, but first let us examine whether or not *Persae* presents the fall of a particular individual, namely Xerxes. Clearly in one sense it does, for Xerxes' condition at the end of the play is much less prosperous than it once was, and he is held to blame for the disaster by Darius. Moreover, he is talked about during the entire play, and his name is especially prominent in the description of the military defeat. It is significant, however, that he figures much less prominently in the descriptions of Persia's prosperity. He is mentioned only once in the parodos (5; cf. 144), and, when the prosperity of Persia is later recalled, it is prosperity under

Darius, not under Xerxes. Xerxes appears on stage only briefly, at the end of the play, after the disaster has been not only announced but also extensively lamented. If Aeschylus' purpose had been to portray the fall of Xerxes himself, he surely would have made more of his role in Persia's former prosperity.[32]

Although in a limited sense *Persae* thus presents Xerxes' fall from prosperity to adversity, a broader view of the dramatic action suggests itself, namely that it is the fall of Persia as a whole, not of Xerxes as an individual. He and the other dramatis personae contribute to the total unity that is Persia, but they themselves are relatively unimportant as individuals and virtually undeveloped as characters.[33] The chorus, for instance, are elders of high standing, but they represent all the people of Persia. Their concerns include the army abroad and the women at home, and, although they are presumably all men, they do not appear to represent only one class or age group or sex. Dramatically, moreover, the chorus is the central figure in the play, for they are present from beginning to end, they converse with each of the other figures, and they are the most nearly identified with Persia as a whole.

The queen[34] also represents or can be identified with the whole of Persia, both because she (like the chorus) is on stage before and after the announcement of the defeat and because she is closely connected with both Darius and Xerxes. This double role as wife of the former king and mother of the present one is emphasized in the chorus' first words to her:

> ὦ βαθυζώνων ἄνασσα Περσίδων ὑπερτάτη,
> μῆτερ ἣ Ξέρξου γεραιά, χαῖρε, Δαρείου γύναι·
> θεοῦ μὲν εὐνάτειρα Περσῶν, θεοῦ δὲ καὶ μήτηρ ἔφυς.

("My lady, of the deep-girded Persian women the most exalted, / mother of Xerxes, venerable lady, welcome, of Darius the wife, / of a god of the Persians the bedmate, and of a god also the mother you were," 155–57). The interlocking of noun and adjective around the diaeresis in 155, the chiasmus in 156, and the balance and anaphora in 157, all lend dignity to the queen's presence. More particularly they show that this dignified position is a result of the queen's dual role as wife and mother of Persian kings. She thus belongs both to the past prosperity and to the present adversity of Persia, and her presence lends an important element of continuity to the play and to its tragic action.

By the same token the relative brevity of both Darius' and Xerxes' appearances on stage suggests that each of these figures represents only one aspect of Persia, Darius its past prosperity and Xerxes its present defeat. The contrast between these two kings is frequently referred to and is an important means of emphasizing the contrast between the past and the present condition of Persia. But insofar as each king represents only one aspect of Persia, neither is the central focus of the play.

This focus is Persia itself, and to the extent that *Persae* is a tragedy, it is the tragedy of Persia. As in any such tragedy, the fall of Persia is the result of certain forces that are implicitly or explicitly said to be governing the action. Moreover, as in the case of individual tragic heroes, some of the same forces that brought about Persia's greatness lead to its downfall. I have suggested that the structure of the play draws our attention more to the condition of Persia after the fall than to the forces causing the fall, but it is nonetheless necessary to consider how these forces are presented in the play. For convenience I will discuss separately the general categories of wealth, war, ignorance, impiety, and divine intervention, though these overlap to some extent.

Wealth (*ploutos*) is a major component of Persian prosperity (*olbos*) before the defeat at Salamis, and the description of the departed expedition in the parodos stresses this wealth, for example, by the threefold repetition of *polychrysos* ("with much gold") in the opening anapests (3, 9, 53). But *ploutos* is by no means an unqualified good, as we learn from the queen, who expresses her fear that the Persians' *ploutos* may in fact cause the destruction of their *olbos* (163–64).[35] In fact her primary worry is not that their *ploutos* itself will be destroyed, for, as she tells us, there is enough *ploutos* (168), but that it may lead to the destruction of the army and Xerxes. The implication here is that wealth contains a potential danger, and this important sentiment is later expressed by Darius, when he warns the chorus to remember Athens, "lest someone scorn his present fortune and being desirous of other goods throw away his great *olbos*" (824–26). A danger of wealth, then, is that it may easily lead one to seek more and more wealth until at last one loses all. This is clearly what happened to Xerxes, for we are told by the queen that he was urged to undertake the expedition to Greece by his advisers, who kept reminding him of the great *ploutos* acquired by Darius (755) and accusing him of cowardice in not increasing the *olbos* handed down by his father (755–56). The advisers, it appears, failed to make a proper distinction between *ploutos* and *olbos* and assumed wrongly that more *ploutos* automatically means more *olbos*. In pursuit of more *ploutos*, however, Xerxes throws away the great *olbos* he already has. In this he is only following Darius' lead, but by going farther than Darius he goes too far and is ruined.

Another factor leading to the downfall of Persia is war. Like wealth, it is ambivalent, though the potential evils of war are more obvious than those of wealth. These evils come not only from defeat but also from any foreign expedition, as is made clear by the description in the parodos of the present conditions at home. Of course, victory produces benefits, as can be seen from the chorus' recital of Darius' military conquests, which added such glory to Persia (852–903). But there are also limits beyond which military action is no longer profitable, and in *Persae* the Hellespont is treated as a sort of natural boundary of the Persian empire. Thus the chorus praise the conquests of Darius,[36] but emphasize that he stayed at home (864–66). Darius criticizes Xerxes for bridging the Hellespont, implying that he himself respected this boundary. Whatever the historical truth of this claim,[37] the point is clear: limited conquest carries few risks and may provide great benefits, but beyond a certain point foreign conquest necessarily brings woe to the city both by the extended absence of its men and by the high risk of defeat. Thus in his military activity, as in his search for wealth, Xerxes continued to pursue the same ends as Darius, but by striving for greater accomplishments than his predecessor he lost all.

Xerxes' defeat, however, is not attributed simply to his making war on Greece; he also made mistakes as a commander. The most important error was his reliance on the navy rather than the traditional land army, a point that is emphasized again and again in the play.[38] Xerxes' failure is also revealed in other references to his intellectual shortcomings. The description of the battle of Salamis, for instance, begins with an account of the Greek trick that Xerxes failed to perceive (*ou xyneis dolon*, 361; cf. 373); in 552 he is said to have acted foolishly (*dysphronōs*; cf. 900–901, where Darius is said to have conquered many Greek cities *spheterais phresin* ["with his wits"]); Darius maintains that Xerxes accomplished evils unwittingly (*ou kateidōs*, 744);[39] he speaks as if Xerxes were ignorant of the oracles predicting the disaster (*ouk eubouliāi*, 749); and finally Xerxes himself naturally calls the defeat "unexpected" (910, 1006, 1027). Throughout the play, then, Xerxes' intellectual failure is stressed as a contributing cause of the disaster.

Another factor mentioned is impiety, often singled out by modern critics as the principal cause of Persia's downfall.[40] The view that Xerxes' impiety caused the defeat is based on Darius' strong criticism of his son (739–52), when he learns the news of his defeat. Darius claims that Xerxes unknowingly (744) accomplished evils that had been foretold and that his particular wrongdoing was the enslavement of the Hellespont, the "river of a god" (*rhoon theou*, 746). Darius continues, "Being mortal he thought to vanquish all the gods, especially Poseidon—not a good plan: surely this is a disease of the mind that came over my son" (749–51). To seek to vanquish the gods is clearly an impiety, and there is no doubt that Darius sees Xerxes' act of bridging the Hellespont in such a way.[41] We should bear in mind, however, that no one else in the play treats Xerxes' action as impious, and none of the other references in the play to the bridging of the Hellespont suggest that impiety was part of that deed (see 50, 69–72, 112–14,[42] 722–25). In fact the queen mentions the bridging approvingly as a salvation for the remnants of the army on their return (736).

Darius does, however, give a rather extended account of the impiety of the army left behind in Greece after Xerxes left, for which they will be punished at Plataea (803–28). In this passage he refers specifically to the *hybris*[43] of the army, and to their impious thoughts and deeds, such as the destruction of altars and temples. He indeed warns of punishment for such wrongs, but he nowhere mentions Xerxes.[44]

Thus Darius' remarks cannot be read as a comment on the actions of Xerxes. The passage is followed by Darius' recommendation that the chorus advise Xerxes to "stop harming the gods with excessive boldness" (*hyperkompōi thrasei*, 831), but this advice refers to the only impiety that Darius has attributed to Xerxes, the bridging of the Hellespont: Xerxes should not try to conquer Greece again.

These two passages (745–51 and 807–31) are Darius' only discussions of impious conduct and the only places in the play where impiety is mentioned. Neither the chorus nor the queen nor the messenger attributes any act of *hybris* or impiety to Xerxes, although both the queen and the chorus hear Darius' accusation. However, they clearly do not accept the old king's view: the queen's immediate reaction is to blame Xerxes' advisers, who urged him to follow his father's example; the chorus praise Darius' military successes but do not attribute his success to any special piety or morally right behavior, only to his remaining within certain territorial limits; and when Xerxes enters, they never speak of his failure in moral terms.[45] We can conclude that, as a cause for Xerxes' defeat and the downfall of Persia, impiety is a relatively insignificant factor and is directly responsible only for the destruction of the rest of the army at Plataea.

But what about Xerxes' impetuosity? Is he not the very embodiment of *hybris*[46] even if this word is never used of him? Certainly the picture we have of Xerxes on stage at the end of the play does not support any such characterization. Nor do the mentions of Xerxes before his appearance support this charge, since the worst that is said of him is that he is overeager and inexperienced. Although these are certainly shortcomings in any commander, they are hardly moral flaws. Consider the words that might be singled out to support the charge of *hybris*, such as *thourios* (73, 718, 754), which means "rushing, eager for the fray."[47] There is certainly a danger in this traditional military virtue, as there is also danger in *thrasos* ("courage," "boldness"), used once, in a positive sense, of the Greeks at Salamis (394) and twice with the implication of recklessness (744, 831). And *neos* ("young") is used of Xerxes by the chorus once (13)[48] and by Darius twice (744, 782), naturally with derogatory implications in the latter case. But these are the only words in the play that describe any such weakness in Xerxes, and they do not indicate moral flaws or an impious or hybristic nature.

Impiety is thus a relatively minor factor in the action of

Persae. Divine influence in human affairs, however, either in the form of a *daimōn* or a *theos* is referred to repeatedly. There are more than a dozen references to a *daimōn* or *theos* causing the defeat of the Persian army,[49] as well as numerous other mentions of the role of divinities in human affairs.[50] Such references are made by all the figures in the play, even Darius (who is himself several times called a *daimōn* or *theos*), and we must therefore conclude that, from the Persian point of view, the activity of some divine force is a major cause of the Persian defeat. Except for Darius, however, no one suggests that there was any specific cause or motivation for these divine forces to work against Persia. The others merely accept these forces as evidently present throughout, working in favor of Persia in the time of prosperity and against it in the time of defeat.

The operation of these forces in the affairs of Persia is first mentioned in the lyrics of the parodos (101–2) where Fate (*Moira*) from the gods (*theothen*) is said to have directed the Persians to carry out their past conquests. The chorus have declared in the preceding mesode (93–100) that no mortal can escape this divine power. Although the primary reference is apparently to the Greek forces, who will not be able to withstand the divinely favored Persian force, the audience would certainly also perceive the ironic applicability of the mesode to the Persians themselves.[51] Just as the gods have favored the Persian triumphs in the past, so the gods will be working against Persia in defeat. Only Darius suggests a human cause for this change in the workings of divine influence, and there is no indication that the chorus or anyone else in the play accepts his view.

But to accept unmotivated divine forces as causing the Persian defeat does not mean that the gods were the sole cause, for clearly Xerxes caused the defeat as well through his own mistakes. Indeed *Persae* presents a convergence of human and divine motivation very similar to what we have seen in Homer; the *daimōn* took away Xerxes' wits and destroyed the army; Xerxes also in ignorance led his army to defeat.[52] This double motivation is well illustrated by the balanced juxtaposition of human and divine factors in 361–62: Xerxes "not recognizing the trick of the Greek man or the jealousy [*phthonos*] of the gods."[53] Just as Agamemnon in the *Iliad* blames Zeus-sent *atē* for his mistake, so Xerxes and the chorus blame the *daimōn* who brought *atē* upon Persia (1007;[54] cf. 653, 1016, 1037). And just as Agamemnon's excuse helps him keep his standing and respect among the Greeks (though it does not relieve him of his liability for punishment), so Xerxes' blaming of the *daimōn* removes some of the disgrace of the defeat from him and helps sustain him through the long lament. If the *daimōn* is to blame for the defeat, Persians can more easily look ahead to the day when a new, more favorable *daimōn* will be influencing the affairs of Persia.

There are thus many forces working to bring about the downfall of Persia. The modern critic is tempted to single out one and designate it the sole cause, but this is clearly a distortion, especially when the factor chosen is the relatively minor one of impiety. Rather, all the factors must be considered together, and we can then see that the issue is much larger than Xerxes himself. He is merely continuing the policies of Darius and the previous Persian kings, and he happens to be the one king in the succession who carries those policies too far.[55] The full cause of the disaster is Persia itself, its wealth grown too great, its military power extended too far, its *daimōn* favorable for too long, and its king too eager to continue the expansionist tradition of his predecessors. These various aspects of the fall of Persia have been discussed separately, but in the play they form a unity, just as the various figures on stage form a unity that is Persia.

From the Persian perspective, then, *Persae* is the tragedy of the fall of Persia, a fall attributed to a complex variety of causes within the general precept that whatever grows too great eventually falls. If we accept this view of *Persae*, however, what can we make of the elements in the play indicating that *Persae* was intended to celebrate the Athenian victory? Must we dismiss these as merely "incidental"?[56] Some such recourse would be necessary if we were to accept the traditional view that "tragedy" and "celebration" (or "propaganda") are essentially incompatible,[57] but, if we put aside this assumption, I think we can see how Aeschylus has blended the two perspectives in *Persae* so that each supports the other in an important synthesis.

In examining this synthesis we must not be misled by the feeling that the internal perspective, from which the play is a tragedy, seems to predominate in the play and may therefore make a stronger impression on the audience than the external Athenian perspective. Remember that Aeschylus' audience had a strong natural bias in favor of the Athenian perspective, and he therefore had to concentrate more on the Persian than on the Athenian point of view if he wanted them to see both. A single verse could evoke feelings of national pride in the audience, whereas a whole scene might be needed to stimulate as much sympathy for the Persian plight. Thus the apparent imbalance of the two viewpoints should not mislead us: the Athenian audience would have learned to understand the Persian viewpoint from the long scenes of lament; they would have been equally inspired to view the action from the Greek perspective by the briefer passages of explicitly pro-Athenian sentiment.

The Athenian audience of 472 would thus have experienced *Persae* from both perspectives during the course of the play. And the two perspectives interact with each other, each affecting the viewer's understanding of the other, to some extent. An Athenian audience, for instance, would probably have been less impressed than a Persian or a neutral audience by Darius' attempt to dissociate his own activity (and that of his predecessors) from Xerxes' actions. The campaigns of 490 and 480–79 were part of the same Persian threat to Athens, and, even if Darius did not himself lead the former expedition, he would have been held responsible for it by the Athenians.[58] Thus Darius' description of the past buildup of the Persian empire (765–81) and the chorus' catalogue of Darius' conquests in the Aegean (864–903) would be seen as part of one long-standing campaign against Greece, which culminated in Xerxes' expedition. Moreover, the fact that Persia was still a threat to the Greeks after Salamis and Plataea and probably continued to be a threat in 472[59] would also have made it easier for the audience to anticipate the survival and future rehabilitation of Xeres and Persia, for which I argued above.

It would thus have been difficult, if not impossible, for the Athenian audience to accept Darius, garbed in Persian splendor and hailed as the king who conquered most of Athens' current allies, as the mouthpiece of their poet, as many critics assume him to be.[60] Rather the Athenians would have seen a basic similarity between the two kings and would have understood the subtle conflict presented not only between father and son but also between father and mother: Darius contrasting, as fathers often do, his son's folly with his own wisdom, and the queen defending her child on the ground that he was merely trying to follow in his father's footsteps. To the Athenian audience Darius would appear not as a model of virtue but as the representative of one traditional point of view, who maintains that point of view so as to present himself and his own reign in the most favorable light. The view of the internal Persian tragedy that I presented above would thus have been even clearer to the Athenians than to a modern reader.

The tragedy may also have affected the Athenian perspective, for, although no explicit warning is given, the spectacle of the collapse of an empire from a position of excessive wealth, power, and foreign aggression may have suggested a warning to those who would extend the power of Athens and the Delian League too far. For instance, certain lines describing elements of the Persian defeat at Salamis, especially such vivid images as the bodies being mangled by fish in the sea (576–78), would have reminded the Athenians of their own losses and thus of the inherent danger of war. And the recognition in the parodos of the distress caused at home by any foreign expedition may have also reminded the Athenians of their own situation, for by this time their fleet was already undertaking wide-ranging overseas campaigns.

If there is a warning, however, it is only implicit. At this time most Athenians probably considered their foreign campaigns fully justified as either retribution, self-defense, or the traditional search for glory. Even if they had already witnessed the suppression of the Naxian revolt,[61] the reality of the extension of Athens' power and the transformation of the league into the Athenian Empire would not yet have been apparent to many. Nonetheless, the presentation of the fall of Persia as an example of the general tendency of power to become overextended and collapse may have somewhat tempered the Athenians' confidence in their superiority, and certainly some may have seen in this a warning against sending their naval forces to distant lands in search of excessive revenge or glory.

These are some examples of how the two different viewpoints, Persian and Athenian, interact in *Persae.* In addition we should look at the obvious way in which victory and defeat in a battle are directly related: the greater the one, the greater the other. Thus, by emphasizing the magnitude of the Persian defeat, Aeschylus was in effect enlarging the Athenian victory. Conversely the Athenians' sense of the magnitude of their victory would have enlarged the Persian defeat. This interaction should not obscure the fact that the two perspectives

are essentially opposed, however, and that the audience would
be presented with a downfall and a triumph simultaneously.

This simultaneous presentation of opposed perspectives is,
I feel, the most significant achievement of *Persae*, for it demonstrates dramatically the view that triumph and disaster, joy
and lament are but two aspects of the same activity, opposed
and yet necessarily linked. There is an inescapable bond between triumph and disaster, whether the two occur simultaneously (Greek triumph and Persian disaster) or consecutively
(Persian triumph and Persian disaster). The same situation
can always be interpreted from opposed points of view as
either beneficial or harmful, as when Xerxes laments the disaster as "painful, a joy to our enemies" (1034).[62]

This comprehension of complementary, opposed viewpoints within a single play is a fundamental aspect of Aeschylus' dramatic technique. Indeed the overall unity or coexistence of opposites is a common element in early Greek
thought, perhaps best expressed by the "paradoxes" of Heraclitus. Such a view does not easily lend itself to logical analysis
or straightforward expression,[63] but it is ideally suited for dramatic presentation, where the poet makes no direct statement
himself but dramatically presents different, often opposed,
positions by means of his characters. *Persae*, it has often been
noted, has no *agon*, no direct dramatic conflict between two
characters, which we find in so many of the great Greek tragedies. But because of its special nature *Persae* can present a
dramatic duality without an *agon*, for the entire play is in a
sense a dialogue between two essentially opposed perspectives.

This may be one reason why it has so little of the imagistic
irony we find in Aeschylus' other plays. We have already noted
the image of yoking, which suggests the similarity of and yet
opposition between military domination and sexual union in
marriage. Also striking is the ironic use of *pelanos*, which can

mean any thick, liquid substance but often denotes specifically a mixture of meal, honey, and oil offered as a sacrifice to the dead. Darius uses *pelanos* to refer to the Persian blood that will flow at Plataea (816), when the word has already been used twice by the queen with reference to her own sacrifices, which are intended to ward off precisely such defeats as Plataea (204, 524). This sort of imagistic irony is common in the *Oresteia* and Aeschylus' other plays but rare in *Persae*, and I suggest that this is because the basic irony or duality of perspective in this play renders further irony unnecessary. *Persae* by its very structure and situation presents the audience with more than one meaning; a description of dead Persians, for instance, could also suggest both the Athenian conquerors and the Athenian dead, and there would be no need for special poetic techniques to convey this multiplicity of meanings.[64]

Finally the fundamental dramatic irony of *Persae* coincides with the basic view of human behavior and universal order that is both explicit and implicit in the play. All human activity follows a certain pattern, a progression from one state to its opposite, from wealth to poverty, from insignificance to triumph, from evil done to evil suffered (*kakōs drasantes ouk elassona / paschousi*, 813–14), in short a pattern of action and reaction. This alternation between opposed states is a pattern long familiar to the Greeks,[65] but Aeschylus has added a new element by demonstrating the close, and in many cases necessary, connection between the two opposed states. *Persae* makes clear, for instance, the relationship between foreign military conquest and troubles at home, between paternal success and filial excess. Aeschylus has further succeeded in dramatizing the necessary connection between the two opposed perspectives in a war: every victory is a defeat, every rise a fall, every extension by one power a weakening of another. These connections are not stated abstractly as principles or theories of the nature of human affairs; they are conveyed through a powerful dramatic presentation. We may not be able to extract a single clear message from this drama, but as members of the audience we surely are brought to a better understanding of our own lives and of social and political behavior in general.

III

The Ethical Pattern in the Oresteia

Besides *Persae* the only complete work of Aeschylus' that survives is the *Oresteia* trilogy. The three other single plays that have come down to us all belonged to connected trilogies whose other plays no longer survive, and without these lost plays our understanding of the three survivors must remain incomplete (see chapter V). The *Oresteia*, however, survives as a single complete work of art,[1] perhaps the greatest work of dramatic art ever created. But the tendency of some recent scholars[2] to single out *Agamemnon* for comment because of its greater complexity and poetic richness has, I think, produced a distorted view of that play and of the trilogy as a whole.

The primary distortion is that, taken by itself, *Agamemnon* appears to be a tragedy in the Aristotelian sense of a man's fall from prosperity to adversity, and this view of the play as a tragedy has prompted critics to focus on a small group of related problems: the character of Agamemnon, the nature of his "crime," and the "justice" of his punishment. When viewed from the perspective of the whole trilogy, however, Agamemnon's death no longer stands out as a single "tragic" event. Rather the killing of Agamemnon is but one step in a larger process, and we can no longer restrict our investigation or our understanding to a single individual or act. Each person in the trilogy emerges on stage and then departs; each is part of the overall process. But the trilogy as a whole is larger than any one of them, and even Orestes hands over his case to Apollo (*Eu.* 609–13), leaves the stage after the verdict (777), and is virtually forgotten by the end of the play.

But, if there is no single hero in the *Oresteia*, there is a center of focus, and this is the family (*genos*) or the house (*domos, oikos*)[3] of Atreus (as it is usually referred to), different aspects of which are represented by Agamemnon, Clytemnestra, Aegisthus, Electra, Orestes and the Furies, much as different aspects of Persia were seen to be represented by the various figures in *Persae*. Furthermore, I will argue, this mythical household, this royal family extending over several generations, becomes identified with the city of Argos as a political community. And, at the end, mythical Argos gives way to the contemporary city of Athens, so that the resolution that finally "cures" the troubles of the house of Atreus and the city of Argos becomes the resolution of conflicts within contemporary Athens also. The unity of the trilogy thus creates an identification of house, family, mythical city, and contemporary city, and these elements are united in the overall movement of the whole. The individuals on stage must be understood as part of this larger unity. This is not to say that they are not also recognizable as individuals but rather that their importance lies more in what they contribute to the overall process of the trilogy than in what they are in and of themselves.[4]

The following discussion of the *Oresteia* attempts to bring out this overall unity by first examining the basic ethical pattern of human action[5] that is described in statements of the chorus and of other characters and is confirmed by the events on stage. This pattern is one of action and retributive reaction, and it continues until the end of the trilogy, where it is modified in such a way that reciprocal action becomes constructive and beneficial rather than destructive. After examining this pattern I look in chapter IV at two especially significant aspects of the action: sexual conflict and political conflict.

The basic ethical pattern or rhythm revealed by the action of the *Oresteia* is one of reciprocity and balance. This pattern is certainly not new; we have seen it in *Persae*, and it is a common element in Greek language and thought. But in the *Oresteia* Aeschylus has left us perhaps the most complex and comprehensive presentation of this pattern in all of Greek literature. In the smallest details as well as in the whole work we are aware of this sense of balance; indeed this may have been one reason for Aeschylus' apparent fondness for writing connected trilogies, where the reciprocal action and reaction of the first two plays could somehow be resolved in a final equilibrium in the third play.[6]

Before considering the overall pattern of action, I want to note some of the many ways in which this basic pattern of balance and reciprocity is present in the minor details of the work. *Agamemnon* begins with the watchman gazing at the stars, which (he tells us) bring winter and summer to mortals (5) in their settings and risings (7).[7] A few lines later he describes the beacon-signal as the "lamp of night, light of day" (22–23), the first reference in the play to the very common day/night (light/darkness) opposition. These small references to common cosmic dualities are not of major importance in themselves, but they give the audience a sense from the beginning that there is an order in the universe that is seen as the coexistence of opposites in a balanced structure. And this universal order is clearly evident in human affairs as well.

It is fundamental to human existence, for instance, that good and evil are mixed, as the chorus sing of Calchas' prophecy (*Ag.* 145, 156–57). A corollary of this view is expressed in the statement that of two alternatives neither is without evil. Agamemnon says this of his decision to kill Iphigeneia (*Ag.* 206–7, 211), the chorus of Orestes' decision to kill Clytemnestra (*Ch.* 1018–20), and Athena of her decision about the fate of Orestes (*Eu.* 480–81). As the herald in *Agamemnon* puts it, "in the long run one would say that some of these things fell out well whereas others are cause for complaint; but who except the gods is untroubled in all things throughout his life?" (551–54).

Together with this sense of mixed good and evil, we find the expression of simultaneous hope and fear, especially in the first two plays. These emotions are expressed by the watchman and the chorus in *Agamemnon* (34–39, 100–3) and the chorus in *Choephoroi* (410–17, 463–65). This sense of the mixture of good and evil, hope and fear, is so strong in fact that, when Clytemnestra prays, "may the good conquer so as not to be seen ambiguously balanced [by evil]" (*Ag.* 349),[8] we are immediately aware that she is asking for something very unusual if not impossible: as a rule, good is always balanced by evil.

Closely linked with this sense of balance in the universe and in human affairs is the necessity for reciprocity. When a harmful act is committed on one side it must be balanced by a reciprocal act; then this new harm in turn requires reciprocation. This basic pattern, action followed by reciprocal reaction, is the most fundamental pattern of action in the *Oresteia* and is referred to again and again by variations of the well-known phrases *pathein ton erxanta* (*Ag.* 1564) and *drasanti pathein* (*Ch.* 313).[9] This maxim is often translated "the doer suffers," but, since *paschō* commonly functions as the passive or opposite of verbs meaning "do,"[10] a fuller translation would be "unto the doer it is done." [11] This rule of reciprocity is demonstrated by the action of the trilogy, as Agamemnon, Clytemnestra (and Aegisthus), and Orestes all kill and in return are killed or at least punished. The herald compares the earlier evil done by the Trojans (*to drama*) to the evil they suffer (*to pathos*) and concludes that the former is not greater than the latter (*Ag.* 533). Both Clytemnestra and Orestes appeal often to this principle of reciprocity: the former speaks of Agamemnon as "having done unworthy things, suffering worthy things" (*anaxia drasas axia paschōn, Ag.* 1527–28;[12] cf. 340, 1397–98, 1658, *Ch.* 888); the latter reproaches her in turn, saying "you killed him whom you ought not, and so suffer what you ought not" (*ekanes hon ou chrēn, kai to mē chreōn pathe, Ch.* 930; cf. 556–57).

Thus, "to the doer it is done" expresses a clear sense of reciprocal action: one wrong leads to another wrong in return. The precise connection between the action and the succeeding reaction is usually unspecified and difficult to determine, but the dominant metaphor used to describe the relation is birth. "The impious deed begets more [impious deeds] like their begettor . . . and an old act of violence [*hybris*] tends to beget a new one," sing the chorus in the first play (*Ag.* 758–60, 763–66),[13] and this view is repeated in similar language by the chorus in the last play: "*hybris* is truly the child of impiety" (*Eu.* 533–34). In both places, moreover, the positive aspect of this process of reciprocal reaction is expressed by the same metaphor, good comes from good (*Ag.* 761–62, *Eu.* 535–37), although this positive aspect is not realized until the very end, when Athena tells the Furies that they should make Athens their home *eu drōsan, eu paschousan* ("doing well, faring well," *Eu.* 868).

The metaphor of one action giving birth to another is by no means original in Aeschylus; it occurs for example in both Solon (6.3 = 5.9D) and Theognis (153). For these earlier poets the metaphor is merely a vivid way of expressing a general truth, but in the *Oresteia* the metaphor of birth is integrally related to the dramatic action, for the abstract pattern of one evil giving birth to another is physically embodied in the successive generations of the house of Atreus. Again and again the familial nature of the action is impressed on us, when the evil in the house is described by such words as *symphyton* ("born in the house and grown one with it," *Ag.* 152),[14] *autophona* ("murdering its own," *Ag.* 1091), *syngonōn* ("in the family," *Ag.* 1190), *homosporois* ("kindred," *Ag.* 1509), *authentaisin* ("through kindred hands," *Ag.* 1573),[15] and *engenēs* ("in the family," *Ch.* 466).[16] Evil breeds in the house just as the family itself breeds. When Orestes says (*Ch.* 1005–6) that he would sooner die childless (*apais*) than take a housemate (*xynoikos*) like Clytemnestra, this is not merely rhetorical hyperbole: the house of Atreus ends with Orestes, so the evil in it ends with him too. Thus, when the chorus sing, "may the old murder no longer give birth in the house" (*Ch.* 806), they are perhaps hoping that the new murderer will refrain from giving birth as well.[17]

This image of an evil innate in the family of Atreus, one evil begetting another, has led some critics to conclude that we have here a pattern of "hereditary guilt"—in other words, that Agamemnon from birth shares in or is tainted by the original guilt of his father, Atreus, and that his subsequent evil actions are, as Lloyd-Jones puts it, "only a consequence of the original guilt inherited from Atreus."[18] The theory that children pay for the crimes of their fathers goes back at least to Solon (13.31–32 = 1.31–32D), but, whereas in Solon the children are blameless (*anaitioi*), in Aeschylus, according to Lloyd-Jones, the children are compelled by Zeus to commit their own crimes for which they are punished.[19] The theory may have a certain attraction, for it provides the "logical" system of causality that is needed if we are to invest Aeschylus with a systematic concept of justice; but there is no support for it in the text.[20] To begin with, it is never maintained implicitly or explicitly that Agamemnon is guilty from birth or is guilty because of the crime of Atreus. Aegisthus, it is true, expresses his own feeling that he had a right to kill Agamemnon in retribution for Atreus' deed (*Ag.* 1577–1611).[21] But Aegisthus' reasoning does not compel us to see Agamemnon as guilty (he could just as easily be an innocent victim in Aegisthus' mind), and, more important, his self-justification is incidental to the main action of the play. Clytemnestra is the actual killer of Agamemnon, and she has her own good reasons, which have nothing to do with Atreus' crime. Aegisthus is only a weak coconspirator (1634–37), and from the perspective of the whole trilogy his role is even less significant. He is rapidly dispatched and forgotten in *Choephoroi*, and throughout *Eumenides* Clytemnestra alone is mentioned as the killer of Agamemnon.

The crime of Atreus, moreover, is introduced only after Agamemnon has already left the stage.[22] It is a manifestation of the evil in the house, and, together with Thyestes' adultery, it extends the sequence of action and reciprocal reaction even further into the past. But it is not a major event in the trilogy, and it is in no way presented as a causal factor in Agamemnon's crime.[23] Indeed, it is absurd to think that the audience would hear about Agamemnon's decision to sacrifice his daughter, deduce that there had to be some further cause, and then wait in perplexity until Cassandra's reference to Thyestes' feast, 875 lines later, gave the clue to what this cause was. Surely, if Aeschylus had wanted us to see Agamemnon's crime as the result of hereditary guilt, he would have mentioned or somehow alluded to this factor when describing the crime. Nor is the general principle of hereditary guilt stated anywhere in the trilogy. There is sometimes thought to be a statement of or reference to it in a corrupt choral passage, *Ag.* 374–75, but this is an unlikely and unsupported guess,[24] and with this possible exception the theory of hereditary guilt is not mentioned.

The metaphor of birth, however, does suggest that there may be more than a merely temporal relation between one crime and the next, and several factors support this suggestion. The preposition *ek* ("from," "out of") is used, for instance, to suggest that one action is somehow the result of the former one (*e.g., ek tōnde, Ag.* 1223; *ek proterōn, Eu.* 934);[25] words emphasizing that one crime is the first (*prōtopēmōn, Ag.* 223;[26] *prōtarchon, Ag.* 1192) may suggest that later actions somehow follow from this first one; and verbal echoes often connect one crime with another in the audience's mind (*e.g., pateō* used of Agamemnon's trampling of the tapestries in 957 and of Thyestes' seduction of Atreus' wife in 1193). But to understand this language, which is metaphoric and imagistic, as indicating a logical cause and effect is to misunderstand not just the *Oresteia* but also poetry in general. Aeschylus certainly makes a deliberate effort to link the various crimes and to equate and identify them imagistically. But a critic cannot approach these poetic connections as a lawyer might and conclude that one act is the simple direct cause of another. The killing of Iphigeneia is clearly motivated by the situation described by the chorus; the killing of Agamemnon is the result of several factors, of which revenge for Iphigeneia's death is surely the most important dramatically. Other motives, including revenge for Atreus' crime, are introduced to broaden the scope of the action and have important poetic and dramatic functions. But to designate such a factor *the* cause of Agamemnon's death is certainly to distort the poet's intentions.

We see, then, in the *Oresteia* a pattern or rhythm of evil succeeding evil that is sometimes spoken of in terms of birth, one evil from another, and that is represented on stage by the members of the house of Atreus. One important factor in the working out of such a pattern in human affairs is, of course, the Greeks' sense of the necessity for reciprocal action, which clearly manifests itself as the spirit of revenge for a wrong done to a person or a member of his or her family. Another factor closely linked to retribution is the notion of pollution, which seems to reach its fullest development in the fifth century.[27] This clearly is a step toward the concept of inner guilt, but in Aeschylus at least it still retains a physical element, and we cannot simply equate pollution and guilt.[28] Rather, the basic effect of pollution is to force some action to be taken in the case of a homicide; the relatives of the victim must obtain some sort of satisfaction, either a retributive killing or a legal settlement or some other compensation that cleanses the situation.

All the killings in the *Oresteia* result in pollution: Agamemnon knows that he will be polluted by killing his daughter (*Ag.* 208–10), and Clytemnestra is clearly polluted after killing Agamemnon (*e.g., Ag.* 1427–28). But in each of these two cases a strongly motivated avenger exists (namely Clytemnestra and Orestes), so that there is little mention of Agamemnon's or Clytemnestra's pollution. Pollution is a more significant factor, however, after Orestes' killing of Clytemnestra, for there are no relatives left who might seek vengeance. Thus the pollution itself becomes important, acting as a kind of magnetic force for the Furies. It is the duty of the Furies to see that satisfaction is obtained for the killing of Clytemnestra,[29] and, although the extent of this duty is challenged by Apollo, even he accepts the fact that Orestes must undergo some purification. The issue in *Eumenides* is whether or not adequate satisfaction has been obtained; the fact of Orestes' pollution and the necessity for purification are accepted by all as part of the basic requirement of reciprocity in human affairs.[30]

The basic pattern of action in the *Oresteia*, then, is that one act of retribution is counteracted or balanced by another. This pattern is perhaps most emphatically stated by the chorus in *Choephoroi*:

> ἀντὶ μὲν ἐχθρᾶς γλώσσης ἐχθρὰ
> γλῶσσα τελείσθω· τοὐφειλόμενον
> πράσσουσα Δίκη μέγ' ἀυτεῖ·
> ἀντὶ δὲ πληγῆς φονίας φονίαν
> πληγὴν τινέτω. δράσαντι παθεῖν,
> τριγέρων μῦθος τάδε φωνεῖ.

("Let hateful tongue be paid out in return for hateful tongue. *Dikē*, exacting what is owed, cries out loud. Let murderous blow avenge murderous blow. It is for the doer to suffer: thus speaks the thrice-old word," 309–14).[31] It is hardly necessary to list in detail the strong verbal balances within the clauses beginning *anti men* and *anti de* and the parallels between these two clauses, all of which emphasize the content of the message. But it is worth noting that the speaker of this "thrice-old word," the law of reciprocal retribution, is *dikē,* usually translated as "justice." The content of *dikē's* statement, however, indicates that *dikē* here is primarily a force of punishment, retribution, and vengeance. As we shall see, it is this aspect of *dikē* that predominates in most of the *Oresteia.*

We saw in our discussion of Homeric values in chapter I that *dikē*-words generally have two different sets of meanings, those concerned with proper behavior and those concerned with legal behavior, and these remained to some extent separate at least until the beginning of the fifth century, though the legal meanings are far more numerous. This same division can be found in the *Oresteia*, where there are clear instances both of *dikē* (*sc. esti*) meaning "it is proper" (*e.g., Ag.* 260, 811, *Eu.* 277; cf. *dikēn* + genitive = "in the manner of")[32] and also of legal meanings, such as "suit," "trial," "decision" (*e.g., Ag.* 1615, *Ch.* 987, *Eu.* 224). But *dikē* in this second sense is also generalized in earlier poetry and sometimes personified as a larger force overseeing human affairs. We find this "goddess" *Dikē* first in Hesiod, where she represents the process for settling disputes, the rule of law as opposed to violence, *hybris* (*WD* 213–85). *Dikē* in this sense of legal process, law, is also found in some of the poets of the archaic period, most notably Solon. In this general sense *dikē* also at times takes on the meaning "punishment for unlawful behavior" (Solon 13.8 = 1.8D; Theognis 207, 330), and punishment becomes an integral part of the overall process of *dikē*, both as the result of a particular settlement (*dikē*) and in return for violating *dikē*.

This sense of *dikē* is further developed by Heraclitus (perhaps influenced by Anaximander), for whom *dikē* is a cosmic principle of order and balance: if the sun strays from its path, "the Erinyes, handmaidens of *dikē*, will find it out" (fr. 94).[33] It is natural that *dikē* comes to include this sense of balance and order, for the Greek legal process from the beginning was always a means of settling disputes between two parties, and *dikē* in such a dispute could be both the plea or case on either side (one person's *dikē* opposed to another's) and the trial and final settlement. The first explicit statement that *dikē* involves a sense of balance, in fact, is in the context of a trial: in the Homeric *Hymn to Hermes*, Hermes and Apollo take their dispute over the theft of Apollo's cattle to Zeus and plead before him in the presence of the "scales of *dikē*" (*dikēs talanta*, 324).

Dikē then has a wide range of meanings: the sense of what is proper; legal meanings including a person's case, the final settlement (and punishment), and the overall trial; the legal process as a whole; and a larger sense of order and balance that incorporates the necessity for reciprocity or retribution (and hence punishment).[34] These various meanings form a complex matrix, well suited for expressing the manifold concerns of the *Oresteia*, from the general laws of balance and reciprocity to the legal settlement at the end. Thus *dikē* is a crucial concept in the trilogy and a complex one.

A major difference between *dikē* in the *Oresteia* and in the earlier poets, Hesiod, Solon, and Theognis, is that, although Aeschylus at times portrays peaceful and law-abiding behavior as they do, the *Oresteia* is more often concerned with violent, criminal behavior. In such situations it is necessarily the element of punishment and retribution in *dikē* that is stressed, both for avenging individual wrongs and for restoring an overall order. The passage from *Choephoroi* (309–14) quoted above is a good example of this emphasis, for it is clear there that *dikē* is seen primarily as a force for retributive punishment,[35] a sense that predominates in the uses of the word in the trilogy.

It is sometimes thought that this aspect of *dikē* designates an archaic principle of justice ("retributive justice"), represented in the *Oresteia* by the Furies, and that the acquittal of Orestes in *Eumenides* represents the triumph of a more advanced concept of justice determined by law ("deliberative justice"). If we examine the matter carefully, however, we find that no such distinction exists. In fact the principle of retribution or punishment, which is the predominant reference of *dikē*, is maintained by everyone in the trilogy (including Orestes, Apollo, Athena, and the Furies), and the Areopagus is created precisely to ensure the preservation of this *dikē* in the future. It is true that the acquittal of Orestes violates the rule of retribution, but the acquittal is necessary for reasons that have little to do with *dikē* or justice (as we shall see in chapter IV). And in spite of Orestes' acquittal, the Areopagus and the Furies will oversee the operation of *dikē* in the future. Of course, in the peaceful and harmonious society that is created at the end of the trilogy, the peaceful and constructive aspect of *dikē* ("rule of law," "peaceful behavior"), whose operation is facilitated by the Areopagus, will be more important. But this is not a new *dikē*; it is the same *dikē* in a different society, a society at peace rather than at war with itself.[36]

The emphasis on *dikē* as vengeance or punishment begins in *Agamemnon*, where both Agamemnon's taking of Troy and Clytemnestra's and Aegisthus' killing of Agamemnon are associated with *dikē*. The herald, for instance, asks the people to welcome home Agamemnon, "the one who utterly destroyed Troy with the mattock of *dikē*-bearing [*dikēphorou*] Zeus" (525–26). *Dikē* here is usually translated as "justice," but it is clearly the element of punishment and revenge that is being stressed in *dikēphorou*, as it is when Aegisthus praises the light of this *dikē*-bearing day (*Ag.* 1577) and when Electra and the chorus hope for the arrival of a *dikē* bearer or avenger (*dikēphoron, Ch.* 120).[37]

Agamemnon himself in his first words gives thanks to the gods for his safe return and for the punishments or penalties (*dikaiōn*) he has exacted from the city of Priam with their help (*Ag.* 812). Clearly Agamemnon considers his own destruction of Troy to be an act of *dikē* (cf. *antidikos, Ag.* 41), and Clytemnestra seems to support this view when she calls upon *dikē* to lead Agamemnon to his "un-hoped-for" home (911, cf. *dikaiōs*, 913). It is clear, of course, that her words here also have an ironic second sense and refer not only to his vengeance in destroying Troy but also to her vengeance, which she is about to exact by killing him. The double meaning of this statement powerfully conveys the similarity of Agamemnon's and Clytemnestra's actions: they are reciprocal acts of vengeance, and both are considered examples of *dikē*.[38]

This use of *dikē* is only one indication of the poetic identity of Agamemnon's and Clytemnestra's actions, of course. That identity is conveyed by many of the images that dominate the first play. Agamemnon sacrifices Iphigeneia and is in turn

"sacrificed" by Clytemnestra; he throws a "net" over Troy and
has a "net" thrown over him in turn; he is the "lion" who de-
stroys Troy and is in turn destroyed by a "lioness." [39] These
and other poetic images, like the ironic use of *dikē*, contribute
to the sense of identity between Agamemnon's and Clytemnestra's actions, which on the surface are opposed.

Clytemnestra also appeals directly to *dikē* in 1432, calling
it the *dikē* of her daughter, that is, revenge for the killing of
Iphigeneia (cf. *dikaias tektonos*, 1406). And Aegisthus refers
several times to his own *dikē*, which is retribution for the
wrong done to Thyestes by Atreus (1577, 1604, 1607, 1611).
Thus in *Agamemnon* Clytemnestra and Aegisthus appeal to
the same principle of *dikē* as does Agamemnon, and all three
consider their own actions to be manifestations of *dikē*. No
one, moreover, disputes any of these claims of *dikē*. It is particularly notable that the chorus, who side with Agamemnon
and reproach Clytemnestra after his death, never dispute her
claim that she acted with *dikē*. In fact after Agamemnon's
death they apparently mention *dikē* only once, [40] and in that
instance they implicitly support Clytemnestra's claim that her
act was a *dikē*, for they say that *dikē* is sharpening itself for
another deed (1535), [41] and they explicitly accept Agamemnon's death as "divinely sanctioned" (*thesmion*, 1564) according to the rule that the doer suffers. Thus the destruction
of Troy and the killing of Agamemnon are both acts of retribution or *dikē*.

So, too, is the killing of Clytemnestra (and Aegisthus). [42]
Electra, Orestes, and the chorus in *Choephoroi* all refer repeatedly to the necessity for this *dikē* (e.g., 148, 497, 805),
and Agamemnon himself is called on to be an avenger of his
own death, so that "those who killed shall be killed in return
with *dikē*" (144). The fact that *dikē* can support two opposite sides is recognized implicitly by the chorus, who speak of
dikē "changing over" (*to dikaion metabainei*, 308), [43] and

explicitly by Orestes in his famous prediction, *Arēs Arei xymbalei, Dikāi Dika* ("Ares will clash with Ares, *dikē* with *dikē*, 461), which means that the might and vengeance on Clytemnestra's side will be opposed by the might and vengeance on Orestes' side. A clearer statement of the reciprocal and nonintegrated[44] nature of *dikē* could hardly be imagined. And the meaning "retribution," which is the primary sense of *dikē* in the trilogy, is reemphasized by the chorus in the fourth stasimon, when they twice equate *dikē* with *poinē*, "blood vengeance" (*Ch.* 935–36, 946–50). In the second of these passages the chorus call *Dikē* the daughter of Zeus, a genealogy at least as old as Hesiod (*Th.* 902), but she is still Retribution, not a higher, divinely sanctioned, Justice. Descent from Zeus gives *Dikē* additional honor and power, but it does not change her basic nature.

In *Eumenides* we find many uses of *dikē* and other *dikē*-words to refer to technical legal matters, such as the trial or the judges. The prominence of a trial in the play means that the senses of *dikē* as legal process or law and of *dikaios* as lawful or behaving lawfully are more prominent in this play. Indeed *dikē* as legal process is in a sense brought on the stage in the form of the court of the Areopagus.

The Areopagus is of great importance, for it provides a means of peaceful compromise and thus enables Athena by skillful manipulation to achieve a harmonious reconciliation at the end. *Dikē* can contest with *dikē* in court rather than through force, as in earlier plays. But the Areopagus does not represent a new or different *dikē* that secures Orestes' acquittal because of his moral innocence. Rather the *dikē* that the Areopagus upholds is basically the same *dikē* as in the earlier plays and includes a strong element of punishment, though it also includes the sense of lawful and peaceful behavior. Moreover, in the conflict in *Eumenides* it is the Furies who stand firmly on the side of *dikē* in all its various senses ("retribution," "overall order and balance," and "legal process") and who support the Areopagus and its principles,[45] whereas Orestes and Apollo pay lip service to *dikē* at first but in fact rest their case primarily on sexual and political considerations and on the power (not the justice) of Zeus. Athena's crucial vote for acquittal is explicitly said to be based on sexual grounds, and after the verdict Orestes praises the political benefits that will result from the decision, whereas the Furies lament the trampling of the old laws and the absence of *dikē*. The sexual and political aspects of the arguments will be taken up in the next chapter, but the legal aspect of the trial and the role of *dikē* in *Eumenides* must first be examined more closely.

Orestes goes to Athens to obtain a decision from Athena (79–83, 243), confident that the power of Apollo will protect him even in a trial. The Furies pursue him there and make it clear to him that they consider themselves agents of *dikē*, not only in his case, but also in general: "and you shall see, if any mortal errs, dishonoring a god or a guest or his parents, that each such offender shall have things worthy of *dikē* [*i.e.,* punishments]" (*tēs dikēs epaxia*, 269–72). That the Furies are agents of *dikē* is no new idea (for Heraclitus, fr. 94, they are "handmaidens of *Dikē*"); indeed they are mentioned in the first stasimon of *Agamemnon* as punishers of those who prosper without *dikē* (*Ag.* 463–65;[46] cf. *Ag.* 1577–82, *Ch.* 646–52). But the extent of their concern with *dikē* is not revealed until *Eumenides*, and the verses just cited (269–72) are only a preliminary indication of this concern: after Athena has assembled the Areopagus to hear the case, the Furies sing the second stasimon (490–565), which could almost be called a hymn to *dikē*.[47]

The Furies warn of the dire consequences if Orestes' case (*dikē*) wins (490–98): then the people will lament, "Oh *dikē*, oh seats of the Erinyes" (511–12); this will be the fall of the house of *dikē* (515–16); but "I tell you to respect the

altar of *dikē*" (539–40); and so on. Many similarities have
been noticed between the sentiments expressed in this ode and
those expressed by the chorus in *Agamemnon* (compare, *e.g.,*
Eu. 533–37 with *Ag.* 758–66 and *Eu.* 538–42 with *Ag.* 381–
84). These similarities have troubled some critics who believe
that the chorus of elders in *Agamemnon* represent the poet's
most profound and advanced thought, whereas the Furies
represent the primitive system of the past. This difficulty cannot simply be brushed aside with the explanation that in this
ode the Furies "appear to speak less for themselves than as
the poet's persona,"[48] for in fact the Furies' concern for *dikē*
here is completely consistent with their similar concern for it
throughout the play (and trilogy). Furthermore this *dikē* of
the Furies, in its basic sense of an overall system of balance and
retribution operating to redress wrongs and prevent unlawful
gain, is exactly the same as the *dikē* of the elders of Argos.

We should also note that the second stasimon is sung by
the Furies immediately after Athena announces that she is
setting up the Areopagus to hear the case, and the first words
they sing are:

> νῦν καταστροφαὶ νέων
> θεσμίων, εἰ κρατήσει δίκα <τε> καὶ βλάβα
> τοῦδε μητροκτόνου

("Now is the overthrow of new ordinances if the plea and the
wrong of this matricide are victorious," 490–92). Different
interpretations of these words have been proposed, and the
text has been emended in order to avoid the apparent meaning
of this statement, which is that the Furies fear the new Areopagus will not survive if Orestes is acquitted. It is clear, however, that they must mean just that.[49] The Furies have faith
that the Areopagus will convict Orestes, for, if it does not,
men may commit all sorts of wrongs without fear of punishment.

The Areopagus is, in short, an instrument for assisting the Furies in their role of punishing offenders, especially those who spill blood (682). For this reason Apollo does not belong at the trial except as a witness for Orestes (574–80), for he has nothing to do normally with deeds of bloodshed (715); these are the concern of the Furies and the Areopagus. And Athena's instructions to the court for its conduct in the future (681–710) provide additional confirmation of the close tie between the Furies and the Areopagus. Athena outlines to the jurors the need for the Areopagus in Athens and their duties in general, and instructs them to give a straight judgment and to respect their oath (*aidoumenous ton horkon*, 710). Her last words echo the Furies' final charge to the jury (*horkon aideisthe xenoi*, 680),[50] and her account of the need for the Areopagus (especially 696–710) is certainly intended to recall the Furies' plea for *dikē* in the second stasimon. She stresses, as they did, the need for fear of and respect for the laws (698–99; cf. 517–25), and she repeats in almost the same words their earlier plea for a political compromise between anarchy and despotism (*mēt' anarkton bion mēte despotoumenon*, 526–27; *to mēt' anarchon mēte despotoumenon*, 696). These similarities confirm the view that the force of law, which in *Eumenides* is embodied in the Areopagus, is a primary concern of the Furies, and that the Areopagus will protect Athens for the future in the same way as the Furies will (once they have agreed to stay)—by fostering respect for the laws and for the rule of law. The Furies, then, as upholders of the principles of order and punishment, stand firmly with *dikē* and with the Areopagus as supporters of the legal process.

It is true that at first the Furies reject the notion of a trial (260–61); they feel that the case is clearly one of bloodshed, for which, as we have been told (*Ag.* 1019–24, *Ch.* 48, 400–402), there is no remedy. The Furies feel that there is no need for a trial unless Orestes claims that he did not kill Clytemnestra and swears to this, which he will not do. When the Furies point this out to Athena, she advises them that true *dikē* is not necessarily decided simply by an oath (429–32), and so they voluntarily ask her to examine the matter and "render a straight judgment" (433). They are confident that they will win, since they have the law on their side, as evidenced by Orestes' refusal to swear the necessary oath.

This question of oaths in *Eumenides* is a complex one.[51] We know that the swearing of oaths by the litigants themselves and by outside witnesses was an important element in the Greek legal process. One possibility was for the defendant to swear that he had not in fact committed whatever crime he was accused of, in which case, if the plaintiff could produce no witnesses, the defendant went free. Orestes clearly cannot swear this; he admits his deed and accepts his liability for it.[52] The dispute, then, must turn on whether the killing of Clytemnestra was lawful or not, as the killing of Aegisthus, the adulterer, clearly was.[53] This is what Orestes maintains when he asks Athena to decide whether his act was lawful (*dikaiōs*) or not (468; cf. 610–11), and he thus rejects the demand that he swear an oath that he did not kill Clytemnestra. What is being disputed (ostensibly) is a point of law, not the facts, and thus the Furies drop their demand that Orestes swear an oath. But they are also concerned with the oath sworn by the members of the jury of the Areopagus, which Athena bids them to respect (483; cf. 486, 710), and in their last words to the court they repeat this appeal to the jurors to respect their oath (680).[54] Thus, the Furies, as supporters of the legal process, demonstrate their respect for oaths in general, and insist on respect for the jurors' oath in particular.

On the other side, Apollo twice scorns the value of oaths. The first instance occurs when he is arguing that the marriage bond is supremely important, as the marriage of Zeus and Hera testifies, "for the bed duly allotted to a man and a woman, when protected by *dikē*, is greater than an oath" (217–18). Although it is unclear precisely how Apollo thinks marriage is greater than an oath, the effect of his words is certainly to depreciate the value of oaths. The second case (614–21) is clearer: having asserted without argument that Orestes acted lawfully, Apollo claims always to speak the truth, since his oracle derives from Zeus. Apollo speaks what Zeus bids him, and the jury should agree with the counsel of Zeus, "for the oath is not stronger than Zeus" (621). The oath here can only be the jurors' oath to judge a straight *dikē*, and Apollo is telling them that his (and Orestes') case (*to dikaion touto*, 619) is so powerful, because it is backed by Zeus, that their oath cannot prevail against it. Apollo's feelings about the legal process are clear. Orestes submits to a trial, backed by Apollo's assurance that he will win, and Apollo intends to win this case even if it means violating the legal process. He has the support of Zeus and thus does not need (and does not waste much time with) legal arguments.

Orestes has in fact no case from a legal point of view. There is no legal provision for the killing of someone merely as an act of revenge,[55] and thus the killing of Agamemnon and the killing of Clytemnestra are both unlawful acts of revenge (though each is a *dikē*). If she deserved to die then so does Orestes, and if Orestes deserves to live then so did she. In the end the only difference Apollo's arguments find between the two killings is that one victim was a man (husband) and the other a woman (mother). Modern readers may perhaps assume the superiority of Apollo's/Orestes' case, but this is in part because they assume Orestes' innocence even before *Eumenides* begins.[56] To us, an innocent mind may compensate for polluted hands, but this was not so to the Greeks, who (at this time) did not separate these two aspects as sharply as we do. Orestes does argue that the killing was lawful because

Clytemnestra was herself polluted (600), but this legal argument cuts both ways and is quickly countered by the Furies. To us, the command of a god is generally understood as a moral imperative, which would thus absolve Orestes of guilt; to the Greeks, a god's command should be obeyed because the god is powerful and one will come to more harm if one does not obey. It is in this sense that Pylades' famous words, "count all men your enemies rather than the gods" (*Ch.* 902), would have been understood: with the gods on your side you will prosper, as Orestes does in fact prosper with the help of Apollo. And, of course, Apollo is supported by the power of Zeus. The situation, then, is one in which Orestes is guilty from the point of view of human law but acquitted by the power of the gods (in particular Zeus), and this seems to be precisely the result of the jury's verdict.

I have argued elsewhere[57] that all the evidence supports the view that the number of human jurors in the trial is odd (probably eleven) and that Athena's vote when added to the others causes a tie vote, which frees Orestes by the rule that a tie vote means acquittal. I will not repeat the arguments here, but it is worth noting that those who feel otherwise (for the most part these are English-speaking scholars) seem to be swayed more by a preconceived notion that it works out better if the human jurors produce a tie that is then broken by Athena's vote.[58] If we accept the clear implication of the text, we must conclude that the human jurors favor conviction (by one vote), and Athena casts the single divine vote for acquittal thereby reversing the human decision. Athena will compensate for this later by restoring the honor of the Furies, but for the moment she has achieved the acquittal of Orestes and thus has obtained the valuable political alliance he offers.

This overall view of the trial, moreover, is confirmed by the reactions of the two sides to the verdict. Orestes does not praise the justice of the verdict and salute the triumph of a new justice as one might expect if his acquittal were a victory for justice. Rather his speech (754–77) is almost entirely political: he thanks the gods (not the court) for restoring him to his homeland and reaffirms his pledge of an eternal alliance with Athens. The only reason he gives for his acquittal is that Zeus saved him because of a sense of respect and shame at his father's death (*patrōion aidestheis moron*, 760).[59] There is not a word about the court, the legal process, or justice. The Furies, however, in their initial outrage at the violation of the laws (778–79, 808–9) appeal directly to *dikē* (*ō Dika Dika*, 785, 815), which they feel has been violated. Athena tries to calm them by assuring them that the judgment was a tie vote (*isopsēphos dikē*, 795), not a victory, and by pointing out that the power of the testimony of Apollo and through him of Zeus was enough to carry the decision (797–99). But she also promises them a lawful seat in a law-abiding land (*pandikōs*, 804; *endikou*, 805), implying that in spite of the verdict in this case, *dikē* will prevail in the future. And she confirms the importance of the Furies in maintaining *dikē*, when she speaks later of the great profit the citizens will receive from the "fearful faces": if they honor the Furies, there will be straight *dikē* (*orthodikaion*, 994; cf. 312) in the land and the polis.

Throughout *Eumenides*, then, the Furies are the upholders of *dikē*, the force of law, order, retribution, and punishment. They plead for *dikē*, they appeal to the members of the Areopagus to respect their oath, they uphold the same values as the Areopagus, they are supported by the majority of human jurors, and they are granted a major role in preserving *dikē* in Athens in the future. Orestes and Apollo, on the other hand, merely state that the killing of Clytemnestra was *dikaios*; they do not offer legal arguments, but simply point to the assurances of Zeus and Apollo; Apollo openly directs the jurors to heed Zeus rather than their oath; and Orestes makes no mention of *dikē* as a factor in his acquittal. The contrast between the two sides is abundantly clear.

Thus *dikē* in all its senses is a keynote of the trilogy and is an important component of the basic ethical pattern of balance and retribution, one act followed by another similar but opposed act, seemingly without end. The process is bound to be seen as a never-ending rhythm, for as each act is answered by a new act, the new act must in turn be answered by another new act. Indeed the feeling that this pattern is unending, that there is no escape or "cure" (the most common metaphor), is often expressed (*e.g., Ag.* 69–71, 1169–71). The impossibility of a cure is especially certain in cases of bloodshed; as Apollo observes, fetters can be loosed, but the blood of a dead man once spilled can never be restored (*Eu.* 645–48; cf., *e.g., Ag.* 1019–24,[60] *Ch.* 48).

In spite of this general conviction, each character hopes that his or her own act will somehow end the chain of bloodshed and will not in turn be avenged. Agamemnon, on his return, clearly feels that his major troubles are over and says he will now cure whatever remains of the disease (848–50). After Agamemnon's death the chorus have a long dispute with Clytemnestra, which ends finally in a stalemate ("reproach has now met with reproach; the matter is hard to decide," 1560–61). They then admit that his death was part of the valid law that the doer suffers (1562–64), and in view of this they wonder "who can expel the seed of the curse from the house? The family is glued to destruction" (1565–66). With these words the chorus accept the process of action and reaction as inevitable and unending. But, although Clytemnestra in reply accepts the truth of their view, she proposes that she herself make a pact with the *daimōn* of the family that there be no more bloodshed, and she is even willing to give up most of her possessions to bring about such an end (1567–76). Clytemnestra's willingness to compromise (now that she has

achieved her purpose), together with the chorus' neutral attitude in 1560–66, seems to suggest the possibility of a reconciliation between the two. Any such possibility is shattered,
however, by the entrance of Aegisthus (1577), who exults
in his victory and is little concerned with what the future may
bring, now that he has achieved his own personal *dikē*.[61] So
Agamemnon ends in a shouting match. The final reminder of
the existence of Orestes (1646–48) confirms the audience's
suspicion that the cycle of vengeance will continue.

The parodos of *Choephoroi* makes it clear that the major
theme of that play will be retribution for bloodshed (48, 66–
69), since bloodshed is as irrevocable as the loss of virginity
(70–74). But again, after vengeance does come, there is a
brief suggestion that this may prove the end of the troubles
for the house. "Rise up, oh house," sing the chorus as Orestes
kills his mother (963); "I see the light" (961 and perhaps
972); "the dwellers in the house [*sc.* the Erinyes?] will be
cast out" (971).[62] After this brief expression of hope, however, the chorus revert to cries of woe and lamentation. Orestes
answers them, "I know not where it will end" (1021), and
as the Furies begin to torment him, we see that the cycle of
retribution is continuing: "Where will it find fulfillment,
where will it leave off and be put to rest, the force of this
atē?" (1075–76). Orestes' killing, like all the other killings,
requires retribution, which the Furies will provide by torment-
ing him until his final acquittal.

I examine some of the reasons for this acquittal in the next
chapter, but I want to note here a mythological parallel to
Orestes' acquittal. The chorus in the third stasimon of *Agamemnon* sing that "once the black blood of a man is shed on
the ground in death, who could call it back by charms?"
(1019–21), and they cite as evidence for this rule the story
of Asclepius, who brought Hippolytus back from death and
was then killed by Zeus as punishment (1022–24).[63] In

Eumenides Apollo is caught in a contradiction on this matter of retribution for bloodshed, for he acknowledges the necessity for Clytemnestra's death as retribution but not Orestes'. Thus, by saving Orestes from death, Apollo is violating a fixed law. This is not the first time he has done so. We are reminded by the Furies that Apollo once persuaded the Fates to let Admetus live beyond his due, thereby "making mortals immortal" (*Eu.* 723–24). This suggests that Apollo, having cheated death once, is perhaps trying to do so again.[64]

Until the end of the trilogy, then, this cycle of retribution seems endless, and every hope for an end is quickly proved false. There is, however, another sort of hope that recurs throughout the trilogy and is often fulfilled, if only to give rise to new fears: the hope of knowledge and understanding. In the very first lines of *Agamemnon* the watchman is looking for a relief from toils that will come from the messenger-beacon (*euangelou...pyros*, 21), and the good news of Troy's capture does indeed arrive to relieve the watchman's ignorance. But the joy brought by this bit of knowledge almost immediately gives way to a new fear, a new uncertainty concerning the future of the house, whose troubles the watchman refuses to discuss (36–37). Similarly the chorus' uncertainty about the fate of the expedition to Troy is eventually dispelled first by Clytemnestra and then finally by the herald, but for them, too, this knowledge only gives rise to new fears concerning the safety of Agamemnon on his return. And when they finally learn of Agamemnon's death inside the house, they are faced with a new set of uncertainties and a new hope for the future, which is not fulfilled until the next play.

These are all specific and rather minor examples of learning, and the knowledge sought throughout the first two plays by the chorus and others is a limited one, a factual knowledge of events to relieve a specific anxiety. Another sort of learning is mentioned, however, in *Agamemnon*: learning one's lesson through punishment. The Greek for this is *pathei mathos*, a phrase commonly translated "wisdom through suffering" and traditionally invested with wide-reaching implications. A detailed examination of *pathei mathos* in the *Oresteia*, however (see Appendix A), reveals that the primary reference of the phrase, which occurs only twice in the trilogy (*Ag.* 177, 250–51), is to the chorus' hope that Troy will learn its lesson by being punished. The only other allusions to this sort of learning come at the end of *Agamemnon* (1425, 1619–20, 1649), where both Clytemnestra and Aegisthus threaten to teach the chorus a lesson, namely to obey. Thus, the lessons learned through punishment are specific and limited ones.

Both of these limited sorts of knowledge, learning of an event and learning one's lesson, are found in the first two plays, but no true or lasting knowledge is gained, since learning always comes after the fact and thus concerns past events. The chorus of elders have knowledge of the past, which gives them authority to speak with persuasion (*Ag.* 104–6), but they are unable to know anything of the future (251–52), as is made abundantly clear in their responses to Cassandra, where they easily understand her references to past events but resist any information about the future.[65] Clytemnestra has arranged to receive early news of Troy's fall and uses this knowledge to prepare Agamemnon's death, but she does not have the ability to foresee Orestes' return and thus is killed in return. Cassandra, who does have knowledge of her own fate and Agamemnon's, has been rendered powerless by Apollo, the same god who gave her this prophetic ability.[66]

In *Eumenides*, however, several of the figures possess a more permanent knowledge, which produces real power and may more truly be called wisdom. Apollo has prophetic knowledge, ultimately derived from Zeus (*e.g.*, *Eu.* 17–19), which unlike Cassandra's gives him real power (*Eu.* 614–21; cf. *Ch.* 558–59). Indeed Apollo's prophetic knowledge is one of his chief arguments to the jury: after he asserts that Orestes killed his mother lawfully, he adds, "being a prophet I will not lie" (615), an apparently successful argument (cf. 797–99). The Furies are said to be wiser than Athena in respect of their greater age (848–49), and once they decide to accept Athena's offer of reconciliation, they prophesy (922) the good they will bring to Athens. Athena, too, is wise, she reminds them (850; cf. 431). She teaches her ordinances both to the Areopagus and to the whole city (571–73), and most important she at last persuades the Furies to accept their place of honor in the city. True, she mentions that she knows where the keys to Zeus' lightning bolt are kept (827–28), but it is certainly the force of her persuasion (*peithō*, 885, 970) more than the threat of punishment that convinces them. And finally the citizens of Athens will "show discretion in time" (*sōphronountes en chronōi*, 1000), thereby demonstrating the positive aspect (discipline, moderation) of a virtue whose negative side (obedience) has hitherto been stressed (*Ag.* 1425, 1620; cf. *sōphronein hypo stenei, Eu.* 521).

Thus the limited and ineffectual knowledge of the first two plays is replaced by a broader and more powerful wisdom in the third. This wisdom results in a reconciliation of forces that have hitherto been in conflict and enables the Athenians to find an end to the cycle of action and retributive reaction. This earlier cycle of each new knowledge leading to a new anxiety and of each act of retribution leading to another finally ends with a lasting stability grounded in true wisdom. *Dikē* still operates at the end, of course, but as law and order (cf. *polin orthodikaion, Eu.* 993–94) rather than punishment, though the fear of punishment will remain as a deterrent. The Areopagus will remain to watch over the laws[67] and preserve fear (690–702), and it will continue to provide a forum for peaceful legal disputes (under the watch of *dikē*), which will replace the bloody strife of the past.[68] Thus the establishment of the Areopagus and the reconciliation of the Furies do not introduce a new kind of justice or a new stage in the development of society,[69] but rather ensure that the positive aspects of the earlier system will prevail. "The doer suffers" is still the law, but now the Furies will bring good to the land and will obtain good in return (*eu drōsan, eu paschousan,* 868).

These are the same forces that existed at the beginning of the trilogy, but, because society has at last achieved an internal reconciliation, the forces that were harmful before are now beneficial for all. This is true not just of *dikē* but of many other factors as well. Two of these, war and wealth, bring to mind *Persae,* where the process is the reverse of that in the *Oresteia.* There we saw that a moderate amount of wealth and limited war were beneficial in the past, but later, when carried to excess under Xerxes, they brought disaster to Persia. In the *Oresteia,* however, war is for the most part evil at the beginning. It does bring Agamemnon victory over Troy, but that victory is short-lived and in a sense causes his defeat. Both the chorus (*Ag.* 408–55) and Clytemnestra (320–47, 861–85) stress the negative aspects of war. After the final compromise, however, Athena predicts that war will be beneficial to all the citizens, and she specifically calls for foreign, not civil, war (*Eu.* 861–66).[70] Closely related to this is a similar change in *eris,* which was the "bloody strife" of the Trojan War (*Ag.* 1460–61, *Ch.* 474), but becomes the beneficial "striving for good things" (*agathōn eris, Eu.* 974–75) after the reconciliation.[71]

The second factor, wealth, undergoes a similar transformation. In *Agamemnon* it is clear (in spite of textual uncertainties) that excessive wealth is spoken of as evil and is directly connected with lawlessness (377–84, 776–80). "The house does not know poverty" (*Ag.* 962) is Clytemnestra's sinister boast, and one of Orestes' stated motives for his matricide is his poverty (*Ch.* 301). With the reconciliation at the end of the trilogy, however, Athens can expect to enjoy the benefits of wealth, since the Furies predict that the citizens will rejoice "in a proper apportionment of wealth" (*en aisimiaisi ploutou, Eu.* 996).

A number of other factors are similarly transformed at the end of the trilogy. Zeitlin has discussed at length what she calls "the motif of corrupted sacrifice"—corrupted because during most of the trilogy the language of sacrifice is applied to the killing of humans.[72] After the Furies are persuaded to accept a position of honor in the city, however, normal and beneficial sacrifices are predicted as part of their future honors (*Eu.* 835; cf. 1007, 1037). The force of *erōs*, which is thoroughly evil in the first two plays (*Ag.* 341, 743, 1478; *Ch.* 597, 600), is at the end directed toward the achievement of glory (*eukleias erōs, Eu.* 865), which will benefit Athens in foreign wars.

Perhaps most important is persuasion (*peithō*), which, as we saw, Athena uses to reconcile the Furies. In the first stasimon of *Agamemnon* (385–86) the chorus sing of the destructive power of *peithō*, the daughter of *atē* ("delusion"), and, although they add a specific reference to Paris, their words apply to many other figures as well: to Agamemnon, who cannot disobey Artemis (*Ag.* 206); to Clytemnestra, persuaded by the beacon fire (*Ag.* 87, 591);[73] and to Orestes, who trusts in the oracles and his own strength (*Ch.* 237, 297; *Eu.* 84). Those who can persuade have power, but it is the power to do harm: Clytemnestra uses persuasion to kill Agamemnon (*Ag.* 943), and Orestes uses "crafty" persuasion (*peithō dolian*) to kill her in return (*Ch.* 726; cf. 781). Only Athena at the end shows how to use *peithō* constructively for compromise (*Eu.* 885, 970; cf. 794).

Finally a similar transformation is represented on stage when the Furies change from spirits of evil and destruction, which they are during most of *Eumenides* (and even from the beginning of the trilogy; cf. *Ag.* 59), into beneficent spirits of fertility at the end. In neither of the first two plays is there any such change. Clytemnestra dominates the dramatic action in *Agamemnon*, as does Orestes in *Choephoroi*: both figures are on stage during most of their plays, leaving briefly to kill their enemies. But, although both plays contain considerably more dramatic action than, say, *Prometheus*, these main figures do not change. Many aspects of Clytemnestra are revealed during *Agamemnon*, but she is essentially the same at the beginning and the end of that play, and indeed in the next two plays as well. The same is true of Orestes.

The first two plays thus portray a situation in which people do not change but either conquer their adversaries or are themselves overcome and eliminated. *Eumenides*, however, presents an alternative: change and reconciliation. The Furies, hideous at first, don the crimson robes of metics for the final procession and are addressed by their new name, Eumenides ("Kindly Ones").[74] This transformation is Athena's last and most important act, and, as Aeschylus' audience watched the final procession of Athenian citizens escort the Eumenides from the stage to their new place of honor in the city, they would be watching a dramatic confirmation of the power of their city's guardian deity to transform the bitter internal feuds of the past into the fertile harmony of the future.

IV

Sexual and Political Conflict in the Oresteia

THE CONFLICT that is finally resolved at the end of the *Oresteia* has many aspects to it, but two that best illustrate the constructive use of opposed forces at the end of *Eumenides* are the sexual and political aspects. Thus an examination of sexual conflict and political conflict in the trilogy will serve to support and elaborate the conclusions of the preceding chapter. In singling out only two aspects of the conflict for consideration, I am aware that I distort the total effect of the play to some extent. All great drama succeeds on several different levels at the same time; certainly in the *Oresteia* it is the simultaneous evocation of so many different aspects of the action that helps make the trilogy such a magnificent work of art. My intention in examining only two of these aspects of the basic conflict is not to detract from the importance of other aspects but rather to add to our understanding of these important themes and thereby increase our appreciation of the whole.

That there is sexual conflict in some sense in the *Oresteia*

is obvious, since the basic pattern of action and retributive reaction (*drasanti pathein*) unfolds in the trilogy as an alternation of male and female agents: Agamemnon, Clytemnestra,
Orestes, and the Furies. This fact in itself might not be very
significant, but, as we shall see, sexual conflict in the form of
debate over male and female values occurs throughout the
trilogy.[1] Particularly notable are the concluding arguments
of Apollo in *Eumenides* (625–28 and especially 657–66)
and the reasons given by Athena for favoring Orestes' case
(736–40), which are based almost entirely on sexual considerations, namely that the male is superior to the female.
These arguments of Apollo and Athena strike most critics as
quite irrelevant to the specific question of Orestes' guilt or to
the larger question of justice which is allegedly being decided
by the Areopagus. Various more or less implausible attempts
have been made to account for the arguments by those critics
who do not simply ignore the problem.[2] But these sexual arguments form the climax of the debate before the court. This is
the one argument by Apollo that the Furies cannot answer,
and it is the only reason Athena gives for her decisive vote for
acquittal. It seems hard to believe that at one of the most important moments of the trilogy Aeschylus would introduce a
completely irrelevant argument and then let the most crucial
decision in the trilogy be based on it.

In order to understand the full significance of this final
argument for male superiority, we must examine all instances
of and references to sexual conflict in the *Oresteia*. As we shall
see, these are numerous. The first mention of Zeus' sending
the Atreidae to Troy, for instance, describes the woes that will
come to both the Greeks and the Trojans "for the sake of a
woman of many men" (*polyanoros amphi gynaikos*, 62).
Throughout *Agamemnon* we are repeatedly reminded that
the war was fought for or on account of a woman (225–26,
402, 448, 823, 1453).[3] Menelaus has lost his wife, and the

Greeks have lost Helen, the ideal of feminine beauty; without her, all Aphrodite is gone (419).[4] But in order to regain Helen and restore Menelaus' marriage they must sacrifice another woman, Iphigeneia, a daughter and innocent virgin, qualities that are emphasized in the poignant description of the scene at the altar (228–47). In short, Agamemnon's decision is to sacrifice one woman, his daughter, in order to regain another woman, Helen.[5]

Before considering the reasons for and the significance of this decision in terms of sexual conflict, it will be helpful to pause briefly and consider the position and relative importance of women in Athens at this time. The evidence is not as abundant as we might wish, yet it is sufficient for us to see that the lives of free-born Athenian women in the fifth century were highly restricted and that, except for a few foreign residents (most notably Aspasia), women had no part in the glory of Greece's "golden age." To borrow a phrase from what is still the best study of the condition of women in Western society, de Beauvoir's *The Second Sex*,[6] we can say that the Greeks certainly saw their women as "the Other," whether praising them, as Pericles does (Thucydides II.45.2), for their obscurity or condemning them for a multitude of faults, as Hippolytus and others do.[7] The Athenian upper-class woman was expected to lead a private life, almost exclusively within her family; except for participation in a few festivals, any public activity by her would likely be condemned.

The basic family unit for the Greeks was the extended household, or *oikos*.[8] All of the *oikos*—women, children, slaves, and other property—was thought of as belonging to the head, or *kyrios*, of the *oikos*. When a woman was married, she was merely transferred from the tutelage of one *kyrios* (normally her father) to another (her husband). The ultimate purpose of marriage was to beget male heirs who would preserve and continue the *oikos* (family and property). Wom-

en were primarily valued in terms of their ability to contribute
to this end. Property was passed down to male heirs, and only
in the absence of a male heir did a daughter become a significant factor in inheritance. Elaborate laws were developed to
provide for the marriage of these "heiresses" to male relatives.[9]
A woman's main functions thus were to bear and raise young
children and to tend to other domestic duties; other activities,
at least for upper-class women, were severely limited. There
was a strong prohibition against adultery, which was considered a violation of the purity of the husband's *oikos*.[10] Of
course there was no such prohibition for men, and prostitutes,
mistresses, and the like were available to them. Clearly the
oikos was a male-dominated institution, existing through and
for its male *kyrios*. A woman's role was to serve the needs of
her *kyrios*; in turn she was protected by him, though the protection might well take the form of further restriction.

Closely related to this family structure was the wide separation between men's and women's lives, which coincided with
the general separation between the public and the domestic
spheres in fifth-century Athens.[11] Athenian men were expected
to participate in public life and normally were out of the
house for most of the day; their wives, on the other hand,
normally stayed at home in the company of female relatives
and slaves.[12] Women probably did attend the dramatic pro-
ductions, which took place during state festivals,[13] but they
did not normally join their husbands in entertaining or being entertained by friends. Any extrafamilial social life was
thus a concern of men only; in particular, *xenia* ("guest-
friendship") was created by and for men; women did not
participate.[14]

Although we have no evidence directly from the women
themselves, we can assume that such a separation of men's
and women's lives led to their having separate concerns and
values (as they still do in many respects today). Women

would be more concerned with home and family and would feel especially close ties to their children, whereas men would be more concerned with and place higher value on public achievement and glory, and would value their children primarily as heirs. Certainly war was a male concern (cf. *Iliad* 6.490–93) and military glory a male value. We cannot say whether women had yet begun to challenge this value, as Medea does when she states (*Medea* 250–51) that she would rather face battle three times than childbirth once, or as the women in *Lysistrata* do when they take control of the normally male administration of the cities. But the hardships that war caused the "single-yoked" women at home are (as we have seen) already suggested in *Persae* and are described at length by Clytemnestra (*Ag.* 855–94).

We find these specifically male or female concerns and values in the *Oresteia* (and in many other Greek dramas). For the most part male and female values are consistently adhered to by members of that sex and thus can be said to form two overall perspectives, one male and the other female. Not every issue, of course, can be divided along these lines, and not every sexual concern fits neatly into such a division; nonetheless, I think an examination of the whole trilogy in terms of sexual conflict will bring out an important aspect of the dramatic action.

In these terms it is clear that, although Agamemnon's decision to kill his daughter is a difficult one (*Ag.* 206–11), it is the only course of action consistent with his role as representative of a strongly male point of view. From the beginning Agamemnon is presented as a king (42–44) and especially as a military leader (45–47) "crying war" (48), who will wage a war harmful to both Greeks and Trojans (63–67) for the sake of a woman (62). The rape of Helen by Paris was a violation of the male institution of *xenia*, presided over by Zeus Xenios, and is a direct violation of the rights of the husband, Menelaus, whose *oikos* is thereby damaged.[15] Helen has in fact been stolen from the Atreidae (399–402), and as property she must be recovered. Not only must Agamemnon recover his lost property, but he and the army must also assess double damages (537), plundering and destroying Troy as punishment for the theft (cf., *e.g.*, 128–29).[16]

The killing of Iphigeneia, on the other hand, which is recognized to be a crime and a religious pollution (*miainōn*, 209), is a less important concern than the male military imperative to regain Helen and punish Troy. Hence Agamemnon decides not to be a deserter (*liponaus*, 212).[17] In his basically male and militaristic set of values, the killing of his daughter is justified by the need to punish a more grievous crime against that set of values. This is not to say that the sacrifice is justified absolutely or ultimately; certainly in the opposing set of female values, represented most strongly by Clytemnestra, it clearly is not justified. Aeschylus makes clear the impiety and brutality of the act, but he also shows how someone like Agamemnon, who in certain respects does fit Fraenkel's description of "a noble gentleman," could be induced through an unusual set of circumstances to commit a crime that under normal conditions would be unthinkable.[18] We cannot necessarily say that the poet is condemning Agamemnon's male set of values, for these may be desirable in many ways. But he does show us that there is a danger, if these values are carried too far, that they will serve to justify actions that are clearly undesirable.

The opposing female perspective in *Agamemnon* is clearly represented principally by Clytemnestra, who is no ordinary woman, as indicated by the first reference in the play to the rule of her "woman's man-counseling expectant heart" (11). We must bear in mind, however, that these and other references to Clytemnestra's masculinity are made by the male characters in the play, who consider it abnormal for any woman to display qualities that they (and many modern critics) feel belong more properly to men.[19] And there is no doubt that Clytemnestra is more powerful and more intelligent than any of the men in the play. She demonstrates her power most convincingly in the brief dispute with Agamemnon about his walking on the tapestries (931–43), where she gains a clear victory over him in spite of the fact that (as he points out) "it is not a woman's part to desire battle" (940; cf. 1236–37).[20] And her intelligence is brought out most clearly in her exchanges with the chorus of Argive old men, who make several scornful remarks about her feminine intelligence (*e.g.*, 479–87) but are proved wrong, as she later points out (590–92). Both her power and her intelligence are further emphasized by contrast with those of Aegisthus.

But, in spite of Clytemnestra's success in playing a role traditionally considered male, she represents the female point of view and certain clearly female values. During the first few hundred lines she is attending to sacrifices,[21] which are a woman's concern (cf. *Ag.* 594–96). She then addresses the chorus with two long speeches, the second of which describes the situation at Troy on the night of the Argive victory, a topic considered by the chorus to be more appropriate to a man (351). But Clytemnestra's account is significantly different from what a man's would be. She begins with only a simple statement of the victory (320) and then describes the woes of the Trojan survivors, who are now slaves (326–29),[22] before mentioning the rather limited joys of the victors (330–37). She follows this with a strong warning that they must behave properly and not seek to destroy what they should not or they will have trouble when they return (338–47). This view of the situation, with its concern for and understanding of the plight of the defeated survivors and its very limited sense of joy at the victory, can properly be called female, as Clytemnestra indicates by pointing out that it is the account of a woman (*gynai-*

kos ex emou klyeis, 348). This is especially clear in contrast
to the herald's speeches announcing the victory (503–37,
551–82), for he mentions the suffering of the army (555–
71) only in order to emphasize by contrast the joy of the
victory. This joy is virtually unrestrained, and even the destruction of holy places at Troy is for him a matter for rejoic-
ing rather than a cause for concern (527).[23]

A more important concern for Clytemnestra is the trouble
the departure of the expedition created for those who remained
home in Argos. These woes are mentioned by the chorus
(429–36)[24] and then described at length by Clytemnestra in
her speech to Agamemnon (855–94). Her list of the troubles
she had to endure as a woman left alone at home by her husband is often disregarded or dismissed as a clever piece of deceit, but, although the end of her speech is certainly deceitful
and is admitted to be so later (1372–73), the description of
her suffering contains probable truths[25] and is never denied
or challenged. Just as the absence of the army has been a general burden on the city ("instead of men the houses receive
only urns with ashes," 434–36), so Agamemnon's absence
has been a particular hardship for Clytemnestra. Thus Agamemnon wrongs Clytemnestra as a mother by killing Iphigeneia, and he wrongs her as a wife by leaving her alone at
home to suffer in his absence for ten years. His absence is an
offense against marriage from a woman's point of view, committed in order to reaffirm marriage from a man's point of
view.[26]

It is thus specifically as a woman that Clytemnestra is
wronged, and in the pattern of reciprocity that dominates the
trilogy this wrong must be redressed. The crime of man against
woman is balanced by that of woman against man, the deceitful (and thus womanly) killing of Agamemnon, husband,
ruler, and leader of the military forces. The male side, originally wronged by the rape of Helen, went to an extreme of

male military domination in order to avenge this wrong; now the balance has swung back to the other extreme, female domination of the male. The punishment of Troy could only be achieved at the expense of the female forces in Argos (represented specifically by Iphigeneia). Now these female forces gain such total domination that all males, Agamemnon, Aegisthus, and the chorus, are subordinated to Clytemnestra's power.

The domination of the female in *Agamemnon* is also represented, though to a lesser extent, by Cassandra, whose intellectual power clearly exceeds that of the chorus, though her power to affect her situation is no greater than theirs. But her knowledge and her powerlessness are important in this context because they are expressly related to her sex: she obtained her prophetic power, we are told, by agreeing to submit sexually to Apollo,[27] but by later refusing to honor her agreement she lost the real power of prophecy, the power to move someone else to action (1202–12). She is thus in an intermediate position; she stands neither with Clytemnestra nor with Agamemnon. Just as she was powerless to prevent the triumph of the latter at Troy, so she is now powerless to prevent the triumph of Clytemnestra, and she herself will be sacrificed in return for the earlier sacrifice of Iphigeneia (1277–78).[28] But the knowledge that Cassandra acquired by almost yielding her virginity allows her to dominate the chorus with her vision, even if she cannot move them to action.

It is in Cassandra's descriptions and prophecies of the crimes in the house that we hear for the first time of the earlier pair of crimes, those of Thyestes and Atreus, and these too fit into the pattern of sexual conflict. The first crime was Thyestes' adultery with his brother's wife (1192–93), and the retribution for this was Atreus' killing of Thyestes' children, whom he served up to Thyestes at a banquet (1217–22).[29] The adultery is, of course, an offense against the male-dominated *oikos*, just as the theft of Helen is. The sacrilege of causing

Thyestes to eat his children in return is an offense against the family and its religious taboos, a violation of female values, just as the sacrifice of Iphigeneia is. Thus both pairs of actions and retributive reactions (Iphigeneia's sacrifice being part of the punitive destruction of Troy) represent the same pattern of sexual conflict: an offense against male domination is followed by an excessive retributive act of masculine power that violates feminine values. The two masculine crimes, Agamemnon's war against Troy and sacrifice of his daughter and Atreus' killing and serving up of Thyestes' children, are in turn followed by the exaggerated dominance of female forces, the killing of Agamemnon by both Clytemnestra and the womanly Aegisthus.

The dispute between Clytemnestra and the chorus after the murder continues to develop this sexual theme. When she rejoices at the deed, the chorus rebuke her for exulting over her husband (1400), which she sees as a criticism of her specifically as a woman (1401; cf. 483–87, 592 ff.). She defends herself as fearless (1402) and in turn accuses the chorus of doing nothing about the sacrifice of Iphigeneia, "the dearest product of my labor" (1414–18).[30] She then criticizes Agamemnon's sexual promiscuity (1438–39) in contrast to Aegisthus' faithfulness and loyalty (1436–37). The chorus in turn lament that Agamemnon, who suffered much "on account of a woman" (Helen), died "at the hands of a woman" (1453–54), another indication of the connected sexual aspect of the action. They continue, moreover, with a denunciation of Helen: from their point of view she was solely responsible for the war, and although Clytemnestra rightly reminds them that the blame is not Helen's alone (1464–67),[31] they continue to blame both sisters for the *daimōn* that has settled on the house (1468–71).

One can see from these remarks that the audience is con-

tinually reminded of the sexual conflict that underlies Agamemnon's murder. This aspect is further brought out in the
numerous references here and in the other two plays to the
shameful and ignoble manner of his death (*e.g.*, *Ag.* 1516–
20). Clytemnestra used deceit, which is characteristic of wom-
en (as Aegisthus points out, 1636). This would be ignoble in
any case, but it is especially disgraceful in the killing of a
military man, who ought to die in battle.[32] Agamemnon has
already been presented as a military leader (cf. 1227, 1627),
and throughout the next two plays he will be remembered as
commander of the expedition. For such a man to die at the
hands of a woman and in a womanly manner is the ultimate
disgrace for the male forces in the trilogy.

Not surprisingly the cycle of action and reaction continues,
and the female dominance in *Agamemnon* is balanced by an
even stronger male dominance in *Choephoroi*.[33] In this play
all women are subordinate to men: the very title of the play,
Libation Bearers, indicates a domestic function of women,
and the chorus of these bearers are not only women but also
slaves, presumably captured in war and taken from their
fathers' homes (76–77). They strongly oppose Clytemnestra's rule over the house; they call her a "godless woman"
(*dystheos gynē*, 46, 525), and they support Orestes' return as
the proper (male) master of the house. Moreover, they sing
one of the most vehemently antifeminine odes in Greek tragedy (585–651), in which they relate the stories of three well-
known crimes committed by women (Althaea, Scylla, and the
women of Lemnos), all of which are attributed to the "unlov-
ing love that overpowers women" (600). These stories are
obviously introduced as mythological parallels to the crime of
Clytemnestra, which is condemned in 623–28 and which leads
the chorus to reflect, "I honor the home and hearth not fired
[by passion] and the woman's unventuresome temper" (629–

30).[34] Thus the chorus of *Choephoroi*, both by their position as slaves and by their utterances, support the almost total male dominance in the play.

The subordination of Electra to Orestes is another element in this strong male dominance in *Choephoroi*. Electra, as a woman, is powerless and can only sacrifice and pray for her brother to return. The relation between these two presents an obvious reversal of the relation between Clytemnestra and Aegisthus in *Agamemnon*. Indeed even Clytemnestra's domination of Aegisthus is reversed (to some extent at least) in *Choephoroi*, for in this play she presents herself as subordinate to Aegisthus. In her first words she says that she can offer the visitors household comforts (the obvious irony of her reference to "hot baths" is the poet's, not hers), but if their business requires further counsel, then it is a matter for men (668–73; cf. 734–37). Her quick recognition of Orestes (887) is evidence that she is still in fact more intelligent than Aegisthus, but she has nonetheless resumed the traditional female role; she recognizes Aegisthus as master of the house (716) and defers to him in any matters requiring deliberation.[35]

Clytemnestra's attempt to resume her subordinate role does not, however, compensate for her excessive dominance in the earlier play, and Orestes is determined to exact vengeance and regain his rightful inheritance. He announces his determination to free the citizens, whom he praises as "the conquerors of Troy," from the rule of these two women (302–4). He also determines to avenge Agamemnon, who died deprived of the honor he would have enjoyed if he had died at Troy (345–53; cf. 354–62). The killing of Agamemnon and the present rule of Clytemnestra (and Aegisthus) are thus seen as a stain on the honor of the men who conquered Troy as well as on Agamemnon's honor.

Orestes brushes off his mother's plea that she nursed him (896–98, 908), that she is a true woman in other words, by pointing to her many offenses against marriage from the male perspective: killing her husband, committing adultery, and casting out her son, the proper heir (906–7, 909, 913).[36] When she brings up Agamemnon's "follies" (918), he replies, "do not reproach him who toiled, you who sat inside [at home]" (919). This remark makes clear the common view that a man's work (out of the house) is greater than a woman's, who sits at home, and that the greater burden shouldered by the man gives him greater rights. When Clytemnestra challenges this double standard by mentioning her own hardships (920), Orestes restates his position, saying, "a man's toil nourishes women who sit at home" (921), and this (it is implied) cancels any possible debt a man may owe for a woman's previous nourishment of him. The male is thus presented as the true nourisher and the female as dependent on him. The obvious conclusion of this belief in male superiority is that the wife's crime against her husband is more serious than the father's against his daughter or the son's against his mother.

As in the case of Agamemnon's killing of his daughter, a normally unthinkable deed is justified according to a set of male values that see the crime as less serious than a previous crime against those male values. Orestes' need to avenge his father,[37] to regain his inheritance, and to restore the *oikos* is greater than the prohibition against matricide. It is true that Orestes appears to be a less extreme representative of the male point of view than his father. Although it may be misleading to compare the behavior of Orestes on stage with the chorus' report of Agamemnon's behavior, Agamemnon seems to display considerably less reluctance in his crime than his son does. Orestes is continually aware of the impious nature of his deed, he acts only after much deliberation and persuasion, and he recognizes the need for some sort of payment (purification) for his act. Orestes' military leadership, moreover, is restricted to the alliance he offers Athens, and in this respect he scarcely resembles his father, the destroyer of Troy. Thus, in spite of the fact that Orestes, like Agamemnon, acts from male values and through his action establishes the dominance of male forces, his is a less extreme act, and the audience may suspect that some sort of compromise is now closer to hand.

An end to the cycle of *drasanti pathein* does not, however, come automatically with Orestes' victory. Clytemnestra's death does not leave her powerless but rather brings on her agents of revenge, the Furies, who appear to Orestes at the end of the play. They are immediately identified as women (1048), and they clearly have some power over Orestes. Their arrival thus indicates that the excessive male dominance in *Choephoroi* is not to be the end of the story. The cycle will continue as the male dominance gives rise to new female forces to counteract it. The killing of Clytemnestra creates another imbalance, this time in favor of the male, and this imbalance must be corrected as the others have been. "Where then will it end?" ask the chorus in their last words (1075–76), and the audience too await the third and final play.

Eumenides opens with a prologue delivered by the Pythia, priestess of Apollo. As the female servant of the male god who had most strongly supported Orestes in *Choephoroi*, the Pythia's mere presence is an indication that the power of the male side has not disappeared. Her prologue, however, suggests that a peaceful settlement of the sexual conflict may be reached in this play, for she relates at length the history of the oracle at Delphi and how it came to belong to Apollo, and her version of this history is significantly different from the standard version, in which Apollo had to fight a monstrous (and female) Python in order to gain possession of Delphi.[38] In the Pythia's account, the oracle at Delphi is handed over to Apollo peacefully as a birthgift from his grandmother Phoebe, who received it (also peacefully) from Themis, who received it from the first possessor of the oracle,

Gaia (Earth). Apollo thus has inherited his oracle from a succession of women. On the other hand, he has obtained his prophetic skill from his father Zeus (17). The prologue, then, suggests that, like Orestes, Apollo represents a more peaceful use of male power than did Agamemnon.

As I have said, the main conflict in *Eumenides* between Apollo/Orestes and the Furies is a sexual one, not just because the participants on the one side are male and on the other female, but also because the point of dispute is in important respects a sexual one. This is apparent even in the preliminary stages of the dispute, where the Furies maintain that Clytemnestra's killing of Agamemnon is less important than Orestes' killing of Clytemnestra, since the latter violated a blood tie but the former did not (210–12). In response, Apollo argues the supreme sanctity of marriage, holding up Zeus and Hera as an example (213–18). We have already seen that from the male perspective the marriage bond is more highly valued than the blood tie: Agamemnon was willing to sacrifice his daughter in order to regain Helen for her husband and punish the Trojans. Here the same set of values is affirmed by the male side and denied by the female.[39] There are, of course, other important aspects to the conflict in *Eumenides* (such as the conflict between two generations of gods), but as the debate progresses the sexual aspect becomes the overriding issue, and the connection between the sexual conflict in this and in the earlier plays becomes clearer.

In her first words to Orestes (436–42), Athena asks who he is and why he is there. He responds that he is the son of Agamemnon, commander of the navy and annihilator of Troy, who was ignobly killed when he returned home (456–61). After this preliminary questioning Athena decides to form the Areopagus to hear the arguments. The debate before this court quickly establishes that Orestes killed Clytemnestra in return for her murder of Agamemnon (587–602). The

Furies press their point that if she deserved to die then so does Orestes. They did not pursue Clytemnestra, they explain, as they now pursue him, since the murder of Agamemnon was not of a blood relative (605). Orestes asks skeptically if he is of his mother's blood (606), and the chorus answer emphatically that she nourished him in her womb (607–8). To this Orestes has no answer, and he turns over his defense to Apollo. The Furies' case at this point is clear: they value the blood tie, especially the tie to a mother, more highly than the marriage bond, and, as we have seen, it was precisely the reversal of this relative valuation that led to the crimes of Orestes and Agamemnon.

Apollo now gives his views on this "matter of blood,"[40] and, after claiming that he does not lie (615), he states openly (625) that the death of a noble man is a different matter (*sc.* from the death of a woman). He continues with a number of remarks that he hopes will "sting" the jury (638): there is disgrace in the death of a noble and honored man, especially if killed by a woman (*kai tauta pros gynaikos*, 627); Agamemnon, moreover, was killed, not in battle by some Amazon, but in his home, deceitfully, in a bath—he, the admiral of the fleet (627–37). And when the Furies again insist[41] that the shedding of a mother's blood, kindred blood, brings pollution (653–56), Apollo resorts finally to the biological argument that the father is the only true parent, the mother merely an incubator (657–66). This scientific theory is generally attributed to Anaxagoras,[42] a younger contemporary of Aeschylus', and it may have been used in Athens at the time to justify the inferior status of women in society,[43] though we have no evidence other than its use in this play.[44]

Here the biological argument is crucial to Apollo's (Orestes') case, since he has been unable to find any convincing reason for valuing the marriage bond more highly than the blood tie. Thus in the end he must deny that there is any such blood tie in this case. Apollo has failed to convince the Furies with his earlier indirect arguments in support of male superiority, and so he must finally resort to this direct statement of the sexual superiority of the male. This is his final argument, followed only by another mention of the political benefits that Orestes' acquittal will bring Athens; with this, Apollo rests his case. The view that the male is the sole true parent is also Apollo's one convincing argument: in reply to it the Furies have nothing to say, and upon it Athena bases her vote for Orestes' acquittal. She is herself evidence of Apollo's argument, since she was born directly from Zeus and has no mother (663–66). Thus she too favors the male in all things (736–40). It should by now be clear that this final argument is in no way irrelevant; in fact it is directed at one of the central concerns of the trilogy, the clash between male and female forces and values.

The debate between Apollo/Orestes and the Furies is finally decided by Orestes' acquittal. In a sense, of course, this is a victory for the male side, but it certainly does not result in the same sort of male dominance we saw in *Choephoroi*. Throughout the debate the two sides appear nearly equal in strength; neither has a clearly superior case, and the net effect is that of a standoff. Aeschylus makes it clear that the arguments are equally strong on both sides by making the decision a tie vote (753), and having Orestes released on the basis of a procedural ruling that a tie results in acquittal (741). The implication of this equal division of the jury is that the arguments on both sides have equal strength. Thus, in sexual terms, the male and female forces are at last equally balanced.

We should note too that the figure who supervises the legal process and who acts as arbitrator in the final reconciliation possesses elements of both male and female sexuality. Athena is, to be sure, female, but she is also a warrior who leads her troops "like a man" (296; cf. 457–58), she was born from

Zeus alone without a mother, and she has never married
(737). But even though she votes for the male side, she is
still a woman; unlike Apollo, she is respectful of the Furies
and neither fears (407) nor denounces them. Thus her bisexuality seems to give her the ability to act as a neutral arbitrator in the sexual conflict and to persuade the Furies that
they were not really defeated (795). A similar bisexuality
is characteristic of another group of women, the Amazons,
who are said by Athena to have camped on the hill of the
Areopagus in a campaign against Theseus and to have given
the hill its name when they sacrificed to the war god, Ares
(685–90; cf. 628). This odd bit of local history is perhaps
included in Athena's account of the court in order to indicate
the sexually neutral nature of the hill and thus to establish
that it is the proper place for a trial that will assist in achieving
a sexual compromise.

In spite of the equal weight of the arguments and the tie
vote, however, a verdict must be rendered, and Orestes is
acquitted. The Furies feel that they have been defeated and
threaten to pour out their wrath on the city, but in the end
they are appeased and persuaded to grant the city their favor
instead. Just as their threatened evil is a barren plague (780–
87, 810–17), so their blessing is one of fertility (921–26,
937–47), a feminine blessing to match the masculine contribution of Orestes' promised military alliance (762–74).
And along with the reconciliation of the female element comes
a complete end to the divisive sexual conflict, for Athena makes
it clear that there will be sacrifices to the Furies at childbirths
and at weddings (835) and that they will be honored by men
and women alike (856). The Furies in turn agree to prevent
men from dying young and to help furnish young maidens
with husbands (956–60), thereby reestablishing the value
of marriage (cf. 835). Male and female elements, which have

been in conflict since before the beginning of *Agamemnon*, are thus reconciled at the end of *Eumenides*. Sexual harmony is established at last.[45]

If the reconciliation at the end of the *Oresteia* is a sexual one, it is also a political one, and it is this aspect that we must now consider. It has been generally recognized, since the publication of Müller's *Dissertations on the Eumenides of Aeschylus* (1833), that there is a close and important relation between this play and the actual political situation in Athens in 458. This has led to extended discussions of such topics as Aeschylus' attitude to the Argive alliance and the nature of Ephialtes' reforms of the Areopagus in 462, but there is little agreement on these matters.[46] Since *Eumenides* is the only play of the *Oresteia* with extended references to contemporary political matters, consideration of the political aspect of this play has tended to isolate it from its two predecessors. The picture we get from such a treatment is of a connected trilogy, in the last play of which Aeschylus rather incidentally includes some references to contemporary politics. Dodds has recently urged an end to the separate consideration of the "morals" in the earlier part of the *Oresteia* and the "politics" at the end, but although his attempt to treat the trilogy as a whole is a step in the right direction, his treatment of political language in the first two plays is inadequate.[47] The following discussion attempts to illustrate the importance of political concerns (in the broad sense) throughout the *Oresteia*.

Even before turning to the text, we should consider the significance of Aeschylus' choosing this particular myth for his trilogy. The story of the return and death of Agamemnon and the subsequent revenge of Orestes would have been familiar to his audience from the references to it in the *Odyssey* and elsewhere in the epic cycle, and perhaps most important, from Stesichorus' *Oresteia*.[48] It seems likely that Stesichorus' work was written in Sparta and presented a pro-Spartan version of the myth; we know, for instance, that he located Agamemnon's palace in Sparta.[49] If this is true, the poem would probably have had the political effect of reaffirming the glory of Sparta's past.[50] Furthermore, the Spartans apparently sought to claim Orestes as their own hero not only by poetic retellings of the myth but also by transferring the supposed bones of Orestes to Sparta in the sixth century (Herodotus I.67–68).

In 462 or 461, Athens made an alliance with Sparta's neighbor and enemy, Argos, and at the same time broke her alliance with Sparta (Thucydides I. 102.4). As a result, by 458 Athens and Sparta were openly hostile. As far as we know, Aeschylus was the first Athenian dramatist to use the myth of Agamemnon and Orestes, and it is significant that he turned to this Spartan myth almost immediately after Athens broke off its alliance with Sparta. The Athenian audience must thus have wondered (knowing perhaps only the titles of the plays) what Aeschylus would do with a myth that traditionally "belonged" to Sparta, and they may have suspected that their poet would present a version of the myth that favored Athens at the expense of Sparta.

The first indication we get of Aeschylus' handling of the myth is ambiguous: the watchman tells us at the very beginning that he is "on the house of the Atreidae" (*Ag.* 3), implying that the house belongs to both Menelaus and Agamemnon. This might suggest that we are in Sparta, which is Menelaus' traditional home, but we are soon informed that in fact the palace is in Argos (24), which may be an Aeschylean innovation.[51] The political effect of this relocation is clear: by making Agamemnon and Orestes Argive heroes, Aeschylus challenges Sparta's claim to the heroes and allows the Athenians to derive the benefit of Orestes' power by virtue of their

alliance with Argos. It is true that this theme is not fully ex-
ploited until *Eumenides*, but the challenge to the Spartan
claim on the two heroes would be evident to the Athenian
audience from the beginning.[52]

The location of the two brothers under one roof is also
important for the political impact of the play, for it makes it
easier for the whole family, the whole *oikos*, to become identified with the polis.[53] There is much emphasis in the *Oresteia*
on the fact that the actions we have observed, crimes on one
side answered by crimes on the other side, all are located in
and belong to one family or house (see chapter III). As a result, the fortunes of individuals become closely tied to the
fortunes of the house, and there is a further tendency for this
house to become identified with the city. In Homer, by contrast, attention is focused entirely on the ruler; the importance
of his city is negligible. But by the fifth century the polis was
a more important concern, and thus, when tragedy draws on
myths from the heroic past, rulers and their cities become
identified to a certain extent and treated as a single concern.

This tendency is evident in the treatment of Troy and its
ruling family in *Agamemnon*. The watchman waits for the
beacon-signal from Troy (9) to announce the capture of "the
city of Ilium" (29). The chorus then enter and sing of the
time when the Atreidae set forth as adversaries of Priam (40),
how Zeus sent them against Paris (61), and so on. It is a
"historical" fact that Paris alone stole Helen, but in the play
the crime is treated as belonging also to his father, Priam,
and to the polis. We tend to consider it an aspect of a different
(perhaps more "primitive") ethical system that a whole city
must pay for the wrong of a single individual, but, to the extent that the rulers and the polis are equated, the crime of the
former becomes automatically the crime of the latter as well,
and thus the city, too, must be punished (cf. 823–24). As the

herald declares, "neither Paris nor his associate city [*syntelēs polis*] can boast that what they did is more than what they have suffered" (532–33).[54]

Similarly the troubles in the house of Agamemnon are troubles for the city of Argos as well. In the first stasimon, for instance, the chorus sing of the troubles in the city caused by the war abroad (403–74). The herald who brings the news of the victory is also aware that the absence of Menelaus is a blow to the whole city (640), just as the victory is a joy to the city (646–47). When the chorus greet Agamemnon, they say he will learn in time "which of the citizens guards the city properly and which improperly" (807–9). Agamemnon addresses Argos first (810), says he will soon tend to the troubles of the city (844–50), and considers briefly the possible public reaction to his trampling of the tapestries of his house (938). Cassandra speaks of *stasis* (1117),[55] often used of political discord, in the family and of a sacrifice "to be avenged by stoning" (1118; cf. 1616), which is an old form of public punishment. And the chorus see Clytemnestra's deed as a step toward tyranny (1355, 1365, 1633) and threaten her with banishment from the city (1410). She pays little attention to them, however, and vows to rule the house well (1673).

All these are indications in *Agamemnon* of the connection between the fortunes of the house and those of the polis. This connection is also evident in *Choephoroi*. Orestes, for instance, gives as one of the reasons for his act of revenge that the citizens of Argos, the "most renowned of mortals," shall be freed from "servitude to two women" (302–4; cf. 1046–47). One of Electra's complaints is that her mother buried her father "without the citizens and without laments" (431–32), and the chorus, while awaiting the outcome of the struggle, see the alternatives as either complete destruction of Agamemnon's house or Orestes' acquisition of the rule of the city and his father's wealth (861–65).[56] The connection between house and polis thus continues in *Choephoroi*, and indeed in *Eumenides* as well, where the issue of Orestes' acquittal clearly has political importance.

Aeschylus' audience would thus be aware of the political aspect of the events in the *Oresteia* from the beginning, not just during a few passages in *Eumenides*. By this I do not mean that they would be seeing references or allusions to specific contemporary political issues, but rather that they would recognize that the pattern of behavior presented in the trilogy also has a political aspect and represents a pattern of political behavior. The effect of this aspect of the trilogy would be to lead the audience to a better and truer understanding of public affairs and political behavior in general. It is in this sense that the *Oresteia* should be considered a political drama, not because of any views it might present on the Argive alliance or the reforms of the Areopagus, for these specific issues are less important in themselves than as illustrations of political activity in general.

Viewed from this general political perspective, the action of the *Oresteia* can be understood as follows: the king of Argos is away, his wife rules, and there is trouble at home (1–39). Ten years earlier, Agamemnon aggressively led his army to punish and destroy Troy in a war that has caused much suffering to both sides (63–67). The sailing of the expedition was held up by winds and opposed by some elements of the city (cf. *Ag.* 799–804), but Agamemnon, bowing to the demand of his troops (212–17) and his own sense of military necessity, sacrificed his daughter so that the fleet could sail. The news then comes from Clytemnestra that Troy is taken, though she adds a warning that this fact does not necessarily ensure a safe future (338–47). The chorus rejoice in the destruction of Troy, but as they sing of punishment and of Paris' crime they remember the difficulties Helen left for Argos (403–5), the sorrow felt at her departure (408–28), and the sorrow caused by the departure of the army to fetch her back (429–55).[57] This suffering of those at home is no small matter; the people "mutter 'for the sake of another's woman' " (448–49), their speech is "heavy with anger" (456), and there is public cursing (457). The chorus themselves are deeply troubled, for they know that the "killers of many" are normally punished by the Erinyes and by Zeus (459–70). For themselves they would prefer to be neither captors nor captives (471–74).

We have seen in *Persae* how war abroad leads to trouble at home. In that play the absence of the army is in itself less important than the fact that it is defeated, but in *Agamemnon* the fact that the expedition is victorious makes it clear that war and the absence of the men are in themselves the cause of trouble at home. Indeed the Argive victory in this play results in considerably more trouble at home than the Persian defeat in the earlier play, where in spite of considerable grief in Susa there is no internal strife and no serious challenge to Xerxes' authority. In Argos, however, the city is split: Agamemnon, the aggressive military commander, leads and represents the forces that would fight an overseas enemy whatever the cost at home; Clytemnestra, who suffers as the city suffers when the expedition has left, is determined to avenge the wrong done to her family and to the home life of the city. In political terms Clytemnestra represents the (more conservative) forces favoring peace and internal order as opposed to external military expansion.

Her counterpart, Agamemnon, is well-liked by the watchman at home (cf. *euphilē chera*, 34), is given a moderately warm reception by the chorus (783–809), and agrees to try to cure the trouble at home (844–50). But in spite of these indications of a more peaceful spirit, Agamemnon is presented primarily as a military commander, not just in the parodos, where he chooses war at the expense of his daughter, but also in the herald's praise of his leadership (524–37), in the primary emphasis he himself places on his destruction of Troy (810–28), and in the many references later in the trilogy to his military position (*e.g.*, *Ag.* 907, *Ch.* 1072, *Eu.* 455–58, 631–37). Agamemnon's military strength is, moreover, reflected in and associated with his incapacity to deal with domestic, nonmilitary affairs. This weakness is ironically pointed up by his own self-deceptive claim to be experienced in judging those who are truly loyal (838–40).[58] However one judges Agamemnon's intentions or his "character" and whatever motives are attributed to him in walking on the tapestries, he clearly is deceived and defeated by Clytemnestra. It also seems clear that this defeat, whether caused by weariness or by secret pride, is directly related to his conquest of Troy (cf. 910–11, 935, 939, 941). By directing all his energy toward external conquest, Agamemnon has neglected the internal affairs of Argos, and thus the victor abroad is in turn vanquished at home.

Just as Agamemnon's weakness at home is related to his strength abroad, so (conversely) Clytemnestra draws strength from the wrongs done her by Agamemnon as military commander. The expedition to Troy and the sacrifice of Iphigeneia are both aspects of Agamemnon's disregard for the internal stability of Argos, but the suffering caused by these actions in the end strengthens the hand of those who suffer. In fact Clytemnestra's strength is such that as soon as she has killed Agamemnon, her rule is spoken of as a tyranny (1355, 1365; cf. 1633, *Ch.* 973), and this description most likely would have been accepted by the audience. In spite of her desire for moderation (1574–76) and her ability to settle petty quarreling (1654–56), she has usurped the throne, or rather she has handed over the throne to the usurper Aegisthus,[59] and their utter lack of popular support is made clear in *Choephoroi*. Clytemnestra had feared that Agamemnon's long absence might lead to internal strife and anarchy (*Ag.* 883);[60] in reaction she creates a tyranny.

From this brief description of political conflict in *Agamemnon* we can see some ties between it and the sexual conflict in the play. It seems characteristic of male values to favor military strength and the forces of external expansion and to be less concerned with internal stability and "domestic affairs." The female forces, on the other hand, favor the traditional stability of home and family and are generally more conservative in their concern for religious values and the maintenance of strong internal order. The extreme result of male values in the *Oresteia* is anarchy, of female tyranny.

The killing of Agamemnon thus results in a shift from one political extreme to the other, and by the law of retribution this shift can only be followed by another reaction, a tyrannicide. The chorus had urged Clytemnestra to go into exile,[61] which would have reduced the extremity of her political crime, but she refused, and so Orestes returns, kills the tyrants, and frees Argos. His act is clearly one of retribution, but in political terms it does not shift the balance all the way to the other extreme (although it leaves Argos temporarily leaderless). Orestes has a legitimate claim on the throne; he also has the support of the people, at least those who appear in the play. And he goes immediately into exile to rid himself of the pollution he has incurred, so that he may properly govern the city when he returns.[62] Thus Orestes' tyrannicide is, in political terms, a more moderate deed than those that preceded it, and it brings us a step closer to the goal of political harmony in Argos. But this goal cannot be reached without some payment to and acknowledgment of the forces that Orestes has defeated.

These forces are represented by the Furies, who in *Eumenides* proclaim their political program. It is "feminine" in its high regard for the value of blood ties and therefore for the home and family; it is strict and even harsh in its emphasis on maintaining order through fear; and it is conservative in its adherence to traditional laws and the old order. These forces receive acknowledgment in the play in several ways: the purification of Orestes, the establishment of the Areopagus, and finally the establishment of the Furies in a position of honor in Athens. Orestes' purification is obviously a payment to the Furies and an acknowledgment that they have a right to punish certain crimes. Although he is subsequently acquitted despite this right, there is no indication that they cannot pursue killers in the future (cf. *Eu.* 932–37). The honorable station granted to the Furies in Athens is also a clear acknowledgment of their power and of the city's need to retain the forces they represent. And the Areopagus, as we saw (in chapter III), is established in order to support and preserve the same forces that the Furies represent. Athena understands that the freeing of Orestes is a political necessity, both for the stability of Argos and for the resultant benefit to Athens. But, rather than make a decision on her own, which might permanently alienate the Furies, she establishes the court to protect their interests. When she then swings the verdict to acquittal, she can point out that this was not her unilateral action but an impartial legal decision. Yet, in spite of Athena's use of the Areopagus against the Furies in this case, the court is in the long run a political concession to the Furies, for it will help maintain their values in society in the future.

Although the Furies' position is essentially a conservative one, and they often maintain their preference for the old and traditional ways (*e.g.,* 172, 778, 808, 838, 871), they also exhibit a certain moderation in their views that suggests a willingness to compromise even before they are persuaded by Athena at the end. Their strong statement of the necessity of fear for both the individual and the city (517–25),[63] for instance, is followed immediately by their famous plea for political moderation, "pursue neither a life of anarchy nor despo-

tism; god gives power to the middle way in everything"
(526–30; cf. 696). This is clearly a less extreme position
than the tyrannical rule of Clytemnestra. Just as Orestes is a
more moderate representative of the same basic forces as Agamemnon, so the Furies are more moderate representatives of
the same forces as Clytemnestra. Therefore the dispute between the two sides can reach a compromise in the last play
that would have been impossible in the first.

I have argued that in the two earlier plays the family and
the house of the rulers tend to be identified with the city of
Argos. This identity is strengthened in *Eumenides*, for example, when Athena questions Orestes about his family and
country (437; cf. 455) and when Orestes thanks her for
saving his house and restoring him to his fatherland (754–
56);[64] indeed by the time of this last speech by Orestes the
city has become the more important entity. The final compromise, however, takes place not in Orestes' house or even
in Argos but in Athens, where the Areopagus is established
and the Furies are honored. This shift of focus from Argos to
Athens may not be entirely logical, but it seems convincing
dramatically, and it is unlikely that the audience would feel
any inconsistency in the fact that the conflict in the house
of Atreus had finally been resolved in the city of Athens.

Athens is not mentioned in the first two plays, but it is
prominent in *Eumenides* from the beginning. Even in the
prologue, when the Pythia relates the history of Apollo's
peaceful acquisition of the oracle, she says that he came to
Delphi by way of Athens and that the Athenians helped him
on his way (10–14).[65] This story suggests a traditional connection between Athens and Delphi and may have provided a
slight clue that Athens would figure in this final play; still it
would probably have been a surprise to the audience when
Apollo directs Orestes to go to Athens to find judges of his
action and a "release from his troubles" (79–83), for this

addition to the myth was (as far as we know) a novelty.[66] These words of Apollo's (*tōnd' apallaxai ponōn*, 83) are certainly intended to recall the watchman's opening line (*tōnd' apallagēn ponōn, Ag.* 1),[67] and this echo would reinforce the feeling that the troubles for which Orestes will seek relief in Athens are the same troubles that have beset the house of Atreus from the beginning. Indeed the audience must have been stirred by Apollo's instructions to go to Athens, curious to see just how the poet would bring about this relief from toils.

After Apollo's instructions, Orestes leaves on a journey that takes him to many cities over a long period of time (239–41, 284–85). When he later reenters an empty stage, he approaches the statue of Athena, which is on stage,[68] addresses it in supplication, and delivers a short request for protection (235–43). The Furies enter in pursuit, and Orestes then states his case at greater length. In the course of this elaboration, he again asks Athena's help, this time promising her in return an eternal military alliance with Argos (287–91). This Athenian alliance with Argos, which is promised again by Apollo (667–73) and confirmed by Orestes after his acquittal (762–74), is almost certainly intended to recall the historical alliance between the two cities concluded only a few years earlier. The last and longest description of the alliance, moreover, occupies most of Orestes' only speech after his acquittal, which makes it clear that the Argive alliance is his contribution to the well-being of Athens in exchange for his acquittal.

The Furies, too, after they accept Athena's offer, promise benefits for Athens. Their benefits are those of internal order and fertility, the preservation of the traditional laws, and the enforcement of traditional punishments, especially for homicide. These benefits are concretely represented by the establishment of the Areopagus, which will oversee not only homicide but also internal order in general. This order is based on punishment for wrong done, imposed by the Furies rather than by human agents, so as not to lead to an unending chain of reciprocal punishments. Indeed the Furies specifically pray for an end to blood feuds (980–83) and internal political factions (976–78). They ask rather for internal peace and a common hatred of others (984–86). They thus provide Athens with internal order, while Orestes brings the city a beneficial external alliance. Internal and external strengths now complement each other in a political harmony rather than working against each other as they did in the beginning of the trilogy.

If we turn briefly to the question of Aeschylus' own political views (in the narrow sense), we can now suggest an answer, but it is necessarily a speculative one, since Aeschylus is not writing as a political partisan. However, since the final reconciliation in *Eumenides* is achieved through a compromise incorporating the benefits of both sides, it is reasonable to conclude that Aeschylus favored such a compromise in contemporary Athens. A frequent assumption in past discussions of this question has been that if Aeschylus favored the "liberal" Argive alliance, as he seems to have, then he must also have favored the "liberal" reforms of the Areopagus, which were supported by the same "party"; conversely, if he opposed the reforms of the Areopagus, he must have opposed the Argive alliance. In my view, however, we must reject this assumption. The clear implication of *Eumenides* is that Aeschylus favored a constructive compromise of both sides: that is, he favored both the "liberal" Argive alliance and the retention and perhaps strengthening of the "conservative" Areopagus.[69] Aeschylus thus does not support the program of one side as opposed to the other but rather a political compromise that will draw on elements of both sides, since both can provide benefits to the city. The victory of one party over the other, as we saw in the first two plays, can be only a temporary and un-satisfactory solution; but a positive compromise can produce the true and permanent benefits that the city and its inhab-itants all desire. The years immediately preceding the produc-tion of the *Oresteia* were turbulent ones: the leader of one party (Cimon) had been ostracized, and a leader of the other (Ephialtes) assassinated. The time for compromise was at hand.[70]

The end of *Eumenides* thus presents us with a general reso-lution of the forces that were in conflict at the beginning and through most of the trilogy. The cycle of *drasanti pathein* has not been eliminated, but is altered from a pattern of doing and suffering evil to one of doing and suffering good (*eu drōsan, eu paschousan,* 868), as the bloody *eris* ("strife") of *Aga-memnon* and *Choephoroi* is transformed into the creative *eris* ("competitive striving") of *Eumenides.* The slow self-destruc-tion, generation by generation, of the family of Atreus is finally halted at the last member, giving way to true harmony in the city. The barrenness that results from destruction of the family by sexual conflict becomes a new fertility resulting from creative sexual harmony. And the political conflict be-tween the forces of traditional law and internal order on the one hand and those of aggressive foreign expansion on the other is resolved by the harmonious coexistence of these forces, each in a more moderate form, in the new city of Athens.

Finally the audience would understand the trilogy and es-pecially the final compromise in relation to their own lives and the affairs of their city. The pattern of action and reaction is a familiar one in human affairs, and the Athenians would surely have observed it in their actual political life. Thus the optimistic conclusion of the trilogy, whether justified by actual conditions or not, would at least suggest hope for a similar political compromise in the city. The "message" (if we wish to call it that) of the trilogy would be the obvious statement that such a compromise involves the balance and harmony of opposing forces, not the victory of only one. This is no deep observation, but depth in poetry is not found in the analytical complexity of a theme. It comes rather from the means by which an idea is conveyed. If Aeschylus has convincingly dramatized a fundamental pattern of life and if the audience has come to understand that pattern better, then the poet has achieved his purpose. The political effect of the *Oresteia* is not that the audience leave the theater intending to vote for or against Pericles, but rather that they leave with a better understanding of human behavior and of the political process and thus are better able to direct the affairs of the city.

V

Septem, Supplices, Prometheus

I N the preceding examination of *Persae* and the *Oresteia* I
have focused primarily on the operation of certain forces
that contribute to the total effect of each work. I have paid
relatively little attention to the characters of individuals in
the plays. Particularly for our understanding of a complete
trilogy, I argued, the character of a single individual such as
Agamemnon is less significant than it might be for an analysis
of one play of the trilogy by itself. The general forces represented by and working through these individuals, however,
usually extend over more than one play and are represented
by several different figures during the course of the trilogy;
thus, only by studying the whole work can we truly understand these forces and their operation. It may consequently
be misleading to draw conclusions about the nature and operation of such forces from the study of a single play, and I
have therefore devoted the major part of this study to the two
surviving works of Aeschylus that in this sense are complete,
Persae[1] and the *Oresteia*.

It would be overcautious, however, to end this work without considering Aeschylus' three other plays, *Septem, Sup-*

plices, and *Prometheus,* even though these were probably all presented as parts of connected trilogies.[2] I thus conclude with a brief discussion of these plays, confining myself to a few major issues, particularly those that relate to issues we have examined in *Persae* and the *Oresteia.* I do not, however, discuss aspects that are only briefly mentioned; a sexual aspect of *Prometheus,* for example, is suggested in the scenes with Io and the Oceanids, but it is unclear what importance this theme may have had in the play or the trilogy. It is possible that its significance would be more apparent if the rest of the trilogy survived, but I will resist speculation along these lines. For convenience I treat the plays in their probable chronological order.[3]

Although *Septem* is often seen simply as a "tragedy of character,"[4] it also presents ethical, sexual, and to a lesser degree political conflicts similar to those in the *Oresteia.* The development of these conflicts can be studied and partially understood even without the evidence of the first two plays in the trilogy, *Laius* and *Oedipus.*[5] On the question of *dikē,* for instance, it would certainly be helpful to know what, if any, information concerning the actions of Eteocles and Polyneices was divulged in the earlier plays; but even on the basis of *Septem* alone, if we do not limit ourselves to the simple acceptance of Eteocles' position, we can gain a relatively clear understanding of the conflict between the two brothers, a conflict in which both sides have a valid claim to *dikē.*

Polyneices' position is revealed in the spy's brief description of him and his shield (631–49). He is attacking Thebes with the hope of killing Eteocles even at the cost of his own life (634–36), or if Eteocles is not slain "may banisher be banished,/ dishonored like me, requited by me" (637–38 [trans. Dawson]).[6] This claim suggests that Aeschylus is adhering to the more common version of the dispute (see Apollodorus

3.6.1), in which Eteocles and Polyneices agreed to share the throne in alternate years, but Eteocles refused to let Polyneices have his turn.[7] Thus Polyneices, who was wronged by his brother, intends to wrong him in return, thereby conforming to the traditional pattern of retribution, which we saw so often in the *Oresteia*. Like the characters of that trilogy, he claims the support of *dikē*, whose figure is emblazoned on his shield and who will restore him to his home and city (646–48). Of course Polyneices' act of revenge may at the same time be a wrong, for which he will in turn pay, but this consideration does not affect his proper initial claim to have the support of *dikē* in his attack.[8]

Eteocles' position is less clear. He vehemently rejects Polyneices' claim to *dikē* (662–71), but he brings forth no specific evidence in refutation or in support of his own position. Instead of directly answering Polyneices' claim to be avenging a previous wrong, Eteocles asserts simply that *dikē* has never supported his brother in the past and thus cannot be supporting him now, since in the first place Polyneices is harming his fatherland (668), and secondly he is a man of reckless daring (*phōti pantolmōi phrenas*, 671). In fact neither of these points would invalidate Polyneices' claim to *dikē*, which is based on the necessity for revenge. Polyneices himself would probably deny both charges,[9] and the accusation of reckless daring can in fact be seen as an ironic foreshadowing of Eteocles' own behavior in the next scene. Eteocles, moreover, never directly claims the support of *dikē* for himself, though he does send out one champion, Melanippus, who is accompanied by *dikē homaimōn* (415),[10] and the chorus twice see the defense of the city as a matter of *dikē* (418, 626). Certainly Eteocles cannot claim the support of *dikē* in the sense of "revenge" or "retribution," but, if he has any other legal justification for his position, he does not mention it. If he were pressed to make his case more explicit, he would probably rely on the necessity for protecting his homeland, regardless of other considerations. In the play he seems to assume without question his status as defender of Thebes. He thinks only of how, not whether, he should defend the city.

Critics of *Septem* have for the most part accepted Eteocles' position and rejected Polyneices' claim of *dikē*.[11] Certainly the figure of Eteocles dominates *Septem*, and Aeschylus is more interested in conveying the full scope of his position and the dilemma he faces than in elucidating Polyneices' claim to the throne. Consequently, it is easy to see the action through Eteocles' eyes alone and to accept his statements without question. There is good reason, however, to reject this one-sided view. Eteocles is not the unambiguously noble hero some critics have made him, as we see in his treatment of the chorus. More significant, however, is the long lament at the end of *Septem*, which seems to confirm the equal status of the two brothers. And we must bear in mind that, if the preceding play mentioned the dispute between the brothers, it may have supported Polyneices' original claim of *dikē*. On this last point we can only speculate, but the quarrel between Eteocles and Polyneices is an important part of the background of *Septem*, and, since it is not mentioned directly in this play, it is likely to have been introduced in the previous play. Certainly no equally important event is omitted from the *Oresteia*.

The last quarter of the play provides the strongest testimony to the equal status of the brothers and their equal claim to the throne, which is indicated by the symmetrical double killing,[12] and is more fully confirmed by the chorus' long lament over their bodies (875–1004).[13] Almost everything said in this lament applies equally to both brothers, and the chorus repeatedly emphasize the equal nature of their situations. They obtained equal lots (*ison lachein*, 907), they are both called "lords" (*toinde duoin anaktoin*, 921), and the balance and equality of their actions are especially brought out in the balanced language of 961–72. It is implied, moreover, that they will receive equal and honorable burials (949–50, 1002–4), and the harm done to their home and land is attributed to both equally (994–95). In fact, in only two brief sections of this lament, 979–81 and 991–92, is it possible to say which brother the chorus are specifically referring to, and in at least one of these they clearly maintain their balanced assessment of the brothers' deeds.[14] Finally, we can only guess at the staging of this final scene, but it would certainly be easy to reinforce the sense of symmetry and balance in the chorus' words by dividing the chorus in two, as most editors do, and by having the bodies of the two brothers symmetrically displayed and equally treated on stage. In sum, although Eteocles is the dominant figure during most of *Septem*, the play as a whole should lead us to see the action from a larger perspective, in which Eteocles' position has a certain validity, but so does Polyneices'. Both brothers, however, are led to wrongful, destructive action, culminating in their deaths, and both are similarly treated by the chorus at the end.

This more balanced assessment of the positions of the two brothers would probably be more apparent if the first two plays survived. In the absence of these plays, however, scholars have tended to concentrate their attention almost exclusively on the figure of Eteocles—the tragic decision-maker, the hero bound by destiny or by a curse, the self-sacrificing ruler, and so on.[15] This intense concern with the question of Eteocles' character has resulted in a regrettable neglect of other elements in the play, in particular the chorus. Critics who do not ignore or dismiss the chorus as insignificant, have generally treated them as a mere foil to Eteocles. The conflict between Eteocles and the chorus, however, is important in its own right, and like the conflict between the two brothers must be understood from the perspective of both sides. Like the conflict in the *Oresteia*, moreover, it has a significant sexual aspect. An examination of the play from this perspective will not only help us understand the unity of *Septem*, but may also provide a clue to the thematic unity of the trilogy.[16]

When Eteocles first confronts the frightened chorus (181–286), he is not so much a cool, rational leader seeking to calm their fears as a harsh and angry military commander who demands their obedience. His scornful references to their being women (188, 195, 200, 256) and his denunciation of the whole female sex (187–90)[17] indicate that he views them from a narrowly male perspective. He values military order and heroic valor and is skilled at commanding troops and arranging the military defense of the city, but he can neither understand nor control the female forces in the city, which the chorus represent. In contrast, their concern is with domestic life, with the religious sanctity of home and city, and with the evils war holds for women and children after men have died gloriously in battle. During the first third of the play, the conflict between these two positions is clearly drawn. Although Eteocles silences the chorus momentarily (262–63), he neither appeases them nor makes any concession to the forces they represent.

When open conflict resumes (677–719) after Eteocles' decision to fight at the seventh gate, we find both parties maintaining the same basic positions as in the earlier scene. The chorus urge Eteocles not to bring this incurable religious pollution upon the city; he maintains that his military duty requires him to fight and that the pollution is unavoidable. The fact that throughout this second confrontation the chorus are asking Eteocles to change his purpose, whereas earlier he had been asking them to change, has led some critics to suggest that the two "appear to reverse roles half-way through this play."[18] Wilamowitz even suggested that the chorus are no longer the young women of the earlier part of the play but now represent the people of Thebes as a whole,[19] and the view that Eteocles changes from the noble defender of Thebes to the accursed son of Oedipus, after he learns of his brother's presence at the seventh gate (653), has found many adherents.[20] This apparent reversal may be misleading, however, for in terms of his conflict with the chorus Eteocles' position remains essentially unchanged. Only the situation has changed, with the result that the weakness of his position, already suggested in the earlier scene, is now made fully apparent. Conversely, the strength of the chorus' position is also revealed more clearly, though it, too, is apparent to the audience, if not to Eteocles, in their earlier confrontation.

By understanding the conflict between Eteocles and the chorus in this way, we can dispense with a problem that has vexed many critics of *Septem*, the question of the play's unity. No longer need we be troubled by a schizophrenic hero, whose transition from cool and rational commander to demented fratricide occurs between two verses. Nor need we worry about Wilamowitz' picture of a poet who took two different heroic legends and managed to make a single play from them by stitching one on the end of the other ("a well-established feature of Greek archaic style," according to Dawe).[21] *Septem* does not present a conflict within Eteocles himself, but between him and the chorus. The play thus reveals how their different attitudes toward life and the city, which are representative of more general sexual values, come into conflict and how the conflict is or is not resolved. It is possible, as Winnington-Ingram suggests,[22] that this conflict between sexual values was related to a similar conflict between Laius and his wife in the first play, but this must remain a matter for speculation.

Although I have discussed the conflict between Eteocles and the chorus primarily in terms of sexual values, a political aspect to the two sides is also suggested, namely the issue of military domination of the affairs of the city. It is true that this aspect of the drama is not emphasized in the play, and no direct connection with contemporary Athens is indicated. Nonetheless, Athens in 467 was supporting a large and active military force, which was justified partly as a defense against the continuing threat of a Persian attack. Thus questions such as how much military activity was necessary for the security of the city or how much influence military men should exert over the affairs of the city may have been discussed at the time. Even if they were not, however, the general political overtones of the conflict in *Septem* may have been apparent to the audience.[23]

Regrettably we cannot be certain what the final outcome of the conflict was meant to be. If the present ending of *Septem* is genuine,[24] then Aeschylus clearly wanted his audience to understand that the conflict had not achieved resolution, since the dispute between Antigone, the woman (cf. 1038) urging the burial of Polyneices, and the herald, who refuses it on behalf of the city council, represents essentially the same conflict between female, religious demands and male, military demands as in the earlier part of the play. The present end thus indicates that the basic conflict will continue in the future. There is no Aeschylean parallel for such an unresolved ending to a trilogy, but it is not an impossible conclusion. Indeed, even if the end of *Septem* is spurious, the conflict may have been presented as continuing after Eteocles' death. It is more likely, however, that the chorus' lament ended the play, and that the death of the brothers was thus presented as the conclusion, if not the resolution, of the conflict between Eteocles and the chorus.

One purpose of *Septem*, then, and perhaps also of the trilogy, is to present a conflict between forces in the city that can be broadly classified as male and female. It (probably) aims to show how, under certain circumstances, such conflict is not constructively resolved but persists from one event and one generation to the next. This is a pessimistic theme, and might represent Aeschylus' earlier attitude, which later gave way to the more optimistic tone of the *Oresteia* and other trilogies.[25] In the sense that both *Septem* and the *Oresteia* give us insight into the nature of such a conflict, however, the lesson to be learned from *Septem*, where resolution of this conflict is not achieved, may be similar in many ways to the understanding gained from the resolution of the conflict in the later trilogy.

We can be less certain of the intended effect of *Supplices*, since it was the first play of its trilogy, and we have almost no knowledge of Aeschylus' treatment of themes in the two subsequent plays. Much effort has been expended in attempting to reconstruct the lost plays, but, as Garvie concluded after a thorough survey of the matter, "Many theories have been developed, some more plausible than others, but none which could not be demolished by a single fortunate papyrus find. At the end we are left with the one certain fact with which we began. Somewhere in the *Danaides* Aphrodite appears and makes a speech praising the power of *erōs*."[26] Though this one fact is by no means insignificant, we must keep Garvie's warning in mind as we look briefly at some of the important issues in the play.

The political situation in *Supplices* and its possible relation to Athenian politics has often been studied.[27] There is general agreement that the play presents the city of Argos in a favorable light and may perhaps recall in particular the city's acceptance of Themistocles when he was a fugitive from Athens a few years earlier.[28] Furthermore, this favorable picture of Argos is thought to be an indication of Athens' friendship with Argos, which was growing stronger at the time of the play's production (circa 463) and resulted in a formal alliance in 462 or 461. But these conclusions are based on the assumption that the favorable picture of Argos in *Supplices* persisted through the rest of the trilogy, although it is quite possible, even probable, that it did not.

At least two events that are generally assumed to have been included in the trilogy would have threatened and might even have destroyed Argos' prosperity. First, in the battle that seems imminent at the end of *Supplices* the Argive forces were almost certainly defeated by the Aegyptians, perhaps before the start of the next play. Secondly, it is probable that forty-nine of the Danaids later killed their husbands on their wedding night, thereby bringing on Argos the very pollution the city was seeking to avoid by accepting the maidens in the first place. Would Argos still have appeared in such a favorable light after these events?

Other questions arise, if we try to see events from this later perspective. Pelasgus, for instance, is usually applauded for his decision that the interests of the city will best be served if it accepts the Danaids and agrees to protect them,[29] but would this decision have appeared so wise in the end? Would his recourse to the local assembly, in which some have seen contemporary political relevance, have appeared politically advantageous?[30] And what would the reaction be to the chorus' great ode (625–709), in which they pray for peace, fertility, and other benefits for Argos? Similar prayers occur at the end of *Eumenides*, where we can confidently expect their fulfillment, but the prayers of the Danaids were certainly not immediately and perhaps never fulfilled. Are the chorus' wishes here doomed to the same fate as their earlier prayer that the Aegyptians be shipwrecked (29–33)?

It is possible, of course, that the trilogy ended with a happy resolution of the issues, in which Argos found the peace and prosperity prayed for by the maidens.[31] Even if this was the case, however, the political aspect of such a resolution may have been quite different from the political situation in *Supplices*. If the constitutional monarchy of the first play was replaced by a foreign tyranny in the second, the third play may have ended with a third, quite different political system for Argos. And the specific question of the wisdom of accepting suppliants into one's city may have been virtually forgotten by the end, so that, even if later events showed Pelasgus' decision to be unwise, the whole trilogy might still have presented Argos in a favorable light.

The suggestion that later events may raise doubts about the decision to accept the suppliants seems to overlook the obvious fact that the maidens have *dikē* on their side, and that a decision to accept them must therefore be correct. Such reasoning is invalid, however, since the Aegyptians may have an equally valid *dikē* on their side. Moreover the Danaids' justification for their position is somewhat ambiguous in *Supplices.* They repeatedly claim the support of Zeus (*e.g.,* 1, 26, 41, 91–93) and of *dikē* (78, 343, 395, 406, 430, 437), and they condemn the *hybris* of their cousins (104, 426, 487, 528). But they are notably evasive when pressed by Pelasgus for specific facts to support their case (336–39), and they use threats of suicide rather than legal or moral arguments to sway his decision. Thus, although their confidence that they are supported by Zeus and *dikē* is impressive, we should hesitate before accepting their view, since their faith in the power of Zeus and his *dikē* (*dikaia Diothen kratē,* 437) may be nothing but wishful thinking, in view of the Aegyptians' later military victory.[32]

The Danaids win our sympathy in this play, however, if not by their appeals to the gods, at least by contrast with the Aegyptian herald, who is clearly portrayed as a barbaric ruffian. But we must remember that he, too, claims the support of *dikē* (916) on the ground that he is merely recovering his lost property (918), and he warns that Ares will judge (*dikazein*) the matter in battle (934–37), a prediction that was probably fulfilled soon afterwards. Of course the question of *dikē* may eventually have been settled in favor of the Danaids, and they may have been suitably rewarded at the end of the trilogy, but here we face another difficulty: who was rewarded—the forty-nine who killed their husbands, or Hypermestra, who spared hers? Or did Aeschylus somehow arrange a final compromise in which all fifty could prosper? Without further evidence, we can only conclude that the Danaids' claim of *dikē* in *Supplices* is an expression of their own feelings but not necessarily an objective statement of fact.

The uncertainty about the outcome of the trilogy is particularly frustrating with regard to sexual conflict, which plays a larger and more evident role in this play than in any other by Aeschylus,[33] and probably continued to play an important role in the rest of the trilogy. From the beginning the Danaids maintain that they are fleeing men and marriage (8–9).[34] They fear that marriage would be slavery (cf. *dmōis*, 335), and this fear seems to be confirmed by the herald's claim that the Aegyptians regard the women as their lost property (918). Indeed the maidens not only flee marriage but also reject all male dominance (392–93), and rather than submit to their cousins they prefer death (787–807). In spite of this extreme rejection of marriage and of Aphrodite (1031–33),[35] however, the women nonetheless uphold the feminine values of fertility (688–93) and childbirth (676–77).[36] Another concern of theirs is to avoid pollution; they reject a marriage that would not be pure (*hagnos*, 228), and they put their trust in the altars to which they cling, claiming, as the chorus in *Septem* might similarly have claimed, that "the altar is stronger than the tower" (190).

In terms of sexual conflict, the Danaids and the female values they represent are victorious in *Supplices*, in that they succeed in obtaining the support of Pelasgus and his city. Like *Agamemnon*, however, the play ends on an ominous note, and it is probable that the Aegyptians, who must have represented the values of male dominance,[37] gained control over the women in the second play, perhaps after a military victory. It is tempting to speculate further that the killing of forty-nine of the Aegyptians in the second or third play (or between the two) represented a movement back to female dominance, and that this action was perhaps balanced by Hypermestra's refusal to participate in the killing. By her refusal Hypermestra would have indicated her submission to marriage and to her husband, and male dominance would thus be reestablished in her case. How the issue was ultimately resolved is quite unclear, but it would have been easier to reach a compromise if Hypermestra's husband was presented as the least brutal and dominating of the Aegyptians, as he was in at least one version of the myth.[38] Perhaps at the end Lynceus and Hypermestra join in a marriage that is more equal, though still, presumably, male-dominated. We do know that in the final play Aphrodite appears and praises *erōs*, the bringer of fertility to the earth (fr. 125 [Loeb fr. 25]). This fragment is scant, but illuminating. It suggests that the Danaids' extreme hostility to the male institution of marriage and to Aphrodite in *Supplices* was modified or abandoned in the last play, since the goddess herself uses the metaphorical language of marriage (cf. *gamos* in verses 2 and 6)[39] in her description of the general fertility of the earth. It thus appears that both fertility and marriage were reestablished at the end of the trilogy.

In terms of sexual conflict, then, we can postulate a probable movement from excessive female dominance in the first play to excessive male dominance in the second. The similarity of this movement to that of the first two plays of the *Oresteia* makes it tempting to assume a similar harmonious resolution of the conflict in the last play, and this is not impossible, as I have indicated above. But the assumption is not supported by any clear evidence, and we certainly cannot rule out the possibility that a strong male dominance was reaffirmed in the final play, not only by Hypermestra's acceptance of marriage, but perhaps also by the marriage of the forty-nine other Danaids. Both of these results could have been brought about by the persuasive force of Aphrodite.

Prometheus is so different in some ways from Aeschylus' six other surviving plays that some critics have questioned its authenticity,[40] and dates ranging from early in Aeschylus' career to the end of the fifth century have been suggested for its production. As in the case of *Supplices*, moreover, uncertainty about the subsequent plays makes interpretation more difficult; in this case our relative abundance of evidence for the lost second play, *Prometheus Unbound*, is offset by our total ignorance of the third play, if indeed there was one.[41] These specific difficulties are not my concern, however, and in the following brief discussion I assume Aeschylean authorship regardless of date, accept what we can surmise with reasonable certainty about Prometheus' relase in *Prometheus Unbound*, and omit any consideration of hypothetical reconstructions of a third play. I have little to add, moreover, to the many discussions of the one problem that has most occupied modern critics of *Prometheus*, namely the presentation of Zeus and its apparent inconsistency with the picture of him in the *Oresteia* and *Supplices*.[42] Let me merely state that, in the first place, I see no reason why the presentation of Zeus in different plays should be completely consistent; Aeschylus is a dramatist, not a theologian. In the second place, Zeus in the *Oresteia* is the god who benefits mortals primarily by punishing those who err, just as he punishes Prometheus' error in *Prometheus*. And in the third place, there is no reason why Aeschylus could not, if he wished, portray a Zeus who changes from one play to the next in a trilogy.[43]

Leaving aside this question, let us turn to the play itself. Perhaps the most striking feature of *Prometheus* is its lack of dramatic action. The binding of Prometheus in the opening scene and his engulfment at the end might be construed as advancing the plot, but essentially the dramatic situation remains unchanged. Aeschylus does not present the conflict between Prometheus and Zeus as a developing or changing one, but as a static situation, a state of rebellion from authority, that remains constant from beginning to end. During the course of the play, a number of other figures encounter Prometheus and react to his situation in various ways; none of them can change it, but each presents us with a different view of it. Indeed it is precisely this dramatic presentation of one basic situation with a range of different reactions to it that is the major interest of *Prometheus.*

Clearly the situation is a political one and is presented as such throughout. As Thomson says, "Zeus is a tyrant, and his rule a tyranny. We learn this from his own ministers, who are proud of it, from Prometheus, who denounces it, from the Oceanids, who deplore it, and from Oceanus, who is resigned to it."[44] Against this tyranny Prometheus is in open rebellion, and, although Zeus has the upper hand at present, we know that Prometheus' secret knowledge will make his rebellion at least partially successful in the long run. As the play proceeds, we learn more about this rebellion, not only from Prometheus' own remarks, but also from the different reactions to it by others, who come forth one after another and present their views: Kratos, the ugly, ruthless henchman, who takes pleasure from his prisoners' troubles; Hephaestus, the sympathetic friend, who nonetheless carries out Zeus' orders; the Oceanids, timid, compassionate maidens, who stick by Prometheus in the end, despite their disapproval of some aspects of his behavior; Oceanus, the pompous counselor, who falters when he himself is in danger; Io, the fellow-sufferer, who cannot see beyond her own lot; and finally Hermes, the sophisticated courier and eager minister of his master's desire. Most important of all, throughout the play we see Prometheus undergoing his punishment, now accepting it, now crying out against it, now defiant, now despairing. Certainly he is an arrogant, stubborn rebel, in some respects similar to the tyrant he is challenging; but he must nonetheless have won the admiration and sympathy of most of the audience, as he has of most audiences since. Some modern critics, perhaps some in the original audience, too, condemn Prometheus and side with Zeus,[45] but these are not, and cannot have been, a majority. Indeed I suspect the chorus would represent the typical reaction of the audience: basic sympathy for Prometheus' cause combined with some disapproval of his manner.

Since the basic situation in Prometheus is a political one, the different reactions to it, either on stage or in the audience, are political reactions and depend primarily on one's general attitude toward power and its use. The rightness or wrongness of his crime and punishment is a relatively minor issue.[46] As in most Aeschylean conflicts, the dispute between Prometheus and Zeus is a matter of *dikē* on both sides. The *dikē* on Zeus' side is the result of Prometheus' theft of fire, which even he admits was an error.[47] It went "beyond the limit of *dikē*" (*pera dikēs*, 30), as Hephaestus, a sympathizer, points out.[48] Prometheus must consequently pay the penalty (*dikē*) for it (9, 614).[49] He does not deny the necessity for some penalty, but he and his sympathizers do protest the severity of the punishment, and, when further punishment is threatened at the end of the play, he accuses Zeus of acting without *dikē* (*ekdikos*, 976, 1093),[50] a charge that the audience would probably also accept as valid. In sum, both accusations, that Prometheus once violated *dikē* and that Zeus is now acting without *dikē*, are valid, but neither has much significance for the political situation.

We do not know whether anything more was said of *dikē* in the second play, nor can we say whether the further events would have substantially changed the audience's reaction to the hero's condition, but we do know that *Prometheus Unbound* was similar to *Prometheus* in several ways. For instance, it apparently had a similarly static dramatic structure, and although the release of Prometheus near the end of the play may have provided some dramatic movement, the basic situation of hostility between Prometheus and Zeus seems to have continued even after his release.[51] We are reasonably certain that here, too, Prometheus was on stage during most or all of the play and was visited by the chorus of his brothers, the Titans, by his mother, Gaia, by Heracles, his deliverer, and perhaps by Hephaestus and others.[52] It is clear from this that Prometheus must have dominated the second play as he does the first. It is important to stress that dramatically Prometheus is the center of attention in both plays, because the attention of scholars is more often directed to the nature of Zeus, and we may consequently forget that it is Prometheus—the rebel who is eventually saved by his own knowledge—who must have been Aeschylus' primary interest, as he is for most readers or viewers of the play.

Although it is possible that the trilogy (or dilogy) revealed the development and resolution of a conflict, as the *Oresteia* does, in the play and fragments that survive, Aeschylus does not seem concerned with presenting any progressive development of the conflict. Instead he makes Prometheus' state of rebellion the constant background against which he presents this one figure who dominates the stage. Indeed the major achievement of *Prometheus* is this powerful picture of a resister, a picture that reveals, among other things, that rebels in their stubborn arrogance often become quite similar to the tyrants against whom they are rebelling (a truth that Sophocles also understood, as we see from his portrayal of Antigone). Furthermore, by showing how different people react when confronted with a state of rebellion, the play reveals further truths about political behavior in general. Similar insights into political rebellion and the reactions to it were probably presented in *Prometheus Unbound.*

We do not know when *Prometheus* was produced, but tyrants had played an important role in recent Athenian history (circa 560–510), and tyranny as a political system was much debated in fifth-century Athens. Rebellion against tyranny was strongly praised by supporters of democracy, and the myth of the Athenian "tyrannicides," Harmodius and Aristogiton, developed rapidly after the Persian Wars, perhaps at the urging of Themistocles.[53] Thus it is not necessary to see, for example, Pericles and Protagoras behind the figures of Zeus and Prometheus[54] in order to argue for the contemporary relevance of *Prometheus*; tyranny and rebellion were common concerns during Aeschylus' lifetime, and one of the effects of the play would have been to enlarge the Athenians' understanding of this political conflict. Since similar political situations have recurred throughout history, moreover, the play has continued to bring insight to later audiences. Indeed the continuing interest in Prometheus and his situation as presented in this play is lasting testimony to the skill with which Aeschylus presented on stage some of the fundamental truths of this common but complex political situation.

As we can see from the brief discussion of these three single plays, any study of forces rather than character, takes us immediately beyond the limits of a single play. Thus, in the preceding discussion it has been necessary to make assumptions about plays that no longer survive. I have tried to remain cautious in these assumptions; new evidence might substantially alter our picture of a lost play and cause us to revise our understanding of the operation of certain forces in a surviving play. This possibility presents less difficulty for those who study the characters of individual heroes, such as Eteocles. Nonetheless, I have tried to demonstrate that the attempt to understand forces rather than characters in Aeschylus' drama is valid, that it sheds light on other issues, including the character of individuals, such as Eteocles, and that it results in both a truer understanding of the plays and a more accurate assessment of their effects on the original audiences. Attic drama shaped the Athenians' attitudes toward life. These attitudes were reflected not so much in their views of individuals as in their perceptions of the city and its political life. Cornford long ago remarked that "in every age the common interpretation of the world of things is controlled by some scheme of unchallenged and unsuspected presupposition,"[55] and he argued that Thucydides' view of the Peloponnesian War was shaped in part by Aeschylean tragedy. Whether this is true of Thucydides or not (and I think it is), it is certainly plausible that Athenians nourished on Aeschylean drama would derive an understanding of political behavior in general that would strongly affect their understanding of actual historical events.

This is not to say that Aeschylus presents a single-minded view of political behavior or human society. Even in his few surviving plays he focuses on a number of different issues and presents different patterns of conflict. But underlying all his dramatic action is a fundamental sense of rise and fall in human affairs, of action and reaction, of reciprocity, and of *dikē*. This *dikē* usually manifests itself in a conflict between individuals, and the modern tendency is to seek a sense of justice in such conflicts: which side is right, are punishment and reward properly distributed, is justice done? Throughout this study I have emphasized that such questions are misleading. In Aeschylean drama there are no Iagos. Each side has some validity, each individual claims the support of *dikē*, each feels he is right and his adversary wrong. Agamemnon and Clytemnestra, Eteocles and Polyneices, the Danaids and the Aegyptian herald, all have confidence in the rightness of their positions. The total effect of Aeschylean drama, however, is or should be to lead us, his audience, to see both sides together and thereby to make us understand that neither side is ever totally right. We should learn, moreover, that the unyielding insistence on one side to the exclusion of the other will lead to disaster and that only through a willingness to grant the validity of both sides can we find a constructive harmony. One may claim the support of *dikē*, but, if one considers this *dikē* to be an absolute right, one will find only the negative side of *dikē*—retribution and conflict. If one admits the existence of *dikē* on both sides, however, one can eventually find the positive *dikē* of balance and harmony, not only for oneself but also for the whole society.

In Aeschylean drama the basic patterns of human action are relatively simple; the actual manifestations of these patterns, however, are varied and complex. It is Aeschylus' genius that he understood the variety and complexity of human affairs, that he saw past the complexity to the underlying fundamental patterns, and that through his poetic and dramatic skill he presented the basic truths of human behavior with a clarity and brilliance that have seldom, if ever, been equaled.

Appendix A

Pathei Mathos

We can begin our examination of the "doctrine" of *pathei mathos* in the *Oresteia* by noting that the words themselves occur together twice in the parodos of *Agamemnon* (177, 250–51) and nowhere else. The first occurrence is in the "hymn to Zeus" (160–83), which interrupts the chorus' narrative of the events ten years earlier, when the expedition gathered under Agamemnon to sail to Troy. At that time the seer Calchas made predictions (from omens) that were both favorable and unfavorable—namely that the expedition would take Troy (126), but that a sacrifice (of Iphigeneia) would be required first (149–50).[1] He further predicted that a "wrath" would remain in the house to avenge the child (*mēnis teknopoinos*, 155), a clear hint that Agamemnon's return might be endangered. Thus, by the end of the epode (159), the chorus have sung at length of their major concern, that the expedition to Troy succeed, and they have more darkly suggested a second concern, that some danger may await Agamemnon on his return. If the "hymn to Zeus" has any specific reference in its context, it must refer to one or both of these concerns, and for several reasons I see the first concern as the chorus' primary reference.[2]

First, the fate of the expedition is their primary concern in the preceding section of the parodos (40–159); their worry about Agamemnon's return is only briefly and indirectly suggested near the end of this section. Secondly, this worry about Agamemnon's return is conditional on their first concern being satisfied. Not until they hear the news from the herald (503 ff.) do they finally accept as certain the fact that Troy is taken. Thirdly, no matter how *pathei mathos* is understood, it cannot relieve the chorus' specific worry about Agamemnon's safe homecoming, whereas, as we shall see, it is easy to understand the chorus' appeal to *pathei mathos* to help relieve their anxiety over the fate of the expedition.

The epode ends with the hope that the good will win out (*to d' eu nikatō*, 159), and this hope leads the chorus to turn somewhat abruptly and address "Zeus, whoever you are" (160). The transition here is underscored by a notable shift from a primarily dactylic meter (especially in 146–59) to the iambo-trochaic rhythm that dominates the great "moralizing" odes of the trilogy. This metrical change emphasizes the fact that the chorus are ceasing their narration of past events and beginning more general reflection. They address Zeus, they say, because there is no one comparable to him "if it is necessary truly to cast off the vain burden of concern from one's thoughts" (εἰ τὸ μάταν ἀπὸ φροντίδος ἄχθος / χρὴ βαλεῖν ἐτητύμως, 165–67).[3] The burden the chorus wish to throw off is not specified, but in the present context it must refer primarily to their ignorance of and worry about the fate of the expedition to Troy.[4] It may have a secondary reference to their anxiety about Agamemnon's safe return,[5] but this burden (as I have said) cannot be thrown off until their primary uncertainty has been relieved.

In the antistrophe (168–75) the chorus continue their

praise of Zeus' power by alluding briefly to his victory over his father (Cronos), who had earlier defeated his father (Ouranos). Neither earlier god is mentioned by name, but the reference to them is clear,[6] as is the emphasis on physical power (*pammachōi thrasei*, 169); Zeus is to be praised as a *triaktēr*, or one who throws his opponent thrice in a wrestling contest, and he who sings of Zeus' victory "shall hit the full mark of understanding" (τεύξεται φρενῶν τὸ πᾶν, 175). The significance of this reference to the establishment of Zeus' reign is not immediately clear, but the fact that Zeus deals out to Cronos roughly the same fate that Cronos dealt his own father suggests that the reign of Zeus has been established by the law of *drasanti pathein* ("to the doer it is done"), and that this rule is valid for one who acknowledges Zeus.[7]

That the force of these verses is to connect Zeus with the law of retribution is in keeping with the general picture of Zeus, who throughout *Agamemnon* and *Choephoroi* is almost always mentioned in the context of punishment, the punishment of Troy during the first half of *Agamemnon*, the punishment of Agamemnon, and then the punishment of Clytemnestra. Moreover the close connection between the reign of Zeus and the law that the doer suffers is explicitly stated by the chorus after Agamemnon's death:

> φέρει φέροντ', ἐκτίνει δ' ὁ καίνων·
> μίμνει δὲ μίμνοντος ἐν θρόνῳ Διὸς
> παθεῖν τὸν ἔρξαντα· θέσμιον γάρ.

("Someone plunders the plunderer; the killer pays the penalty; and it remains, while Zeus remains on his throne, that the doer suffers: for this is the [divine] ordinance," 1562–64). These considerations lend support to the view that in this middle section of the hymn to Zeus (168–75) the chorus are celebrating Zeus' power as the enforcer of the law that the doer suffers. This conclusion in turn reinforces the view that

the chorus primarily have in mind the expedition to Troy, for
they would thus be expressing their faith in Zeus specifically
as the punisher of Troy.[8]

In the third and final stanza of the hymn to Zeus (176–
83) the chorus describe in some detail how Zeus' power operates in human affairs:

> τὸν φρονεῖν βροτοὺς ὁδώ-
>   σαντα, τῷ πάθει μάθος
> θέντα κυρίως ἔχειν·
> στάζει δ' ἀνθ' ὕπνου πρὸ καρδίας
> μνησιπήμων πόνος· καὶ παρ' ἄ-   180
>   κοντας ἦλθε σωφρονεῖν·
> δαιμόνων δέ που χάρις βιαίως
> σέλμα σεμνὸν ἡμένων.

("[Zeus] who put men on the road to understanding by estab-
lishing *pathei mathos* as a valid principle; but toil, recalling
woes, drips before the heart instead of sleep, and discretion
comes even to the unwilling. There is, I think, a favor with
violence from the gods [who are] seated on high benches").[9]
There has been much discussion of these difficult lines and
their importance for the play and trilogy, but little agreement
has been reached. We can begin by inferring from the first
clause that the understanding that men are led toward is apparently the law of *pathei mathos*. We can further surmise
that it is by means of this law that Zeus provides the chorus
in particular, as well as men in general, with the means for
casting off the burden of anxiety mentioned in the first stanza
(165–67).

Leaving aside for the moment any discussion of the precise
meaning of *pathei mathos*, let us consider the next clause: "instead of sleep there drips before the heart *ponos* (toil), recalling woes." The emotional state described here seems to cor-
respond to the burden of anxiety (165) that the chorus are
trying to throw off. Parallels elsewhere in the play indicate

that it is precisely the sense of fear and worry that these words refer to.[10] Moreover, *ponos*[11] sounds one of the keynotes of the trilogy, the search for deliverance from toils and troubles. In the opening line of the play the watchman asks for a "release from these toils" (*tōnd' apallagēn ponōn*), and the repetition of these words halfway through his speech (*apallagē ponōn*, 20) would fix them in the audience's mind. The *ponoi* of the watchman are in one sense merely his labors as a watchman, which will end when the news comes of Troy's capture. But it is clear from the rest of his speech that his troubles also include his fear and anxiety for the house and that he is looking for deliverance from these as well. These *ponoi* remain in the house until the final play, when Orestes goes to Athens seeking to be "released from these toils" (*tōnd' apallaxai ponōn*, *Eu.* 83). This echo of the watchman's words in *Eumenides*[12] indicates that Orestes' troubles are basically the same ones that have beset the house from the beginning, and it is this whole climate of trouble that is suggested by the chorus in *Ag.* 180.[13] Their primary worry is, as we have seen, the fate of the expedition, and their anxiety is a toil; they remember their woes and cannot sleep. It is clear from this that *de* (179) must be adversative: they have confidence in the law of *pathei mathos, but* they still have their anxiety.

The next two statements, however, are again spoken in confidence, or at least in hope. The word *sōphronein*, which I have translated "discretion," is applied to the ability to know one's place and stay in it. I will argue below that in this trilogy (and elsewhere) it implies not just discretion but also obedience, and the chorus' view here that it will come even to the unwilling is certainly consistent with such a meaning. Finally, the "favor" of the gods, who are in command, comes somehow violently, as would be necessary if it brings obedience to the unwilling. But what is this favor? *Charis* is a common word in the *Oresteia*, with several senses, but the only other mention of the *charis* of a god that seems relevant here[14] is when the herald says that the *charis* of Zeus, which has accomplished the overthrow of Troy, shall be honored (*kai charis timēsetai / Dios tad' ekpraxasa*, 581–82). Here the *charis* of Zeus is certainly a favor for the Greeks, but it has also come violently on the Trojans. Thus the conquest of Troy is clearly an example of the sort of *charis* of the gods that the chorus have in mind at the end of the hymn to Zeus. To confirm that the *charis* they sing of refers specifically to the fall of Troy, we need only look to their reaction to Clytemnestra's announcement that Troy is taken: there they rejoice that a worthy *charis* has been accomplished for their *ponoi* (*Ag.* 354).[15]

Thus the "violent favor" that the chorus hope for at the end of the third stanza must refer to the fall of Troy; it could hardly refer to the safe return of Agamemnon, since this would presumably not be violent, and the same is true of their confidence that "discretion" or "obedience" will come even to the unwilling. These considerations thus lend further support to our conclusion that the primary reference of the hymn to Zeus is the chorus' anxiety over the fate of the expedition to Troy, an anxiety they wish to cast off. As is typical of them, they are torn between conflicting feelings of worry over their toils (179–80) and confidence that Zeus' law and the favor of the gods will dispel this worry (176–78, 180–83). Of course, the audience would probably also have in mind Agamemnon's fate on returning and might note that he will feel the violence of the god's favor, just as the Trojans have. From this perspective all of the chorus' hopes for the punishment of Troy have an ironic secondary application to Agamemnon himself, and this irony reinforces the validity of the law that the punisher is punished in turn. But it seems unlikely that the chorus themselves are aware of this ironic sense at this moment.

What then, we must now ask, is the meaning of *pathei*

mathos, and how does it bear on the chorus' anxiety about the fate of the expedition? If we translate the phrase "learning through a suffering,"[16] what is learned, and by whom? In answer to the second part of this question, one would certainly expect that the sufferer himself is the one who learns, and this is confirmed by the second reference to *pathei mathos* at the end of the parodos (see below). This interpretation is also in keeping with a Homeric expression that many consider an earlier version of *pathei mathos*. The phrase occurs first in a passage where Euphorbus is killed by Menelaus after being warned not to face him in battle, for "the fool learns when it happens to him" (*rhechthen de te nēpios egnō*, *Il.* 17.32; cf. 20.198).[17] Of course we need not restrict Aeschylus' meaning to that of Homer and Hesiod, and many would argue that these examples are of little or no relevance. But later echoes of this sentiment are similar in meaning and indicate that the expression "learning through suffering" continued to have this Homeric meaning. Oedipus, for instance, warns Teiresias that if he were not such an old man, he would "learn through suffering what sort of thoughts you have [*sc.* disobedient ones]" (*pathōn egnōs an hoia per phroneis*, *OT* 403), and Alcibiades warns his listeners to learn from his own example "and not, as the proverb goes, like a fool learn through suffering" (*kai mē kata tēn paroimian hōsper nēpion pathonta gnōnai*, Plato, *Symp.* 222b). It is especially clear in this last example that the proverb means that the learner is himself the one who suffers; he does not learn from the suffering of others.[18]

What does the sufferer learn? In the *Iliad* Euphorbus learns only that he was wrong. He "learns his lesson" as we say in English, giving no implication that a general lesson is being learned, other than that one should not have done what one did. This is learning in a rather limited sense, and it is difficult for most people to believe that this is all Aeschylus means by *pathei mathos*. Before looking for a larger sense, we must note

that this restricted meaning of *pathei mathos*, that the suffering is its own lesson, can certainly be applied to several important events in the trilogy. Troy "learns its lesson" by being
destroyed. Agamemnon "learns his lesson" by being killed. In
both these cases (and in the case of Clytemnestra's death) it is
difficult if not impossible to find any larger sense in which the
sufferer learns.

Before considering other cases, let us look at the only other
place in the *Oresteia* that explicitly refers to the law of *pathei
mathos*. After the sixth strophe of the parodos in *Agamemnon*
the chorus break off their description of the sacrifice of Iphigeneia and begin the final antistrophe:

> τὰ δ' ἔνθεν οὔτ' εἶδον οὔτ' ἐννέπω·
> τέχναι δὲ Κάλχαντος οὐκ ἄκραντοι.
> Δίκα δὲ τοῖς μὲν παθοῦ-
> σιν μαθεῖν ἐπιρρέπει· τὸ μέλλον
> ἐπεὶ γένοιτ' ἂν κλύοις.

("What followed I neither saw nor do I tell of it; but the art
of Calchas is not without fulfillment. And *dike* weighs out to
those who suffer to learn; but the future, when it should come,
you would learn of it," 248–52).[19] As in the hymn to Zeus,
the primary reference of these lines is to the capture of Troy.
The chorus did not see anything of the events after the fleet
left Aulis and cannot tell of the fate of the expedition (hence
their anxiety). But they also have confidence in the prophecy
of Calchas, the main thrust of which was that Troy would fall.
And they know that *dike*, the force of retribution, brings
"learning" to those who suffer. The chorus are reasonably confident about the punishment of Troy, but still they warn that
the future is known only when it comes.

Because the chorus break off their description of the sacrifice
of Iphigeneia before the actual blow is struck (though they
leave no doubt that the sacrifice took place), some have seen
a different reference in these lines. *Ta enthen* ("what fol-

lowed") is taken to refer to the blow itself, which the chorus did not see (we must assume that they covered their eyes at the last moment). The prophecy of Calchas then refers to the warning that a wrath remains in the house, and the chorus are worried that *dikē* will teach Agamemnon a lesson when he returns. I have several objections to this view. First, if the chorus, who have given such a detailed account of Iphigeneia's sacrifice in the preceding verses, had in fact covered their eyes at the last minute, they would certainly have made a more direct reference to this action. Secondly, it seems unlikely that the chorus would register such a strong objection to the sacrifice either when it occurred or ten years later, since they elsewhere express only mild qualms about it. Thirdly, it is more plausible for the expression "*dikē* teaches people a lesson" to refer to the lesson taught the Trojans than to the one taught to Agamemnon since the chorus are less likely to speak of Agamemnon's potential punishment as a lesson. Finally, the later reference to "what remains" (*ta epi toutoisin,* 255) would have little meaning if the chorus had already spoken of the possible fate of Agamemnon on his return, whereas if they have spoken of the fate of Troy, "what remains" easily refers to affairs at home and Agamemnon's return. Thus, the primary reference of *pathei mathos* here is to the punishment of Troy, but, as in the hymn to Zeus, it is certainly likely that Aeschylus meant to suggest the secondary reference to Agamemnon's fate: his triumph and his death would thus ironically be seen by the audience (though not consciously by the chorus) as examples of the same process.

This second explicit reference to *pathei mathos,* moreover, makes it certain that it is the sufferer himself and not someone else who "learns." Whether these lines refer to Troy or to Agamemnon, they give us no further evidence for a broader interpretation of the learning that comes through suffering. There are, however, two more significant references to someone learning something through suffering, and these may suggest a slightly broader interpretation of the lesson learned.[20] The first of these occurs in 1425, after Clytemnestra has told the chorus that she is willing to abide by their rule if they should conquer her by force. "But if a god brings about the opposite," she continues, "then you will learn discretion, though being taught late" (*gnōsēi didachtheis opse goun to sōphronein*, 1425). This is clearly a threat: if the chorus lose a battle with her (as she expects they will), they will have to "learn discretion." Later Aegisthus makes a similar threat: if the chorus do not obey him, they shall be taught the error of their ways, by prison if necessary (1619–23). When they do not obey, his final threat, "you shall soon learn" (*gnōsēi tacha*, 1649), leads both sides to draw their swords, until Clytemnestra calms them down.[21]

These threats by Clytemnestra and Aegisthus do not suggest that the chorus are in for any moral instruction. The lesson to be learned is in one sense simply the punishment they will suffer. In a larger sense, however, both Clytemnestra and Aegisthus are threatening not just an immediate punishment but also a punishment that will make the chorus obey in the future. Such a punishment would teach them the general rule that they should obey their superiors (or else they will be punished again), and it is this general lesson of obedience that is indicated by the verb *sōphronein* ("be discreet," 1425, 1620; cf. 181, discussed above). Clytemnestra and Aegisthus are not urging general wisdom on the chorus or even a sense of moral self-control; their concern is simple, pragmatic obedience.[22]

If the chorus are to learn to obey, it may be thought that their lesson is an even more general one, such as that the weak should obey the strong, or that disobedience is always punished. It is even possible that they would learn the law of Zeus and *dikē*: that wrongdoing in general is punished. But the intention that they should learn this sort of general lesson, if present at all, is certainly not uppermost in the minds of Clytemnestra and Aegisthus when they threaten the chorus, and there is no indication that the chorus do or would learn such general lessons by suffering. In fact, the chorus already know the general law that wrongdoing is punished. The lesson they have not learned is to obey their new rulers.

Thus, in two examples of the law of *pathei mathos* (the destruction of Troy and the death of Agamemnon) the lesson learned is only the punishment itself, and in the third case (the chorus), where the sufferers survive, the lesson to be learned is obedience. Clytemnestra's case is similar to Agamemnon's (though there is no reference to *pathei mathos* in connection with her death), and Orestes certainly suffers, but does not appear any wiser (or any different at all) after his suffering. Cassandra and the Furies might also be said to suffer, but neither seems to derive any knowledge or understanding from the suffering.[23]

In short there is no evidence in the *Oresteia* for a broader sense for *pathei mathos*, nor should we expect to find one.[24] The expression occurs only in the parodos, where the chorus needs the comforting certainty that Troy will learn its lesson because of the inevitable operation of the law of Zeus that the doer suffers. What is perhaps surprising is the preoccupation of modern critics with *pathei mathos* and their exaggeration of its importance in the trilogy.[25] The reason for this lies in their focus on Zeus in Aeschylus or Aeschylus' concept of Zeus, a focus caused ultimately, I believe, by the more or less unconscious association of Zeus with the Judeo-Christian God.[26] In the *Oresteia* Zeus' activity seems largely concerned with punishment, and critics therefore look for some higher benevolent aspect of the god. The only benevolent doctrine they are able to discover is the law of *pathei mathos*, and they therefore exaggerate the importance and distort the meaning of this simple phrase. What these critics overlook is the possibility that, in the hymn to Zeus, the chorus are expressing their conviction that Zeus is benevolent, that he is man's greatest hope and comfort, precisely because he is Zeus the punisher. The law of retribution, weighed out by *dikē*, is Zeus' law (*Ag.* 1562–64), and it is the primary law for mankind, at least through the first two plays. The chorus in *Agamemnon* (and *Choephoroi*) sing over and over of the necessity for retribution: this is the one law they can have confidence in, and, since it is Zeus' law, he is the one god they have confidence in. He will relieve their burden of anxiety because as Zeus the punisher he will teach Troy a lesson. It is the sure knowledge of this punishment that the chorus seek in the law of *pathei mathos*, not any higher wisdom.

Appendix B

Eteocles and the Chorus in Septem

As we saw in our discussion of the conflict between the two brothers in *Septem* it is a common mistake to accept at face value Eteocles' own view of the dispute. There is a similar tendency among critics of *Septem* to accept Eteocles' view of the chorus as objective truth. Certainly general admiration for the heroic character of Eteocles has led to a corresponding depreciation of the chorus. In fact, a number of scholars have remarked how the calmness and rationality of Eteocles as a commander is emphasized by contrast with the hysterical panic of the chorus.[1] To see the chorus as a mere foil to Eteocles, however, leads not only to a misunderstanding of their position and the values they represent, but also to a serious distortion of the conflict between them and Eteocles. In the following examination of this conflict I attempt to understand the chorus in their own terms, as an equally significant party to the conflict. I try to show that their opposition to Eteocles results not from hysteria but from a set of values, broadly characterized as female, that are in direct conflict with his own male, military values.

The conflict between the chorus and Eteocles is developed

mainly during two scenes of direct confrontation, one before he knows he will fight Polyneices (181–286) and the other after his decision to do so (677–719). Before examining these scenes, however, we must estimate the impression the chorus make in their first appearance (78–180). The lyrics of the parodos are predominantly dochmiac, a meter that indicates heightened emotion but not necessarily hysteria or panic. In fact all the lyrics before Eteocles' exit in 719 are primarily dochmiac, even when the chorus are explicitly trying to calm him (686–708). Thus the dochmiac meter undoubtedly serves to characterize the chorus, but it does not in itself indicate hysteria or panic.[2] There is no evidence, moreover, to support the view of some editors that these verses were divided among individual members of the chorus or that the *choreutae* enter one by one and dash wildly around the stage.[3]

When the chorus enter in 78, they are certainly afraid, and they intend to sing of their "frightening, great troubles" (*phobera megal' achē,* 78), which are caused by the presence of the enemy at the walls, preparing for a final assault. Some critics have felt that the chorus' description of the danger that threatens the city is greatly exaggerated, if not imaginary,[4] but a comparison of this description of the situation (79–84) with the spy's earlier description (59–61) indicates not only substantial agreement on the facts but even a number of echoes in the language.[5] Thus the chorus' fear for the city is the natural result of their estimate of the military situation, which is the same as the spy's, and, although their sense of danger is high, it is neither extreme nor unjustified.

Eteocles, of course, is also concerned for the safety of the city. But, whereas the chorus seek protection primarily from the gods, repeatedly praying for their help in the parodos, Eteocles' primary concern is the army's defense of the city, and he makes it clear that his faith in the power of the gods is limited. True, he does show some concern for the gods in his opening address, calling on Zeus (8), mentioning the gods' altars (14–15), acknowledging the help of his prophet (24–27), and calling again on god (21, 35) or the gods (69–70). But these appeals seem official and pro forma. They are certainly less important to him than his primary interest, the military defense of Thebes. Many critics, moreover, have noted a certain cynicism in his observation that the gods get credit in victory but he himself would be blamed in defeat (4–7). The overall impression of Eteocles after the opening scene (1–77) is thus of an effective military commander who is somewhat cynical about the ability of the gods to help the military cause but is willing to maintain a proper attitude of respect toward them.[6]

When Eteocles returns, after the parodos, and addresses the chorus, he expresses his concern for the safety of the city and its army (183–84). He criticizes the chorus for their excessive attention to the gods (185–86) and for arousing the fear of the citizens (191–92). These remarks express sentiments that we have attributed to Eteocles from the opening scene, but his reaction to the chorus after the parodos also reveals a quality that we did not see earlier, his scornfulness. This is clear from his first words to them, "insufferable creatures" (*thremmat' ouk anascheta*, 181), and from his description of their song as the "shrieking and howling" (*auein, lakazein*) of those who are *sōphronōn misēmata* (186). The usual translation of these last two words is something like "hated by all sensible people," but the additional sense of discipline and obedience, often present in *sōphrōn* (see Appendix A), is undoubtedly in Eteocles' mind here. He is angered by the chorus' failure to be properly disciplined and obedient to his command, and considers such behavior "hateful to those who are disciplined." From such statements it is clear that, rather than calm their fear, he angrily and aggressively tries to force them to submit to his will.

After his opening attack, Eteocles does not, as might be expected, explain why the chorus is wrong or how they should behave, but instead proceeds with a denunciation of the entire female sex:

Neither in bad times nor in wished-for prosperity
may I share my home with the female sex [*tōi gynaikeiōi genei*].
For when she's in control,[7] her insolence is unapproachable,
but, when scared, she harms the home and city more.

                                                            [187–190]

Eteocles' desire never to share a house with women is perhaps understandable in view of his own family background,[8] but his sweeping condemnation of all women should raise some doubts about his own state of mind. After pointing out the ill effects of the chorus' fear, he repeats his general denunciation of women: "such would be one's lot, if one lived with a woman" (195). This ruler apparently does not live with women and knows only one way of treating them—to demand their obedience. He accordingly threatens that anyone who disobeys him, "man or woman or something in between" (197),[9] will be put to death. Most commentators remark on this unusual expression and see it as a sign of Eteocles' anger at the chorus,[10] but they tend to treat it as an isolated remark rather than as part of an emerging pattern: his scornful rebuke of the chorus, his repeated denunciation of all womankind, and now his partially incoherent demand for total obedience. These remarks, taken together, suggest that Eteocles is at least as "hysterical" as the chorus. To confirm this impression, moreover, he first renews his demand in sexual terms, telling the women to remain indoors and not involve themselves in men's affairs outside the house (200–201), and then ends his tirade with an exasperated and illogical shout, "do you hear me or do you not hear me, or are you deaf?" (202).

Both the demand for obedience and the attitude toward women revealed here by Eteocles are consistent with the picture we had of him in the opening scene. From the first he is not simply the ruler of Thebes but also its military commander. The army is his primary concern, and he treats the women of the city as he would an army, demanding the discipline and obedience he expects of soldiers. As a male, he has no understanding of the women's position and no appreciation of the values they uphold. Thus, like Agamemnon, he can deal adequately with a military situation, but he is less able to cope with domestic affairs. When confronted by the women of the chorus, he resorts to scornful language and traditional misogyny, and makes demands backed by partially incoherent threats. Whatever the justification for his demands, he reveals in these remarks that his competence as a military commander is matched by a corresponding incompetence in dealing with the women of the city.

There follows an exchange between Eteocles and the chorus, first in an *amoibaion* (203–44), and then in stichomythia (245–63). At the end they agree to submit to his demand that they be silent (260–63), but until this point there is no progress toward agreement and the exchange serves mainly to amplify or reinforce aspects of the conflict. The chorus continue to emphasize that they are frightened by the sounds of battle, which they hear in spite of Eteocles' request that they "not hear too much" (246). They repeatedly stress their belief[11] that they must turn to the gods for help, not only for themselves but for the entire city, including the army (219–22; cf. 214–15, 233–34[12]), and they make no apology for this behavior, not even in their final statement of submission ("I'll accept my fate," 263).

Similarly Eteocles continues to restate his demand that the chorus cease their cries, and he is now openly critical of their belief in the power of the gods. Walls protect the city, he asserts (216), but the gods desert a captured city (217–18).[13] When the chorus again pray for help, he responds with an angry command, "don't give me bad advice, calling on the gods" (223). In fact the chorus have not been advising but disobeying, and this, as we have seen, he finds intolerable. For Eteocles "obedience is the mother of success" (224–25).

He also reiterates his view that the women should remain in their homes (232) and adds that sacrifice is the duty of men when the city is under attack (230–31). Not that he wants any men to begin conducting sacrifices at this time, but he does want the women to stop doing so. Sacrificing in the city on behalf of the army, however, is one activity that, in Aeschylus, is a prerogative of women: both Atossa and Clytemnestra, for example, supervise the citywide sacrifices for the army, one after defeat and the other after victory. Eteocles' denial of that prerogative would surely be seen as unwarranted, as he himself seems to acknowledge in his next response, when he grudgingly allows the chorus to honor the "race of the gods" (*daimonōn genos*, 236).[14] The dispute finally ends when the chorus call on Zeus for help (255), and Eteocles replies in traditionally misogynistic fashion, "Zeus, what is this race of women you have provided us?" (256).[15] This remark seems to demoralize the chorus, for they answer it with a resigned reflection on the wretched lot of women (257), and shortly thereafter they capitulate.[16]

For the moment Eteocles has won. The chorus are silent and presumably obey his order to move away from the statues of the gods (265). This allows him to give an extended address in which he demonstrates the proper way to pray to the gods. His prayer is formal and consists primarily of a pledge to sacrifice and set up trophies to the gods in the event of victory (274–78). After recommending this sort of unemotional (*mē philostonōs*) prayer to the chorus (279–80), Eteocles leaves to arrange for the defense of the seven gates by himself and the six champions.[17]

Eteocles has now turned his attention back to military operations, where he can be effective, and when he returns to the stage (372) he will be in full control of the military situation. But this first confrontation with the chorus has nonetheless revealed certain of his limitations, and the audience may suspect that the basic conflict between Eteocles and the chorus has not ended. The women have been temporarily silenced, but they and their concerns have been neither eliminated nor adequately answered.

This is made clear in the first stasimon (287–368), which the chorus sing immediately after Eteocles' departure.[18] In this ode they express the same emotions as they did in the parodos and in their first confrontation with Eteocles—fear for the city and a desire for the gods' help. They also elaborate on several earlier themes, such as their specific fear of slavery (cf. 111) and the wretched lot of women (cf. 257). The ode begins with a statement of their fear, which is compared to a dove's fear of snakes:

> as the all-timorous dove
> fears on behalf of her children
> the snakes, evil companions of her bed.
> [292–94]

The female dove is at the mercy of male snakes, who not only threaten to destroy her young but also, it is implied, violate her sexually.[19] The simile thus introduces the theme of sexual conflict, which runs through the ode, and in particular foreshadows the description at the end of the stasimon, where slave girls must satisfy the sexual desires of their captors after the city is taken (363–68).[20] The chorus continue with a prayer on behalf of the fertile land of Thebes (304–9), a concern that is echoed when they later sing of the infertility that results from war, specifically the destruction of crops and the wasting of the earth's gifts (357–62). After further prayer, they sing in detail of the evils that befall women, young and old, in a captured city (321–35), when they are part of the booty to be dragged off into slavery by their captors, along with their suckling babes, whose "bloody bleatings" fill the air (348). A man who is killed in battle fares better than these captive women.[21]

In this ode the chorus are gradually creating their own picture of war, a distinctly feminine one, in which suffering and destruction are emphasized, especially as they affect women, and the glory of victory or of heroic defeat is rejected. The climax of this picture comes at the end of the second antistrophe in one of Aeschylus' most striking images, that of Ares polluting piety (*miainōn eusebeian Arēs*, 344). The expression is bold, but easily understood in its context:

> One man drives another back, kills him,
> sets fire to things; with smoke
> the whole city is defiled,
> and raging,[22] people-destroying,
> he breathes his spirit into them,
> Ares, polluting piety.
>
> [340–44]

This last phrase expresses the essence of the women's view that war is in itself a pollution to the city and to their sense of piety. *Miainōn*, moreover, has a sexual as well as a religious sense,[23] which connects this image with those at the beginning and end of the stasimon, reminding us that one aspect of women's inferior position is that they are frequently sexually violated in war. Thus, the crazed male god of war, the people-destroyer, fills the warriors with his spirit and pollutes piety, which is both feminine in gender and also the particular concern of the women in this play.

This central image of Ares polluting piety is the keynote of the ode and indicates precisely the conflict between Eteocles and the chorus. The male military commander sees the city primarily as an army to be ordered and arranged for military defense. He values the gods and religious feeling in general only in a formal and restrained way and insists that religious feelings not interfere with the operations of the army. The women, on the other hand, see the city primarily as a collection of homes inhabited by women and children and protected by the gods. They value the fertility of the land and pray for the safety of the city and its army, but they reject the absolute demands of military authority. They understand the destructive side of military valor, and they reject the value of military glory, so esteemed by Greek men since Homer. Men, they acknowledge, may achieve a glorious death even in defeat, but for women there remains only a wretched servitude and for their city only the religious pollution inherent in war.[24]

In the first third of the play, these two opposed positions are maintained in sharp conflict. When Eteocles returns to the stage in 372, however, the conflict is suspended, while he gives his full attention to the disposition of his troops. Although the chorus continue to sing of their own concerns[25] in brief lyrics following each pair of speeches in the famous central scene,[26] they do not oppose Eteocles again until after his decision[27] to face his brother at the seventh gate. This decision immediately renews the conflict, however, and leads to a series of exchanges between them (686–719) quite similar in form (*amoibaion* followed by stichomythia) to their earlier exchanges (203–63). The chorus' immediate concern is that Eteocles not fight his brother, and they state this concern clearly and rationally in trimeters (677–82). They first ask him to calm his temper and then point out that, whereas blood shed in war can be cleansed, pollution (*miasma*, 682) from the killing of kinsmen has no end. In the lyrics that follow they continue to express their concern for this "unlawful bloodshed" (*haimatos ou themistou*, 694), and they repeatedly try to calm the fury that is urging Eteocles on.

It is clear that the situation at this point is precisely what the chorus had feared: "the crazed war-god, polluting piety,

breathes his spirit into them." The maddened spirit of war is
indeed in Eteocles, driving him on to a pollution (*miasma*,
682; cf. *miainōn*, 344) that will never grow old. He fully
realizes what is happening and does not deny that killing
Polyneices will be a pollution, but rather he insists that he
cannot do otherwise, for the god irresistibly drives him to the
deed (*episperchei theos*, 689).[28] In accordance with his military values, Eteocles must commit the pollution, because the
alternative is intolerable. Not to enter battle brings shame on
a warrior, and for him there is no glory in shameful deeds
(685), whereas to die gloriously in combat is the highest
personal achievement—indeed the only success for a dead
man (*monon gar kerdos*, 684). From this perspective death
is no evil. Thus, even though Eteocles foresees his own death,
he refuses to make any accommodation to it: "why then should
we cringe any longer at our fated death?" (704). The demands
of war and of his military ethics bring Eteocles to this act of
pollution, just as Agamemnon bows to similar demands and
accepts the pollution (cf. *miainōn*, *Ag.* 209) of sacrificing
his daughter.

The chorus answer Eteocles' arguments directly, pointing
out the seriousness of the religious impiety involved and denying the importance of his traditional, military values. "You
will not be called a coward if you fare well in life [*i.e.,* if the
city is saved without your fighting]" (698–99), they argue.
They also maintain that the god will honor even a cowardly
victory (716), that is, even one in which Eteocles himself
does not fight. But as a soldier he will not tolerate any mention of the word "cowardly" (717), and the chorus' plea is in
vain.[29] Eteocles also refuses to try to alter what he sees as
the will of the gods. The chorus suggest that a sacrifice to the
gods will rid the house of the Erinys (699–701), but he
answers that he is already abandoned by the gods and adds
ironically that "the favor [*charis, sc.* of a sacrifice] that they

admire is that of my death" (703).[30] And when the chorus again maintain that the *daimōn* may change its temper, Eteocles again replies that it is too late (705–11). Both sides thus keep the same attitudes toward the gods that they have held from the beginning of the play. The chorus put their faith in prayer and sacrifice and urge the avoidance of pollution even at the cost of cowardice; Eteocles argues that the god's decisions cannot be influenced by human actions, so men should attend to human affairs and deal with these as best they can, whatever the situation. "When the gods give evils, you cannot escape them," he concludes (719), and leaves the stage to meet his death.

This final stichomythia, we should note, presents an exact reversal of the end of the earlier stichomythia (260–63). There Eteocles asks the chorus to grant him one small request (260); when they ask what it is, he answers, "shut up, you wretch" (262), which they agree to do. Now the chorus ask Eteocles to obey them as women (712); when he asks what they have in mind, they ask him not to go to the seventh gate (714). He refuses to let them "blunt his whetted purpose" (715), however, and so again, at least temporarily, Eteocles is the victor. But this victory, like his earlier one, does not resolve the matter. Although the city is saved (793), the conflict between the two sets of values represented by the chorus and Eteocles has not been resolved and may even be continued in the dispute over the burial of the two brothers.[31]

From this analysis it should be clear that Eteocles does not change after 653, as so many critics have maintained.[32] Indeed it is precisely his refusal to change, his refusal to abandon his male, militaristic set of values, that causes his death. The same intolerance toward women and their feminine values that he displayed at the beginning of the play leads him to reject the chorus' demands at the end. Thus, even those who wish to study only Eteocles' character must take a more objective view of the conflict between him and the chorus. Only by seeing his actions from the chorus' point of view can we properly understand certain qualities that make up a significant aspect of his character.

More important than insight into Eteocles' character, however, is the general understanding of the sexual conflict itself, especially if this conflict in fact was present in some form from the beginning of the trilogy.[33] If so, we would need to have the complete trilogy to understand the full dimensions of the conflict, but even in this play alone we can see that the conflict between Eteocles and the chorus is based to a significant extent on two sets of values which, as in the *Oresteia*, are upheld by male and female figures and can be traced in part to the different lives of men and women in Athens at this time (see chapter IV). From this play, then, and also from *Supplices* and the *Oresteia* it is clear that Aeschylus saw sexual conflict as a major social issue. Although *Septem* apparently reveals no resolution of the conflict, it does provide a better understanding of the two positions and offers a warning against adherence to only one side.

Notes

NOTES TO CHAPTER I

1. Bruno Snell, *Aischylos und das Handeln im Drama* (1928), and *The Discovery of the Mind* (1953; German edition 1948); E. R. Dodds, *The Greeks and the Irrational* (1951); A. W. H. Adkins, *Merit and Responsibility* (1960); Albin Lesky, *Göttliche und menschliche Motivation im homerischen Epos* (1961); E. A. Havelock, *Preface to Plato* (1963); Hugh Lloyd-Jones, *The Justice of Zeus* (1971).

2. For some very sensible remarks on this question of "character" in Aeschylus, see P. E. Easterling, *G&R* 20 (1973), 3–19.

3. I use the term *hero* for the sake of convenience, though Aristotle himself never uses it. John Jones, *On Aristotle and Greek Tragedy* (1962), 12–20, argues rightly that the modern emphasis on the "tragic hero" is misplaced. He is mistaken, however, in his view that Aristotle never entertained "the concept of the tragic hero" (13), for, although no word for hero appears in the *Poetics* and although plot is given the place of highest importance, when Aristotle discusses plot, he always does so (as we shall see) in terms of a single character whose rise or fall forms the plot. It is this single character whom we call the "tragic hero."

4. On the moral sense of *epieikēs* in 1452b34, see D. W. Lucas (note *ad loc.*) and Adkins, *CQ* n.s. 16 (1966), 79–80.

5. *E.g.*, Lucas (p. 140): "nothing could be less 'manifest' than the truth of this extraordinary statement."

6. See Lucas (p. 141). For *Republic* 392a–b, see below, note 75. We might compare a similar situation: in his treatment of the views of the pre-Socratics, Aristotle often draws conclusions about their views in terms of his own system rather than on the basis of direct evidence from their

writings. See, for instance, his attribution of the concept of material cause to Thales, Anaximenes, et al. in *Metaphysics* 983a24 ff. Cf. Harold Cherniss, *Aristotle's Criticism of Presocratic Philosophy* 218 ff.

7. *Philanthrōpon* seems to include the two senses of "desire for justice" and "sympathy for others" (see J. M. Bremer, *Hamartia*, 14, especially note 7). D. de Montmollin (*Phoenix* 19 [1965], 15–23) understands the word to mean what men approve of (because it is just) and therefore sympathize with. There seems to be no adequate English equivalent.

8. Also unacceptable is a third plot that Aristotle mentions, a bad man passing from bad fortune to good: this is neither *philanthrōpon* nor pitiable and fearful, but the least tragic of all (*atragōidotaton*, 1452b37). The fourth possibility is never mentioned: the passage of a good man from bad fortune to good. This would presumably be *philanthrōpon*, but not pitiable or fearful. Whether Aristotle omits this possibility because it is too obviously unfitting or for some other reason, we cannot know.

9. For a thorough treatment of the evidence for and previous opinions on the meaning of *hamartia*, see Bremer, *Hamartia*. He concludes that the arguments for a nonmoral interpretation of *hamartia* outweigh those for a moral interpretation, but he allows that "for a short moment Aristotle falls victim to the popular need for poetic justice" (14–15). Kurt von Fritz ("Tragische Schuld," 2–5) has some good remarks on the difficulties of both the English "flaw" and the German "Schuld" as translations of *hamartia*. In his view, Greek tragedy presents "objective Schuld" not "subjective Schuld."

10. See Thomas Gould, *Arion* 5 (1966), 513–23.

11. Even if one allows for gradations of moral guilt and innocence, the dilemma remains, since if tragedy is to be morally acceptable the punishment of the hero should fit his crime. Thus, even if we consider Oedipus, for example, to be "a little bit guilty," we would nonetheless see his punishment as excessive and therefore unjust.

12. See, *e.g.*, von Fritz ("Tragische Schuld," 15): "Die antike griechische Tragödie hat daher nicht nur nicht die sogenannte poetische Gerechtigkeit zum Ziel, sondern sie schliesst sie geradezu aus."

13. For the first of these two approaches, see, *e.g.*, Gould (*Arion* 4 [1965], 377): "it is a remarkably common feature in both religious and non-religious stories to have a figure who is made to suffer unjustly; and ... *one* of the reasons why such stories do not depress us but, on the contrary, thrill us in a distinctly pleasant way may be that we like to be convinced that monstrous injustice is possible after all." For the second

approach, see, *e.g.*, C. H. Whitman (*Sophocles*, 41): "Evil in Sophocles is nonrational. For him the importance, even the very existence, of man's moral life depends in great part on the absence of any teleological scheme of cosmic justice."

14. Thus Gould's conclusion that Oedipus is innocent is based to a large extent on arguments that he is not guilty—a perfectly logical conclusion in our way of thinking. But, in assuming that such a decision between guilt and innocence must be made, Gould is attributing to Sophocles a systematic moral view of human behavior not found before Plato.

15. These two tendencies are, of course, related in that moral judgments are made about human agents and their actions, and not about an action per se. Indeed, implicit in the title of Aristotle's *Ethics* is the assumption that it is a study of the human character.

16. One could argue that the early Greek world view was nonmoral if one were to stipulate a fairly narrow definition of the word *morality*. It is possible, however, to apply the term *morality* in a wider sense to, say, the heroic code of behavior in the *Iliad*, where success in battle seems to be the most important "virtue." It seems to me important to stress the basic difference between such a code, which values primarily external success and shows little or no concern for internal character, and Aristotelian and most Western moral thinking, which values primarily internal character. However, I will refrain from calling the latter moral and the former nonmoral. In our own world, of course, both standards exist and indeed often conflict. Theoretically we value character and "doing the (morally) right thing," but in practice we often value success more highly (*e.g.*, "it's all right as long as you don't get caught," or "the road to Hell is paved with good intentions").

17. I will use the words *right* and *wrong* as both nouns and adjectives in a nonmoral sense except when qualified by *moral*. In general, any discussion of moral behavior is made more complicated by the overlapping of moral and nonmoral meanings of many common English words. R. M. Hare (*The Language of Morals*) is very thorough on this point.

18. Pelasgus' decision to protect the Danaids is generally considered the right one, but it is quite possible that the remainder of the trilogy would have shed a different light on this decision, which in fact leads to the defeat of Argos. See chapter V.

19. Julius Kovesi in *Moral Notions* argues convincingly that some of the accepted beliefs about moral judgments (such as the distinction between "evaluative" and "descriptive") are inadequate. But Kovesi ex-

plicitly stops short of delineating moral notions from "other notions that are about ourselves in so far as we are rule-following rational beings, like 'clever,' 'consistent,' 'learned,' etc., which are not necessarily moral notions" (147). R. M. Hare, who is currently the most influential British moral philosopher, is able to distinguish between "a good hygrometer" and "a good man" on the grounds that the former judgment is applied to a "functional" noun and is therefore nonmoral, whereas the latter is applied to a "nonfunctional" word and *may* therefore be moral. But Hare cannot clearly distinguish moral from nonmoral judgments within this latter category, and indeed the basic distinction between functional and non-functional words or uses of words seems to break down as he examines it more closely (see *Essays on the Moral Concepts*, 34–38).

20. The fact that this distinction between voluntary and involuntary is a necessary factor in moral evaluation is first made explicit in Book Three of Aristotle's *Ethics* (1109b30–1115a3). We may also say that acts that fall within the proper sphere of moral judgment are also generally acts for which the motives are open to doubt; conversely, if the motive of an act is questioned, the act is usually subject to moral judgment. If a person makes an error on a math problem, for instance, it is generally assumed that this error is involuntary; if, however, there are grounds for suspecting that the error is intentional (*e.g.*, a favorable miscalculation on one's income tax return), then the error may be a moral one. Although Hare never explicitly discusses this factor, he does (like virtually all later moral philosophers) follow Aristotle in insisting that the moral judgment that a man is good must be based on a consideration of his inner state of mind or motive: *e.g.*, "It is a commonplace that to say that a certain act was right is not to say that it was a good act; for to be good it has to be done from a good motive, whereas to be right it has merely to conform to a certain principle, from whatever motive it is done" (*The Language of Morals*, 185).

21. *Responsible* and *responsibility* are words with many meanings, most of which involve no moral sense. A waitress, for instance, is responsible for all the tables in a certain area, a military commander is responsible for the success or failure of his troops, and an elected politician is responsible to the people who elected him. These uses differ from the moral and legal uses of the words, according to which someone is responsible for an action only if he or she has in some way "caused" that action to take place. For the purposes of this study it is sufficient to say that moral responsibility is the principle according to which a person

is morally accountable for those actions and only those actions intended by him or her. H. L. A. Hart (*Punishment and Responsibility* 264–65) discusses the connection between different applications of the word *responsibility*, and he concludes that the moral and legal sense of causal responsibility or liability-responsibility is primary. Cf. Richard Robinson (*Philosophy* 37 [1962], 277–79), who lists several different meanings of *responsibility* and makes some valid criticisms of Adkins for his loose use of the term in *Merit and Responsibility*.

Perhaps an illustration from recent American politics will be helpful. The congressional hearings on the Watergate affair during 1973 and 1974 focused principally on the guilt or innocence of President Nixon— that is, whether he knowingly and intentionally directed the burglary or participated in an illegal cover-up. If his participation was purely inadvertent, he would be considered innocent in a moral and legal sense, though he might still be accused of political incompetence and failure. In one of his own speeches (April 30, 1973), Mr. Nixon accepted "responsibility" for Watergate, by which he clearly meant political and administrative responsibility but not moral or legal responsibility, since at the same time he asserted his innocence. Mr. Nixon also made it clear that his political responsibility was less significant to him than his moral and legal innocence, an opinion with which most Americans apparently concurred. For the early Greeks, however, the question of political competence would have been of greater interest, and they would have considered the narrower question of moral responsibility relatively insignificant.

22. On this complex question of responsibility in legal systems, see the excellent collection of essays by Hart, *Punishment and Responsibility*, especially 113–35 and 210–37.

23. Cf. Hart, *Punishment and Responsibility*, 226:

The hypothesis that we might hold individuals morally blameworthy for doing things which they could not have avoided doing, or for things done by others over whom they had no control, conflicts with too many of the central features of the idea of morality to be treated merely as speculation about a rare or inferior kind of moral system. It may be an exaggeration to say that there could not logically be such a morality or that blame administered according to principles of strict or vicarious responsibility, even in a minority of cases, could not logically be moral blame; none the less, admission of such a system as a morality would require a profound modification in our present concept of morality, and there is no similar requirement in the case of law.

24. See Adkins, *Merit and Responsibility*, 52–53.

25. Cf. G. M. Calhoun (*The Growth of Criminal Law in Ancient Greece*, 11): "In the Homeric poems . . . homicide is a simple wrong against the individual or the family; it is not looked upon as morally reprehensible, or as an offense against the common welfare."

26. A similar nonmoral treatment of homicide appears in a story related by Elspeth Huxley in *The Flame Trees of Thika*, the autobiography of her childhood in Kenya at the beginning of this century. A native foreman on a neighboring estate is killed one night, and the settlers naturally seek the killer in order to have him tried and punished. The author, being a child, gains the confidence of the natives and learns (but does not reveal) that one of her own family's servants, Njombo, is the killer. Every native knows that Njombo is the killer, but no one turns him in to the English authorities. He is required, however, by his own tribal law to pay many goats to the dead man's father, and this large debt lowers Njombo's status and also prevents him from buying the wife for whom he had been saving the goats. The English demand that Kupanya, the tribal leader, deliver up the murderer, but he does not do so until threatened; then he turns over a different young man, who willingly confesses to the murder, since his father owes a debt to Kupanya. (Njombo could not go to prison, he explained to the author later, for "if I had done so, who would have paid the debt?") The self-confessed defendant is then acquitted (probably on grounds of self-defense), and Njombo continues in service, poorer but otherwise no less valued or respected. The native attitude toward homicide revealed here seems very similar to that of the early Greeks, and the difficulty the English have in understanding it illustrates the difference between this attitude and the modern view.

27. Phemius has in fact done Odysseus no wrong and would be able to do him much good in the future, as he points out. At question is his vicarious liability for punishment because of his singing for the suitors, and as a bard he is allowed to dissociate himself from their behavior. But his case is exceptional; a good suitor, for instance, cannot escape (see below, note 33). Phemius is also called *anaitios* (*Od.* 22.356) by Telemachus (see below, note 28).

28. The Homeric uses of *aitios, anaitios,* and *aitiaomai* show that the words are usually applied to situations that even we would not consider moral, that it is always a person in the poem (never Homer) who puts the blame on someone (usually other than himself), and that the issue is always blame or fault, never credit in a positive sense. The words ap-

parently refer to external blame rather than inner responsibility, and *aitios* should be translated "blameworthy" and not "guilty."

29. For Agamemnon, see Dodds, *The Greeks and the Irrational*, chap. 1, and Lesky, *Motivation*, 40–42; but cf. below, note 52.

30. We are never told whether the second part of this punishment is fulfilled.

31. The only major unpunished wrong in the epics is Odysseus' killing of the suitors (killing of non-Greeks or enemies in war is no wrong). Compensation ought to be given for this killing, but in fact Odysseus is so powerful, especially with Athena at his side, that the relatives of the suitors finally accept their (shameful) weakness and drop their demand for compensation.

32. By *moral justice* I mean the distribution of punishment (and *mutatis mutandis* of reward) to those who are morally responsible for wrongdoing, as distinct from punishment merely on the basis of wrong action regardless of moral responsibility.

33. Amphinomus is killed because he does not recognize Odysseus' warning ("Athena set fetters upon him to be slain by the spear and hands of Telemachus," 18.155–56). Note that earlier Athena induces Odysseus to gather bits of bread from the suitors "and so learn which of them are *enaisimoi* ['decent'] and which *athemistoi* ['lawless'], but even so she was not going to save any one of them from ruin" (17.363–64).

34. Although Adkins' discussion of competitive virtues in Homer is thorough and convincing, his treatment of his other category, cooperative virtues, is less satisfactory, for in equating these cooperative values with our own moral values Adkins seems to be making the same mistake as those he is attacking, that is, reading our own moral values into Greek words. A. A. Long (*JHS* 90 [1970], 121–39) offers some good criticism of Adkins' "two exclusive categories" of values. Cooperative words, he feels, evaluate results of a different kind, not intentions; intentions are not completely absent from Homer, but they are unimportant "in the sense of moral will, decision or purpose, where explicit judgments of value are concerned" (124, note 9).

35. It is quite consistent, for instance, for us to speak of a court decision as "unjust" or to see a conflict between the legal process and "true justice." In such cases we have in mind a higher, moral justice, which the judicial system perhaps ought to represent but sometimes does not.

36. *Dikē* is also found in the *Odyssey* in the sense of "characteristic behavior" or "mark" (but not "right" or "due"). The legal meanings are

all found in Homer and Hesiod. See Gagarin, *CP* 68 (1973), 81–94 and *CP* 69 (1974), 186–97. The following discussion of *dikē* is based on these articles.

37. *Dikē* is little valued in Homer, where peace itself has relatively little value. Hesiod and Solon emphasize the necessity of a stable and well-functioning legal process for a peaceful and prosperous society, and thus *dikē* has a larger place in the works of these authors.

38. Long, *JHS* 90 (1970), 136. He suggests a standard of "appropriateness," but I find "propriety" a more convenient term. Adkins' reply to Long (*JHS* 91 [1971], 1–14) adds little to the discussion of this point.

39. There are some excellent remarks on the effect of Homer's style in Adam Parry's "The Language of Achilles," *TAPA* 87 (1956), 1–7: *e.g.*, "The formulaic character of Homer's language means that everything in the world is regularly presented as all men (all men within the poem, that is) commonly perceive it. The style of Homer emphasizes constantly the accepted attitude toward each thing in the world, and this makes for a great unity of experience" (p. 3).

40. See Havelock, *Preface to Plato*, especially chap. 3.

41. Snell, *The Discovery of the Mind*, chap. 1.

42. The validity of the step from "did not have a word for" to "did not have a concept of" is certainly debatable, but there is no indication in Homer of anyone trying to talk about a "soul" but lacking the word for it. Even Lesky, who believes that the *psychē* is more important than any of the other psychological organs in Homer and contains the "raw material" for the later concept of the soul, admits that Homer tells us nothing about the nature of the *psychē* in the living person (*Motivation*, 7).

43. Snell, *Aischylos und das Handeln im Drama*, 20–26.

44. Cf. Havelock, *YCS* 22 (1972), 9, note 23: "The Socratic self-dialogue . . . is the lineal descendant of such Homeric expressions as *kradiēn ēnipape* and *thymos anōge me*, with the important difference that the 'subject' and 'object' in the expression have been identified with each other, by an act of integration, the conceptual result of which is most conveniently expressed by extending the significance of the term *psychē*."

45. The Homeric view of human behavior I have outlined here suggests an interesting parallel with some aspects of modern behaviorist theory, especially the work of B. F. Skinner. In *Beyond Freedom and Dignity*, Skinner argues that such hypothetical states of mind as "free-

dom" are not only misleading in discussing human behavior but also dangerous. The only valid statements are those made about external observable behavior, and we should concentrate on trying to change this behavior rather than any untestable (and therefore unknowable) inner states of mind. Skinner's position can be called nonmoral (and has been strongly attacked for being so) in that the question of moral responsibility is for him irrelevant; his only concern is observable behavior. The parallels with the Homeric view are not exact, but the two views are similar enough, I think, to shed some light on each other.

46. Cf. what A. P. D. Mourelatos calls "the naive metaphysics of things." He coins the term *character-power* to designate the complex perception of an object or thing together with its component characters or powers, and he observes of them (*Studies Vlastos*, 32–33), "The fact that the world of character-powers is essentially a world of things in physical space means that in principle everything will lie open to view, that everything can be visualized. The genius of the world of character-powers is thus akin to the genius of *parataxis*, the dominant principle of order in Homer, in Archaic art, and in Archaic composition. Each thing will be complete by itself, and the plurality of things will form a whole (harmonious nevertheless) in which all relations are external and explicit." Plato indicates explicitly that the fundamental axiom of his moral philosophy, that a man's actions have internal consequences (affecting his soul), is a new idea in Greek thought, when he has Adeimantus say to Socrates, "All you who profess to sing the praises of right conduct, from the ancient heroes whose legends have survived down to the men of the present day, have never denounced injustice or praised justice apart from the reputation, honours, and rewards they bring; but what effect either of them in itself has upon its possessor when it dwells in his soul unseen of gods or men, no poet or ordinary man has ever yet explained. No one has proved that a soul can harbour no worse evil than injustice, no greater good than justice" (*Rep.* 366d–e [trans. Cornford]). Later Socrates summarizes their achievement in the dialogue: "we have not introduced those rewards which . . . Homer and Hesiod hold out to men who have acquired a reputation for justice. We have found that, apart from all such consequences, justice is the best thing for the soul, which should do what is right" (*Rep.* 612b [trans. Cornford]).

47. It is true that in another case Patroclus, before he dies, tries to taunt Hector by claiming that Apollo and Euphorbus had more to do with his death than Hector himself (*Il.* 16.849–50), but this taunt in no way

diminishes Hector's responsibility for the deed, as is made clear by Achilles' demand for Hector's death as retribution.

48. Lesky's discussion of this phenomenon (in *Motivation*) is excellent; he examines some cases where divine and human forces seem to work together and others where one or the other is emphasized. But his attempt (44) to equate this double motivation with our own feeling that occasionally there is a superhuman force at work in our own activity is less convincing and seems to result from his desire to diminish the difference between the outlook of the Homeric Greeks and our own. This is apparently why he rejects (29 ff., 44) Dodds' term *overdetermination*, although Dodds (*The Greeks and the Irrational*, chap. 1) in fact analyzes this phenomenon in very much the same way as Lesky does.

49. "Dass aber ein und derselbe Akt wie des Achilleus Heimfahrt oder sein erneuter Eintritt in den Kampf in gleicher und ungeschiedener Weise vom Menschen wie vom Gotte verursacht wird, das steht in einer Einheit, die sich einer Analyse mit den Mitteln unserer Logik entzieht." Lesky, *Motivation*, 30.

50. The view that freedom of moral choice and determinism may coexist has been held in various forms by Hobbes, Hume, J. S. Mill, and others and is commonly referred to (following William James) as "soft determinism." It is presently rather out of fashion in moral philosophy, though in my own opinion it is the only sensible solution to the problem. See Richard Taylor "Determinism," 368.

51. We must try not to think of this duality as illogical or self-contradictory, since it did not appear so to the Greeks (in part because they never developed as clear a view of cause and effect as ours). Double motivation is a perfectly sensible way of understanding behavior, and we must not conclude, because it is a nonanalytic view, that it is therefore confused or unintelligent. We ourselves are not confused if someone says, for instance, "The Devil got into me, and I . . . ," though we (unlike the Greeks) might consider such language to be purely figurative.

52. Lesky is wrong to conclude (*Motivation*, 38), "dass der göttliche Anstoss zu einer Handlung oder die göttliche Mitwirkung bei ihr dem Menschen nicht das Geringste von seiner Verantwortung abnimmt." He does not examine this sense of responsibility (though *Verantwortung* clearly has a moral sense) but apparently assumes it is the same as ours. Lloyd-Jones follows Lesky in this error, concluding that "human characters are free to decide and are responsible for their decisions" (*Justice*, 10). "Liable (in a strict sense) for their actions" would be more accurate.

In a recent review (*TLS* for 14 March 1975, 273) Lloyd-Jones indicates that he is upset by those who deny the early Greeks our sense of moral responsibility because (he feels) to do so is somehow the same as to "abolish the concept of responsibility" and "to blame 'society' for crime." But, if we distinguish clearly between "moral responsibility" and "strict liability" (which we may call "responsibility" if we wish), then we can deny the early Greeks our sense of *moral* responsibility and still agree with Lloyd-Jones that they insisted "that a man must be held responsible for his actions, whether or not he is guilty in the sense in which we use the word."

53. J. K. Campbell's distinction between guilt and shame, which is quoted by Lloyd-Jones (*Justice*, 25), seems to me too narrow as well as confused and misleading. Dodds (*The Greeks and the Irrational*, 17) makes the proper distinction between internal conscience and external approbation: "Homeric man's highest good is not the enjoyment of a quiet conscience, but the enjoyment of *timē*, public esteem."

54. It should be noted that this approval is manifested in material terms. *Timē* ("honor") is not simply an abstract feeling of respect, but also material goods, slaves, women, political and military power, etc. Men give *timē* to the gods when they give them sacrifices, not prayers. Thus Achilles cannot be satisfied by merely knowing that he is the best fighter, but must have a concrete manifestation of his ability, which is why he withdraws from the fighting in Book One.

55. There can hardly be a better illustration of the nonmoral shame-culture of the Homeric Greeks than the story of Ares and Aphrodite (*Od.* 8.266–366). Their adultery brings shame upon Hephaestus as well as upon the lovers themselves, and it requires monetary compensation, but there is no moral judgment anywhere in the tale.

56. *Justice*, 164.

57. Havelock's views are most fully stated in *Preface to Plato*; see also *Prologue to Greek Literacy* (1971), where he looks more closely at the conditions of preliteracy. Havelock's work ultimately relies on the conclusions of Milman Parry and others about the oral and formulaic nature of Homer's poetry (see *The Making of Homeric Verse*).

58. See Joseph Russo and Bennett Simon, *JHI* 29 (1968), 483–98.

59. Cf. Havelock (*Preface to Plato*, 159): "You [the preliterate Greek] did not learn your ethics and politics, skills and directives, by having them presented to you as a corpus for silent study, reflection and absorption. You were not asked to grasp their principles through rational

analysis. You were not invited to so much as think of them. Instead you submitted to the paideutic spell. You allowed yourself to become 'musical' in the functional sense of that Greek term."

60. The theories of Marshall McLuhan (see especially *Understanding Media*) about the connection between modes of communication and modes of thought are interesting in this regard, though his arguments for the connection between literacy and "linear" (*i.e.*, analytic and logical) thought leave something to be desired as far as clarity and cogency are concerned. See the sensible words of G. M. A. Grube on this matter (*How Did the Greeks Look at Literature?* 20–21).

61. The principle that the path to knowledge lies outside society still underlies our concept of the university (the "ivory tower") and is ultimately traceable to Plato's *Republic.* In Plato's ideal state the guardians are removed from society and trained to contemplate the Forms, which are the realm of truth, rather than the phenomenal world, which is only the realm of opinion.

62. The Bible is, of course, a written book, but in the societies (such as early Puritan New England) where it has exerted the greatest influence it has generally been learned and communicated to others by oral recital, both at home and in church.

63. Cf. Havelock (*Preface to Plato*, 167–68), "If the saga is functional, if its purpose is to conserve the group mores, then the men who act in it must be the kind of men whose actions would involve the public law and the family law of the group. They must therefore be 'political' men in the most general sense of that term, men whose acts, passions, and thoughts will affect the behaviour and the fate of the society in which they live."

64. Snell, *The Discovery of the Mind*, chap. 3, "The Rise of the Individual in the Early Greek Lyric." The traditional notion of the "individuality" of the early monodists has recently been questioned by K. J. Dover ("The Poetry of Archilochos") and Russo (*Arion* n.s. 1 [1973/74], 707–30).

65. See especially Stesichorus, *P. Oxy.* 2735, which D. Page continues (*Supplementum*, p. 48) to ascribe to Ibycus (cf. M. L. West, *ZPE* 4 [1969], 142–49); and Ibycus, *PMG* 282 (cf. J. P. Barron, *BICS* 16 [1969], 119–49). For the combination of political and mythical material in Alcaeus, see Lloyd-Jones, *GRBS* 9 (1968), 128–29.

66. The question of the origin of tragedy is still much disputed, but most would, I think, go at least as far as T. B. L. Webster (in the second

edition of A. W. Pickard-Cambridge, *Dithyramb, Tragedy and Comedy*, 112), who says, "The hypothesis that the style and language of early tragedy was influenced by Peloponnesian choral lyric is highly likely."

67. Concerning Pelasgus, Snell says, "Nowhere in early poetry does a man go through a similar struggle to arrive at a decision, nowhere does he, as in this scene, reflect 'downward into the depth' of his soul in order to make up his mind. For the first time in literature someone toils hard for the sake of responsibility and justice, for the purpose of warding off evil. This is the birth of concepts destined to lie at the heart of all drama thereafter, concepts which have become increasingly important even outside the province of tragedy" (*Discovery*, 102).

68. Cf., *e.g.*, Lesky, *Motivation*, and Lloyd-Jones, *Justice*.

69. Snell's claim (see above, note 67) will not survive one look at the text, for Pelasgus thinks nothing of his "soul," and his natural desire to ward off evil from his city has no necessary connection with justice or responsibility. See chapter V.

70. Dodds sees the transition from shame-culture to guilt-culture as taking place before Aeschylus, but the guilt he associates with the concept of pollution is not a moral guilt, as he makes clear by contrasting it with sin (*The Greeks and the Irrational*, 36–37):

The distinction between the two situations is of course that sin is a condition of the will, a disease of man's inner consciousness, whereas pollution is the automatic consequence of an action, belongs to the world of external events, and operates with the same ruthless indifference to motive as a typhoid germ. Strictly speaking, the archaic sense of guilt becomes a sense of sin only as a result of what Kardiner calls the 'internalising' of conscience—a phenomenon which appears late and uncertainly in the Hellenic world, and does not become common until long after secular law had begun to recognise the importance of motive [that is, at the end of the fifth century].

Dodds is thus saying that there was still no moral understanding (as I have defined it) of wrong behavior before the end of the fifth century. Because of the ambiguous nature of the word *guilt* (which surely is a moral concept for most people), I prefer not to use it in a nonmoral sense, as Dodds does.

71. Even Phaedra in *Hippolytus* (428 B.C.) is most easily understood in terms of shame-culture. See David Claus, *YCS* 22 (1972), 223–38.

72. Gagarin, *CP* 68 (1973), 91–92.

73. Cf. Gagarin, *CP* 69 (1974), 190–92.

74. Cf. the passages from the *Republic*, quoted above, note 46.

75. "We shall find both poets and prose-writers guilty of the most serious misstatements about human life, making out that wrongdoers are often happy and just men miserable; that injustice pays, if not detected; and that my being just is to another man's advantage, but a loss to myself. We shall have to prohibit such poems and tales and tell them to compose others in the contrary sense" (*Rep.* 392a–b [trans. Cornford]).

NOTES TO CHAPTER II

1. For the rather scant information we possess about pre-Aeschylean tragedy, see Pickard-Cambridge, *Dithyramb, Tragedy and Comedy*, 63–89; Lloyd-Jones, "Problems of Early Greek Tragedy," and Lesky, *Tragische Dichtung,* 49–64. The testimonia and fragments are collected by Snell in *TGF*, pp. 61–84.

2. The classical Greeks (perhaps wisely) never separated history and myth as sharply as we do; they seem rather to have viewed myth as early, fairly remote history. Thus, Herodotus begins his *History* with the Trojan War and ends it with the Persian Wars, and Aristotle distinguishes between fourth-century comedy, whose characters are invented, and tragedy, whose characters are with a few exceptions real (*Poetics* 1451b 11–19).

3. The recently discovered Gyges fragment has been thought by some scholars (mostly English) to date from this period, but others (mostly German) assign it to the Hellenistic period. See Lloyd-Jones, "Problems of Early Greek Tragedy," 24–30; Lesky, *Tragische Dichtung*, 536–37, especially note 30; and most recently Snell, *ZPE* 12 (1973), 197–205, who favors the earlier date.

4. See the hypothesis to *Persae*, where this information is attributed to Glaukos of Rhegium.

5. We know that Themistocles was the *chorēgos* for a victorious tragedy by Phrynichus in 476 (Plutarch, *Them.* 5.4), and it is extremely tempting to accept the conclusion that this play was *Phoenissae*. Cf. W. G. Forrest, *CQ* n.s. 10 (1960), 235–36. Most other scholars also accept 476 as the probable date for *Phoenissae*.

6. It seems likely that Phrynichus' earlier play, *The Capture of Miletus* (produced perhaps in 492), also supported Themistocles. See Lloyd-Jones, "Problems of Early Greek Tragedy," 22; Lesky, *Tragische Dichtung*, 60.

7. H. D. Broadhead, whose recent commentary on *Persae* (1960) is

the fullest, is preoccupied with showing that in spite of "occasional lapses" *Persae* is a "genuine tragedy" (xv–xxxii).

8. The attempt to combine both views of the play has been made before by, *e.g.*, Gilbert Murray (*Aeschylus, The Creator of Tragedy*, 121–30); cf. H. W. Smyth (*Aeschylean Tragedy*, 67): "The *Persians* is at once patriotic and religious." But no one to my knowledge has sought to understand the total effect of combining these two perspectives.

9. Cf. Pickard-Cambridge's description of the Greater Dionysia (*The Dramatic Festivals of Athens*, 58–59):

> The importance of the festival was derived not only from the performances of dramatic and lyric poetry but from the fact that it was open to the whole Hellenic world and was an effective advertisement of the wealth and power and public spirit of Athens, no less than of the artistic and literary leadership of her sons. By the end of March the winter was over, the seas were navigable, and strangers came to Athens from all parts for business or pleasure. After the founding of the Delian League the allies of Athens brought their tribute at this season; Isocrates asserts that it was displayed in the theatre. At the same period, before the performance of the tragedies began, the orphaned children of those who had fallen in battle for Athens, such as had reached a suitable age, were caused to parade in the theatre in full armour and receive the blessing of the People . . . . The festival was also made the occasion for the proclamation of honours conferred upon citizens or strangers for conspicuous service to Athens; and it was a natural time for the visits of ambassadors from other states for business requiring publicity.

10. In the competition between Euripides and Aeschylus in the *Frogs*, a mixture of "literary" and "political" criteria for judging tragedy are introduced, and these are, I feel, a more valid indication of the fifth-century audience's reaction to Greek tragedy than the more purely "literary" criteria set forth in the *Poetics*.

11. Cf. Herodotus' account of the battle, in which he praises at some length Artemesia, a Persian ally (8. 87–88).

12. The verbs in the chorus' description of the new Greek freedom are all in the present tense, which Broadhead and others interpret as "prophetic" presents looking to the future. This may be correct from the Persian perspective, but the Greek audience would undoubtedly understand the verbs as referring to the present state of affairs in Greece.

13. This point is made by Lattimore, "Aeschylus on the Defeat of Xerxes," 91–93.

14. Cf. A. Sidgwick's note on *Persae* 349: "The Persian's speech here as elsewhere is coloured with Athenian sentiment. The poet writ-

ing a patriotic drama for Athenian ears cannot help making the enemy's narrative turn to the glory of Athens."

15. The slaughter on Psyttaleia was apparently the work of Aristides; the major architect of the victory at Salamis was Themistocles. A. J. Podlecki is probably right, then, in contending that Aeschylus was not supporting one of these politicians against the other but was implicitly giving them both credit (*The Political Background of Aeschylean Tragedy*, 23–25).

16. Outside the description of the battle, Salamis is mentioned by name in 273, 284, and 965. It is also identified by certain periphrases, such as "island of Ajax" (307, 596–97); cf. 570, where "Kychreian shore" may be an allusion to the alleged appearance of the mythical Salaminian king Kychreus in the form of a serpent during the battle (Pausanias I.36.1), and 895, where Salamis is called "mother-city" of the Cyprian Salamis, perhaps an allusion to the Athenian view of Athens as mother-city of the Ionian Greek cities. (On the pro-Hellenic position of Cyprian Salamis, see Russell Meiggs, *The Athenian Empire*, 39, 482.)

17. Words referring specifically to the naval defeat are not only frequent but often made more emphatic by their position in a lyric ode. Note, for example, the threefold repetition of *naës* in 560–62, corresponding to the threefold repetition of Xerxes' name in the same place in the corresponding strophe (550–52), and the occurrence of such words in an emphatic position at the end of a stasimon: 680, *naës anaës anaës*, and 907, *pontiaisin*; cf. 1076, *barisin olomenoi*.

18. It may well be significant that Pericles was *chorēgos* for *Persae*. We know nothing about his political activity or views at this early date, but it is attractive to speculate that he already favored the strong naval policies of Themistocles. See Forrest, *CQ* n.s. 10 (1960), 233–36.

19. A few of the early members of the Delian League were Aeolian cities (*e.g.*, Lesbos) but the league as a whole was predominantly Ionian.

20. The chronology of the period immediately after the Persian Wars is notoriously difficult. The first attempt to secede from the league, the revolt of Naxos, occurred sometime between 474 and 466, but it seems impossible to determine a more precise date. If we assume an early date for the Naxian revolt, this may indicate that, for some cities at least, Persia was no longer a threat by 472. See Edouard Will, *Le Monde Grec et l'Orient*, 136–37. Meiggs, however, argues for a later date for the revolt (*Athenian Empire*, 80–83) and suggests a possible link to a Persian attempt to retaliate against Greece, a threat only finally removed

by Cimon's victory at the Eurymedon (which Meiggs dates to 466).

21. If the treasury of the Delian League had by this date been transferred to Athens (see W. K. Pritchett, *Historia* 18 [1969], 17–21, for a rejection of the traditional date of 454 for this transfer), then the audience would have witnessed a procession of their Ionian allies bearing tribute at the opening of the City Dionysia only a few days earlier (see Pickard-Cambridge, *Festivals*, 67).

22. One should also note the reference to democracy in 242, where the chorus inform the queen that the Athenians are "slaves to no mortal." The Athenians' pride in their democracy as opposed to the Persian monarchy would perhaps also be evoked by the queen's earlier warning to the chorus that Xerxes would still be king even if defeated (213–14).

23. See above, note 15.

24. Forrest (*CQ* n.s. 10 [1960], 221–41) assumes the traditional division between the (aristocratic) followers of Cimon and the (democratic) followers of Themistocles and later Pericles. This division may be a valid one for certain issues, such as Athens' relations with Sparta, but it seems less valid for the issues presented in *Persae*. Cimon supported Themistocles' policy of evacuating Athens and fighting at Salamis and also led many naval expeditions for Athens until his ostracism in 461.

25. The opening anapests (1–64) form a unit; the chorus focus on the expedition until verse 60, where *oichetai* echoes *oichomenōn* in 1, and then shift to the situation at home for the concluding four verses.

26. The other examples of a similar movement from concern for the army to concern for those at home all occur after the announcement of the defeat, and so they naturally bring out the connection betweeen the defeated expedition and the suffering at home (see 256–89, 532–45, 568–83). But the parodos makes it clear that domestic suffering results from the mere absence of the army, whether or not it is defeated, a theme that recurs in *Agamemnon*.

27. Cf. two later references to yoking: Xerxes in the queen's dream yokes the two women to his chariot (191), and the Persian women are said to yearn to see their "recently yoked" husbands (541–42).

28. R. D. Dawe has recently argued, not very convincingly, that the purpose of 529–31 and 849–51 is to create dramatic tension and movement, since the audience's expectations would be twice frustrated (*PCPhS* 189 [1963], 27–30).

29. Darius' own clothing must have presented a sharp contrast to Xerxes' rags, if (as seems likely) the chorus' reference to the rich clothes

Darius will wear when he appears (660–62) is an accurate stage direction for his costume. Unlike Shakespearean ghosts, there is nothing ghastly about the "Ghost of Darius."

30. Harry C. Avery's theory (*AJP* 85 [1964], 181–83) that Xerxes receives new clothing on stage at about verse 1001 from an attendant (or even perhaps from the queen) must be rejected, since such a major stage action would certainly be referred to in the text.

31. The first part of the exodos (909–1001) is sung in lyric anapests with exchanges of several lines each; the second part (1002–77) is sung in lyric iambics, and most of the exchanges are of one line each.

32. One might compare Agamemnon, who also appears only briefly on the stage but might be considered a tragic hero. During Agamemnon's stage appearance, however, we see both his triumph and his fall, whereas Xerxes is seen only in defeat.

33. It is always possible to select certain utterances by a person and infer from these a "character," but such a procedure with respect to Aeschylus not only leads to false conclusions but also is fundamentally misleading. Broadhead, for instance, concludes from the chorus' ability to answer the queen's questions about Athens (231–43) that "they are well informed about Athens . . . as behoves members of a Privy Council" (xxiv). But he ignores an equally necessary conclusion of such reasoning—that the queen must have been kept in complete ignorance of the affairs of Persia for the last ten years or more. He also ignores the fact that these "worthy representatives of the noble class" are completely blind to the obvious meaning of the queen's dream. But primarily he misleads us by implying that scenes such as these are intended to shed light on a character rather than to produce a particular dramatic effect. P. E. Easterling (*G&R* 20 [1973], 3–19) is right, of course, to warn against going too far in denying character to Aeschylus' personae; the personae must be consistent enough in their words and actions to be believable. But her warning against asking "What kind of a person is Agamemnon?" (7) is even more applicable to the personae in *Persae*, for in this play there is even less indication of character than in Aeschylus' other plays.

34. The name Atossa does not appear in the text, and thus the audience would never hear it. If Aeschylus had intended us to think of her as Atossa, he would have had someone refer to her by that name.

35. The sense of 163–64 is clear if we distinguish properly between *ploutos*, "wealth, riches," and *olbos*, "general prosperity, well-being,"

which includes a certain amount of *ploutos* but is not identical with it
(cf. Herodotus 1.32.5–7). In 250–52, for example, the messenger can
speak of Persia, "great harbor of *ploutos*," whose great *olbos* has been
destroyed, for even though *ploutos* remains, *olbos* can be destroyed by
the loss of some other element of prosperity, in this case the Persian
army. (In 755–56 no distinction between the two terms is specified, but
this does not mean that none exists; see p. 45.) In 163–64, moreover,
ploutos is not only separate from *olbos* but it is *ploutos* itself that causes
the destruction of *olbos* by stirring up the dust on the plain. The language
here suggests only one image that makes sense in the context, the assem-
bling of a military force. This interpretation was suggested by Page (see
Broadhead's commentary on *Persae*, p. 72, where it is rejected) and is
supported by *Septem* 60, the only other occurrence of *koniō* in Aeschylus,
where the verb refers to the besieging army preparing for its attack. (In
several Homeric passages, cited by Groeneboom on *Persae* 161–64, *koniō*
indicates swift flight; however wealth cannot be said to cause the flight
of the Persian army except indirectly.) In this play then, great *ploutos*
has induced Persia to send off the expedition, and this stirring up of the
dust may, the queen fears, destroy the Persian *olbos*.

The division of *olbos* into two main components, wealth and man-
power, must be the reference of the queen's "double concern" (165),
whatever the precise meaning of 166–67. She expresses the same double
concern later when questioning the chorus about Athens: what is the
size of the Athenians' force, she asks (235), and what is their wealth
(237)? (The ms. order of 235–37 should probably be retained.)

36. Some have argued from the presence of *nomismata* in the corrupt
lines 859–60 that the chorus also praise Darius as a lawmaker. But for
the sense of the passage it seems that some reference must be made to the
military activity of the army before the men return, and thus Keiper's
polismata is a likely emendation for *nomismata* (and is accepted by Page).
Douglas Young (*GRBS* 13 [1972], 12–14) wants to keep *nomismata*,
but he does not explain what is meant by his translation, "and towered
law codes sped over all things."

37. There is some truth to the claim that Darius stayed at home. We
know that he did not accompany the expedition to Marathon, and it seems
that he entrusted many of his campaigns to his subordinate commanders.
However, Darius himself led the disastrous Scythian expedition, during
which he and his troops did in fact cross the Hellespont.

38. On the contrast between sea power and land power in *Persae*, see

A. E. Wardman (*Historia* 8 [1959], 54), who concludes that the emphasis on the Persians' defeat at sea is the result of "the workings of Athenian panegyric, attempting to claim all the glory for the final result of the Persian wars" (cf. above, note 17).

39. In 744 (παῖς δ' ἐμὸς τάδ' οὐ κατειδὼς ἤνυσεν νέῳ θράσει) Broadhead and others maintain that *tade* (*sc. kaka*) goes with *ēnysen* and not with *ou kateidōs*, which is used absolutely. But it seems natural and easier to take *tade* with both verbs: "not perceiving these evils he accomplished them." There is certainly no evidence that *ou kateidōs* refers to Xerxes' unawareness of divine law (as expressed in, *e.g.*, 742), though some scholars would change the order of the lines to produce such a sense (see Broadhead *ad loc.*).

40. See, *e.g.*, Broadhead (xxiii): "In the *kommos* the harvest which *hybris* reaped (822) is made visible in the person of Xerxes, whose sin had brought about the terrible catastrophe." Broadhead's reason for equating Darius' view with Aeschylus' is that Darius attributes the calamity to "*the transgression of divine law,*" and he concludes (xxix) that Darius' words represent "the concentrated essence of the poet's philosophy." More recently R. P. Winnington-Ingram (*JHS* 93 [1973], 218) comments that "the religious thought of Darius . . . is also the poet's."

41. That Xerxes' failure is spoken of in intellectual terms (*ouk eubouliāi*, 749) is in accord with the view of behavior described in chapter I. Since everyone, it is assumed, wants to succeed, failure results not from wrong intentions but from some physical or intellectual weakness. Note that Darius' famous claim (referring to Xerxes), that "when someone himself hurries along [toward disaster], god also lends a hand" (742), does not necessarily imply impious or immoral behavior on the part of that mortal agent, as Lesky claims (*Motivation*, 50). Xerxes was hastening toward disaster by his ill-conceived military strategy more than anything else.

42. The chorus in 113–14 describe how the Persians have learned to look upon the sea "trusting in slender ropes and people-conveying devices." From the preceding context (109–12), this phrase must designate seafaring in general, but the language is undoubtedly intended at the same time to suggest the bridge over the Hellespont, and we need not insist on one reference exclusively (see Winnington-Ingram, *CR* n.s. 12 [1962], 123–24).

43. Xerxes himself is never spoken of in terms of *hybris*, and the only

two occurrences of *hybris* in *Persae* are in this passage (808, 821).

44. It is true that Xerxes was in command of the Persian army when it sacked Athens, and the audience might therefore think of him when Darius mentions the destruction of temples (811–12). But there is no specific reference in the passage to Athens or to Xerxes' presence with the army, and, since the punishment for the deeds mentioned comes at Plataea, the implication is that Xerxes is not involved. Furthermore, *pros taut' ekeinon* (*sc.* Xerxes) in 829 introduces a new topic and indicates that Darius here turns his attention from the rest of the army back to Xerxes.

45. *Megalate* in 1016 (now accepted by most editors) is usually taken to mean something like "struck by a great calamity" (Groeneboom). Even if we take the sense of *atē* to be "folly, delusion," it can refer to any kind of mistake that leads to the disaster. These two different meanings, "ruin" and "delusion," are in fact often both present and would not have been thought of as totally separate. We should thus understand *atē* to include both the final outcome and the prior state of mind necessarily leading to a disaster.

46. I use *hybris* in the traditional modern sense here of "overweening pride." Lattimore is correct to point out that the word is never used this way in Greek tragedy. His discussion of the word is valuable (*Story Patterns in Greek Tragedy*, 23–24 and notes, pp. 80–85), although he erroneously states that *hybris* is charged to Xerxes in *Persae*.

47. See Fraenkel on *Ag.* 112: "in Aeschylus, *thouros* and *thourios* always refer to the onrush of battle, just as they do in Homer." *Thouros* is used favorably of the Persian warriors in *Persae* 137.

48. The reading of 13 is a notorious crux. Page accepts the ἐόν of a few late mss. and posits a lacuna after 13. If the more usual νέον is correct, we would expect a verb meaning "follow" not "complain about" (see Wilamowitz' *apparatus criticus ad loc.*).

49. 294, 345, 347, 362, 373, 454, 495, 514, 515, 904, 911, 921, 942, 1005.

50. *E.g.*, 158, 472–73, 532, 601–2, 724–25, 740, 742.

51. This mesode (93–100) has troubled many critics, who have questioned whether it is in its proper place and whether the text needs emending. In answer to the first, I accept the conclusion, if not all the arguments, of W. C. Scott in *GRBS* 9 (1968), 259–66, who contends that the primary reference of the mesode is to the Greeks. This sense seems to me obvious if the mesode is taken closely with the preceding

antistrophe, in which the chorus maintain that no one shall resist the Persian might (87–92). They clearly have the Greeks in mind in these verses, and this confidence that the Greeks will not escape leads them to the general observation that no mortal can escape his ordained destruction. The third strophe then continues to explain why the Greeks are doomed, "for" (*gar*) divine Fate has held sway in Persia (101 ff.). The chorus' worry and concern for their own army are not expressed until the fourth strophe (115 ff.), where the switch from ionics to lyric iambics underscores the change from confidence to worry. However, the ironic application of the mesode to the Persians themselves would undoubtedly have been clear to the audience.

As to the need for emendation, I see no compelling reason to attempt to construct a responsive strophic pair out of the mesode. Nor have any convincing emendations been proposed for some of the unusual and difficult expressions in these lines. The mesode should therefore be left as it is in the mss. with only Hermann's two corrections *metri gratia*. Against these corrections, Young (*GRBS* 13 [1972], 5–6) defends the metrical scheme of the *paradosis*, but Young's mixture of major and minor ionics (with a choriamb thrown in) seems very doubtful after the strong and regular rhythm of the preceding thirty verses.

52. On 726 ("The evil he accomplished [*ēnysen*] is evident"), Broadhead says correctly, "It is not clear whether *daimōn* or Xerxes is the subject of *ēnysen*." This may well be an intentional ambiguity, and it is best not to select one of the two as the sole agent but rather to understand both Xerxes and the *daimōn* as agents.

53. Broadhead (on 362) rejects any nonmoral interpretation of *theōn phthonon* (cf. Fraenkel, *Agamemnon*, vol. 2, pp. 349–50). But both these scholars rely primarily on the statements of Darius for their view that this *phthonos* is the just retribution for hybristic action.

54. This parallel between the *atē* ("ruin") of Persia and the *atē* ("delusion") of Agamemnon supports the view (see above, note 45) that these two meanings are present simultaneously in *atē*.

55. Darius' account of the previous kings of Persia (765–79), which has seemed out of place to some, makes it clear that Xerxes' rule is the continuation and culmination of a long tradition.

56. See H. D. F. Kitto, *Greek Tragedy*, 36.

57. Cf. ibid.: "if one critic says 'This is a religious play about the punishment of *hybris*' and another, 'This is a patriotic piece celebrating the victory,' they are not saying the same thing, and it is perhaps possible

to prove that the one is substantially right and the other substantially wrong."

58. That the Athenians held Darius responsible for the Persian attack at Marathon is indicated by the chorus' reply to the queen (244) that the Greeks are capable of destroying Darius' fine large army. Whatever the precise construction of the infinitive in 244 (see Broadhead, *ad loc.*), this reply must have been taken to refer to Marathon.

59. But see above, note 20.

60. See above, note 40.

61. See above, note 20.

62. Because of the dual perspective, certain words that normally have two fairly distinct meanings could be understood in one sense from one point of view and in another sense from the other. Thus *daïois* (286) designates the Persians, who are "wretched" from their own perspective but who are "enemies" for the Athenians (see Broadhead's note *ad loc.*).

63. The absurd conclusions that can be reached by a logical exploration of the consequences of the coexistence of opposites are fully displayed in the *Dissoi Logoi*, written ca. 400 B.C. (see Diels-Kranz, §90).

64. Cf. the ironic overtones of the mesode in the parodos (above, note 51).

65. Archilochus (130 = 58D) says the gods often raise up men who are beset by evils, and they also overthrow those who are faring well. It is this pattern of rise and fall, of good followed by evil, that Archilochus refers to when he says elsewhere (128 = 67aD) that a *rhysmos* ("rhythm") holds men, so that they should neither rejoice nor grieve excessively during a high or low point in their lives. Cf. Hesiod, *WD* 5–6.

NOTES TO CHAPTER III

1. The satyr play, *Proteus*, which deals with the fortunes of Menelaus in Egypt, was probably related to the trilogy (see H. J. Mette, *Der verlorene Aischylos*, 76–77), but would not have affected the dramatic unity of the three tragedies.

2. I have in mind particularly the commentaries of Fraenkel and of Denniston and Page (hereafter cited simply as Page).

3. *Oikos* and *domos* in Greek both carry the same breadth of meaning, "dwelling" and "family," as the English "house" (though *domos* in the sense of "family" is found only in tragedy). One of the many virtues of John Jones' treatment of the *Oresteia* is his emphasis on Aeschylus'

concern with the *oikos* (*On Aristotle and Greek Tragedy*, especially 82–111). The political implications of this emphasis on the *oikos* will be considered in chapter IV.

4. P. E. Easterling's remarks on the question of "character" (*G&R* 20 [1973], 3–19) strike a sensible balance between the extremes of excessive concern with and total denial of character in Aeschylean drama.

5. I use the words *ethical* and *ethic* to apply to patterns or standards of behavior without the further implications of the words *moral* and *morality*, which may suggest an absolute sanction for the standards of behavior and imply a sense of moral responsibility (see above, chapter I).

6. Such a pattern is generally assumed for the *Supplices* trilogy and is often postulated for the *Prometheia* too; see below, chapter V. C. J. Herington (*Arion* 4 [1965], 387–403) sees this pattern as a late development in Aeschylus' career, after the production of *Septem* in 467.

7. Page is quite right (against Fraenkel) to keep *Ag.* 7.

8. I have overtranslated *dichorropōs* in order to bring out the sense of balance in the root **rep-*, compounds of which occur frequently in the trilogy: *e.g., epirrepō*, Ag. 251, 707, 1042, *Eu.* 888; *antirrepō*, *Ag.* 574.

9. In *Ch.* 313 I follow the ms. reading, *drasanti*. Page emends to *drasanta*, which does not substantially affect the sense.

10. See L-S-J, s.v. *paschō* I.

11. It is especially important not to read a Christian sense of suffering (with its implications of redemption) into the words "the doer suffers."

12. The text of 1527 is often altered (following Hermann) to *axia drasas* (see Fraenkel). This emendation strengthens the basic sense of reciprocity in the words.

13. In *Ag.* 750–60 the chorus disagree with the view that evil is born from good. Rather it is evil that comes from evil (like from like). This view may seem to be contradicted in 1001–4, where the chorus apparently speak of excess health leading to disease (see George Thomson's note *ad loc.* for parallels for this view) and excess wealth leading to financial disaster (if no precautions are taken). One can reconcile these two views by saying that great wealth or health is likely to lead to an act of *hybris* (excess health or wealth), and this *hybris* breeds another evil in turn. That excess wealth is a violation of *dikē* seems to be the meaning of *Ag.* 376–78.

14. This full translation of *symphyton* is Fraenkel's; see his note *ad loc.*

15. In 1571–73 Clytemnestra is in fact praying for the *daimōn* to wear out a different family "with kindred murders," but her words clearly apply also to the troubles in her own family.

16. At the end of *Eumenides*, after the familial evil has been eliminated by Orestes' acquittal, Athena asks the Furies not to instill civil war (*Arē emphylion*, 862–63) in the city (Athens). *Emphylion* suggests a link between the elimination of evil in the family of Atreus and in Athens.

17. We do not know if the later story of Orestes' marriage to Hermione, who bore him a son, was current at the time of the *Oresteia* (see P. T. Stevens' edition of Euripides' *Andromache*, 1–5). If it was, Aeschylus never so much as hints at it.

18. Lloyd-Jones, *CQ* n.s. 12 (1962), 199.

19. Fr. 273.15–16 (Loeb fr. 277) from Aeschylus' *Niobe* is often quoted (Lloyd-Jones, *CQ* n.s. 12 [1962] 192) in support of this view: "god sows in mortals an *aitia* [cause for blame] whenever he wishes to ruin a house utterly." But in the first place this fragment seems to picture the god as acting at first without any cause, and secondly, if he has a cause, the situation is likely to be something like that of Odysseus' companions (discussed in chapter I), who are virtually forced to eat the cattle of the sun, thereby insuring their own doom. Certainly there is no hint in the fragment of hereditary guilt or punishment.

20. Indeed Lloyd-Jones does not argue his case directly from the text. His reasoning is as follows (to oversimplify): Zeus sent Agamemnon to Troy to punish Paris; Agamemnon was thus forced to kill Iphigeneia, for which crime he must pay. But a just Zeus never would punish an innocent person, and, since Zeus must be just, Agamemnon must have some original taint of guilt. The crime of Atreus then gives us the clue we are looking for: hereditary guilt.

21. Cassandra (1223–25) tells the chorus that Aegisthus is plotting the killing of Agamemnon for the slaughtered children (*ek tōnde*, 1223). Thus we can accept this as Aegisthus' true motive. Cf. *Ag.* 1338–40, where *proterōn* (1338) seems to refer to the children of Thyestes, though it may also include Iphigeneia.

22. Cassandra first alludes to the children of Thyestes (1096–97) as testimony to the evil in the house.

23. Likewise the curse of Thyestes, often referred to in discussions of hereditary guilt, is only mentioned once by Aegisthus (1601), and is

disregarded by everyone else. Clytemnestra once tells of the curse in the house (*Ch.* 692) but this is a general spirit of evil similar to the *daimōn* or *alastōr* or Erinys (cf. *Eu.* 417).

24. Page feels that a statement of hereditary guilt is likely in 374, since the reference is to Paris, who "is driven to his crime by supernatural powers against his better judgment; he is paying for the corruption of the society from which he comes, he is an example of the visitation of fathers' sins upon children's heads." Nowhere in the trilogy, however, is there an indication of or interest in the reason for Paris' crime, and nowhere is there a suggestion that Trojan society is corrupt or that Priam has ever done wrong. Cf. Fraenkel *ad loc.*

25. Lloyd-Jones translates *ta ek proterōn aplakēmata* (*Eu.* 934) as "crimes born from those of long ago," and sees these as crimes caused by inherited guilt. But he is letting his own view intrude, for these words mean only "crimes arising out of earlier ones." All the crimes in the *Oresteia* (except Paris' rape of Helen and Thyestes' adultery) arise out of earlier ones in some sense, but this does not mean that "men cannot help committing" them (Lloyd-Jones *ad loc.*).

26. Page (note to *Ag.* 223) interprets *prōtopēmōn* as the "first cause . . . of the disasters which are to follow," but "cause" is not in the Greek.

27. Lloyd-Jones' arguments (*Justice of Zeus*, 70–78) that the notion of pollution was just as strong in Homeric times as in the fifth century are quite unconvincing and only confuse the issue. The plague at the beginning of the *Iliad* is sent by Apollo in anger because Agamemnon dishonored his priest, but Agamemnon himself is not polluted; he can and does lift the plague by appeasing the god. Oedipus, in contrast, is himself polluted; he cannot lift the plague by any act except by removing himself from Thebes. What is important in the fifth century is this "personal" pollution, which attaches itself to an individual automatically when that person commits an act (most notably homicide), and there is no suggestion of anything like this in Homer. Certainly it is hard to believe that if Theoclymenus (see pp. 8–9) had been purified after killing his kinsman, he would not mention this fact to Telemachus when he asks to be taken along in his ship (it was notoriously dangerous in the fifth century to take an unpurified killer aboard; cf. Antiphon, *De Caede Herodis* 82).

28. See Chapter I, note 70.

29. The killing of Aegisthus is relatively insignificant and does not incur pollution (*Ch.* 989–90). It belongs to a category of permissible

homicides, the killing of an adulterer (see D. M. MacDowell, *Athenian Homicide Law*, 77). Strictly speaking, the adulterer should be caught in the act, but Aegisthus' adultery is clear to everyone.

30. When Orestes reaches Athens, Athena accepts him as purified (*Eu.* 474), but the Furies still smell blood on him (253).

31. On the reading *drasanti*, see above, note 9.

32. This adverbial use of *dikēn* with the genitive is rare in all poetry before the *Oresteia*, where suddenly it occurs more than twenty times. It seems reasonable to assume that Aeschylus' fondness for this expression is related to the importance in this trilogy of *dikē* in its other senses. See E. G. O'Neill, Jr., *TAPA* 72 (1941), 295, note 9.

33. Cf. fr. 80, where *dikē* is said to be *eris* ("strife").

34. I have intentionally avoided making a division between a divine *dikē* and a human *dikē*, which is popular among some scholars: see, *e.g.*, Friedrich Solmsen, *Hesiod and Aeschylus*, and Dieter Kaufmann-Bühler, *Begriff und Funktion der Dike in den Tragödien des Aischylos*. There is no textual evidence for such a distinction, and not only is it unnecessary but it also hinders us (I feel) in arriving at a true understanding of Greek *dikē*.

35. The sense of punishment in *dikē* in *Ch.* 311 is reinforced by *prassousa*, since *prassō* can be used in both middle and active voices (cf. *Eu.* 624) to mean "exact" a penalty or "avenge." See L-S-J, s.v. *prassō* VI.

36. I do not mean to imply that society at the end of the trilogy is a different kind of society, a polis instead of a tribal society, as some have suggested, for the strife in the first two plays is civil strife just as the harmony at the end is civil harmony. Cf. Thomson (*Aeschylus and Athens*, 292), who speaks of the Furies' role in a "new order, which is not new in the sense that it supersedes the old, but in the sense that in it the conflicts of the old are blended and reconciled."

37. In this last case (*Ch.* 120) it is particularly clear that *dikēphoron* means an avenger, since Electra asks whether the chorus want a *dikēphoron* or a *dikastēn,* a judge. They reply that they want one who will kill in return (*antapoktenei*, 121) on the age-old principle of doing harm to one's enemies (123), and this clearly means they want an avenger, not a judge.

38. Page's note on 911 (ἐs δῶμ' ἄελπτον ὡs ἂν ἡγῆται Δίκη) is instructive: "The hidden meaning is: 'that Retribution (for Iphigeneia) may lead him to a home far different from the one he expected'; the surface meaning, 'that Justice may lead him to the home he never expected to

see again.'" This represents a common view among commentators and translators, that Clytemnestra's *dikē* is mere "retribution" whereas Agamemnon's *dikē* is some higher "justice." There is no justification for such a distinction. The point is rather that it is precisely the same sense of *dikē* that leads Agamemnon to punish Troy (and thus kill his daughter) and that leads Clytemnestra to kill him in return. Cf. H. D. F. Kitto, who sees the *dikē* of Clytemnestra and Aegisthus as the "same in kind" as Agamemnon's and "different only in degree" (*Form and Meaning in Drama*, 37–38). I see no evidence in the text for this difference in degree, nor am I persuaded by Kitto's notion of Zeus and Apollo as "progressive" (see chapter IV, note 27); but his arguments that both sides in *Eumenides* are both right and wrong and that *dikē* as retribution is still present at the end (82) have considerable validity.

39. These poetic images have been studied by others, though there is still more to be said about how they operate in the trilogy. See Anne Lebeck, *The Oresteia: A Study in Language and Structure*; on the image of sacrifice, see F. I. Zeitlin, *TAPA* 96 (1965), 463–508, and *TAPA* 97 (1966), 645–53; on the lion cub, see B. M. W. Knox, *CP* 47 (1952), 17–25.

40. In an earlier passage (1509–12) the chorus may offer direct support for Clytemnestra's claim of *dikē,* but this depends upon the uncertain emendation of *de kai* to *dikan* in 1511. If we accept this emendation (as Page does but Fraenkel does not), then the chorus acknowledge that *dikē* had to be paid for the killing of Thyestes' children. See Page's note *ad loc.*

41. Reading (with Page) Δίκα δ' ἐπ' ἄλλο πρᾶγμα θήγεται in 1535. The general sense of 1535–36 is clear whatever text one adopts. Cf. *Ch.* 805, where the implication of calling for a "fresh" (*prosphatois*) *dikē* is that the previous killing was also a *dikē.*

42. The similarity of Orestes' and Clytemnestra's deeds is reinforced by the imagery, for as Lebeck notes (*The Oresteia*, 14), "In avenging a serpent's crime, [Orestes] too becomes a serpent."

43. The sense of "change," always present in *metabainō,* is often ignored by translators or rendered ambiguously as "the turning of Justice" (Lattimore). It is acknowledged by Sidgwick (note on *Ch.* 308), although he is troubled by the illogicality of the phrase. He is quite correct to be troubled if *to dikaion* is thought to mean "Justice." H. J. Rose, note *ad loc.,* in fact finds *metabainei* incomprehensible: "To the Chorus, there is but one possible 'path' for Justice to go upon; how then can she be said to 'change' or 'pass over'?" These remarks show how thoroughly

commentators have misunderstood the Greek sense of *dikē* by equating it with our unified and integrated concept of justice.

44. By "nonintegrated" I mean that one instance of *dikē* may conflict with another instance without there necessarily being any means of reconciling them. In most post-Platonic thought we can (theoretically) weigh one injustice against another and decide on the lesser of the two according to an ultimate concept of justice, but Greek *dikē* provides no such absolute standard. See above, note 43, and chapter I.

45. On the connection between the Furies and the Areopagus see Lloyd-Jones, *Justice*, 92–95.

46. It is clearly implied that "the one who prospers without *dikē*" (464) is the same as the "killers of many" in 461, which must refer to Agamemnon (among others).

47. Page capitalizes *Dika* five times in the seventy-five verses, and the word occurs emphatically as the last word in both the second strophe and antistrophe.

48. E. R. Dodds, *PCPhS* 186 (1960), 23. Dodds (23, note 2) also lists additional parallels between the Furies' second stasimon and the odes in Agamemnon.

49. See K. J. Dover, *JHS* 77 (1957), 230–32. *Thesmiōn* in 491 must refer to the Areopagus, which Athena has just referred to as a *thesmon* (484). The text of 483–84 is corrupt, and in Page's version, for example, the jurors respect the "ordinances of their oaths," whereas Wilamowitz and others (following Casaubon) have Athena appoint the sworn jurors to be an "ordinance." But in either case *thesmon* refers directly or indirectly to the Areopagus, as it does also in 615 and 681 (cf. 571, where the plural *thesmous* apparently refers to the "ordinances" of the Areopagus). Note also that the only use of *thesmos* in *Eumenides* other than these references to the Areopagus is when the Furies describe their own duty (punishing offenders) as a divinely appointed *thesmon* (391).

50. The lines 679–80 are sometimes assigned to Apollo and 676–77 to the Furies. Both couplets are assigned to the chorus in the mss. (and Douglas Young in his translation retains this *paradosis*), but most editors divide them between Apollo and the chorus. For the order I follow, see R. P. Winnington-Ingram (*CR* 49 [1935], 7–8), who argues that (a) Apollo has just given several speeches, and it is slightly more natural if he speaks first here; (b) the switch from the plural to the singular in 676–77 is easier if we assign the lines to Apollo; and (c) the metaphor

of archery in 676 is more suitable for Apollo. These reasons are sufficient to make his case likely, even without his further argument that the appeal to the juror's oath in 680 is more suitable for the Furies. A further point is that a scribe might have mistakenly assigned 676–77 to the chorus instead of Apollo because of the first word *hēmin*, whereas there seems to be no such easy explanation why such an error would have occurred in 679–80. Page now restores the correct distribution of speakers, as do P. Groeneboom and Thomson. Thomson also compares *Il.* 19.259–60, where the Erinyes are said to punish violators of oaths; cf. Hesiod, *WD* 803–4, where they are said to have helped at the birth of Horkos (Oath).

51. On the question of oaths in taking testimony, see A. R. W. Harrison, *The Law of Athens*, vol. 2, pp. 150–53. On oaths in *Eumenides*, see H. J. Dirksen, *Die aischyleische Gestalt des Orest*, 53–54.

52. In keeping with the Greek sense of double motivation or over-determination (see Chapter I) Apollo can be *panaitios* (*Eu.* 200), and yet this does not detract from Orestes' responsibility or deter the Furies from their pursuit of him.

53. For a good summary of the circumstances under which homicide was lawful in the fourth century, see MacDowell, *Athenian Homicide Law*, 73–79. The only circumstance that might possibly be applied to the killing of Clytemnestra is the provision that it is lawful to kill a tyrant, but Orestes never mentions this justification. For the killing of Aegisthus see above, note 29.

54. See above, note 50.

55. See above, note 53.

56. To many modern critics the major difference between the two killings is that Orestes acted reluctantly at the command of Apollo and is therefore innocent, whereas Clytemnestra acted out of her own (malicious) desire and is therefore guilty (see, *e.g.*, William Arrowsmith, *Tulane Drama Review* 3, no. 3 [1959], 31–57). But, although Orestes' reluctance is clear in *Choephoroi*, no mention is made of it during the trial in *Eumenides*. We must therefore conclude that it is of little or no relevance to the final dispute and settlement, although it is important in other respects (see Chapter IV).

57. Gagarin, *AJP* 96 (1975), 121–27.

58. Cf. Sidgwick's revealing note on 741.

59. The phrase *patrōion aidestheis moron* (760) indicates the sense of respect Zeus has for Agamemnon and the shame he felt at his ignoble

death. We see in chapter IV how the shameful manner of Agamemnon's death is a vital aspect of Orestes' revenge and acquittal.

60. The preceding strophe (*Ag.* 1001–18) is partially corrupt, but the chorus seem to say that, for other crimes short of bloodshed, punishment may be avoided if due moderation is restored.

61. Aegisthus' willingness to die, now that he has accomplished his desire (1610), recalls a similar willingness on the part of the herald (539), another suggestion of the similarity between the two opposed actions, the conquest of Troy and the killing of Agamemnon.

62. The text of these lyrics (*Ch.* 961–72) is quite corrupt. In particular 971–72 are open to different readings and interpretations.

63. The precise text and meaning of *Ag.* 1022–24 are disputed, but it is generally agreed that the reference is to Asclepius. See Page and Fraenkel for two quite different interpretations.

64. Karl Reinhardt (*Aischylos als Regisseur und Theologe*, 152–53) sees the duping of the Fates by means of wine (*Eu.* 728) as a mythological paradigm for the trial and concludes that Apollo's arguments at the trial are intended to trick the Furies just as he once tricked the Fates. I argue in chapter IV, however, that Apollo's arguments at the trial must be taken seriously, although the Furies may nonetheless feel they have been tricked.

65. Cf. the contrast between *toutōn* and *ekeina* in 1105–6 (cf. 1242–45).

66. Cassandra demonstrates her impotence by shedding her prophetic robes (1264–72) so that even the chorus seem to understand the special misery that is produced by knowledge of one's own fate: "Oh, very wretched and very wise" (*ō polla men talaina, polla d' au sophē*, 1295). Note that it is Cassandra's knowledge of her fate that causes her suffering, not her suffering that leads to knowledge.

67. The precise function of the Areopagus is much disputed, in part because of textual uncertainty in *Eu.* 693. See Dover, *JHS* 77 (1957), 232.

68. Nowhere is it said that the Areopagus itself will punish offenders. This duty is explicitly assigned to the Furies (934–37), who will presumably be helped by judgments of the court.

69. The *Oresteia* has been seen by some as a dramatization of the change from primitive tribal society to the society of the polis (see above, note 36). But nothing about the organization of the polis would in it-

self bring an end to the cycle of crime. It is only by reconciling the Furies that internal strife is banished (862–64). Otherwise, it is implied, the polis will be no better off than the house of Atreus was.

70. Cf. above, note 16. The Trojan War was a foreign war, but because it required the sacrifice of Iphigeneia, it produced civil strife also. Athena undoubtedly means to imply that foreign wars should be fought with the support of all factions at home, a lesson the United States should have learned before fighting the recent war in Vietnam.

71. This dual nature of *eris* in the *Oresteia* has obvious roots in Hesiod's two *erides* (*WD* 11–26).

72. Zeitlin, *TAPA* 96 (1965), 463–508, and *TAPA* 97 (1966), 645–53. On *pelanos* in *Persae*, see above, 54–55.

73. Cf. the exemplum of Scylla, "persuaded" to her crime by a golden necklace (*Ch.* 618).

74. It appears from the hypothesis and from Harpocrates (see Page's *apparatus criticus* on *Eu.* 1027) that Athena explicitly gave the Furies their new name at the end of the play, but this is not in the preserved text. That the Furies put on crimson robes for the final procession is generally assumed, but not explicitly stated.

NOTES TO CHAPTER IV

1. The only scholarly attempt at a full-scale treatment of the sexual aspect of the *Oresteia* is R. P. Winnington-Ingram's article, "Clytemnestra and the Vote of Athena," JHS 68 (1948), 130–47. His interpretation is in my view too narrowly psychoanalytical: "The thesis of this article— and it is supported by the continual emphasis which the dramatist places upon the sexual antithesis and upon the anomalous personality of Clytemnestra—is that she hated Agamemnon, not simply because he had killed her child, not because she loved Aegisthus, but out of a jealously that was not jealousy of Chryseis or Cassandra, but of Agamemnon himself and his status as a man" (132). But Winnington-Ingram does make a serious effort to connect the sexual arguments in *Eumenides* with the sexual conflict in *Agamemnon*.

2. Among the explanations given are that Athena's justification of her vote is intentionally irrelevant in order that she avoid deciding the judicial issue ("pure chance, if there be such a thing, would be the most appropriate arbiter," notes Verrall in his edition of *Eumenides*, xxvii); that Athena "must decide for acquittal. Yet, she cannot risk offending

the powerful Erinyes by openly proclaiming that . . . she is on the side of the younger generation of the gods" (Lloyd-Jones' translation of *The Eumenides*, p. 58); that "Athena's somewhat illogical reason . . . is what [Aeschylus] thinks Athena would have said" (Dover, *JHS* 77 [1957], 236); or that the entire trial is "a caricature of Athenian legal procedure" (Lebeck, *The Oresteia*, 137). See also Reinhardt's view (chapter III, note 64). A serious explanation of Athena's justification of her vote is given by George Thomson, who contends (*Aeschylus and Athens*, 288) that her argument "touches the crucial point at issue," for "Aeschylus perceived that the subjection of woman was a necessary consequence of the development of private property." Thomson's views, interesting as they are, are based on the theory of primitive matriarchy originally developed by Bachofen in *Das Mutterrecht* (1861) and elaborated by Engels in *The Origin of the Family, Private Property and the State* (1891). This theory is now almost universally discredited by scholars. See, *e.g.*, Bamberger, "The Myth of Matriarchy," 263–80, and, for the Greek tradition, Simon Pembroke, *Journ. Warb. & Court. Inst.* 30 (1967), 1–35. (It still crops up in some feminist writings, however: cf. Kate Millett on the *Oresteia* [*Sexual Politics*, 112–15].) On the seriousness of Apollo's and Athena's arguments, see also Brian Vickers, *Towards Greek Tragedy*, 414–17, and Gustav Grossmann (*Promethie und Orestie*, 226–28), who sympathizes with the male side more openly than most critics.

3. Cf. Semonides 7.118. Lloyd-Jones notes (*Females of the Species*, 92) that this view is a commonplace, but it is significant that Aeschylus, like Semonides, emphasizes that the Greeks fought for "a woman" rather than for Helen. In *Ag.* 800 and 1455–57, Helen is singled out by name as the cause of the war.

4. *Errei pas' Aphrodita* (*Ag.* 419) certainly suggests that love is gone for all the Greeks, even if the primary reference is only to Menelaus. For Aphrodite's connection with marriage, see *Eu.* 215.

5. The juxtaposition of *thygatros* and *gynaikopoinōn polemōn* in 225–26 emphasizes the connection between these two events.

6. Simone de Beauvoir, *The Second Sex* (1953), xvi–xviii. The original French edition was published in 1949.

7. Eur. *Hipp.* 616–68. Hippolytus' remarks may of course reveal more about his own abnormal psyche than about the Athenian attitude toward women, but his views are part of a long tradition going back to Hesiod (*Th.* 570–612, *WD* 57–104) and Semonides (7). Similar

misogynist remarks occur so often in drama that we can assume at least some Athenians felt this way. For a study of this misogynist attitude toward women in Greek myth and society, see P. E. Slater, *The Glory of Hera.*

8. For a full discussion of the *oikos* and women's role in it, see W. K. Lacey, *The Family in Classical Greece.* Though the picture I give of women's place in society is based to some extent on Lacey's study, it is certainly a more negative one than his. In part this is undoubtedly the result of different attitudes toward the matter in contemporary society; here I acknowledge my indebtedness to recent feminist literature and discussions, which have convincingly shown that many benefits women enjoy in their position as "the Other," such as freedom from hard labor, are in fact restrictions that reinforce their subordinate position. For a similar reaction to Lacey's views, see Caldwell, *Arethusa* 6 (1973), 225, note 6. For an excellent brief estimate of the restricted position of women in fifth-century Athens see Joseph Vogt, *Von der Gleichwertigkeit der Geschlechter,* 7–8. Vogt also has a brief discussion (14–15) of sexual values in the *Oresteia.* Sarah Pomeroy's *Goddesses, Whores, Wives, and Slaves,* which contains a useful survey of Greek (and Roman) women, reached me only when this book was in press.

9. See Harrison, *The Law of Athens,* vol. 1, pp. 9–12, 132–38.

10. Ibid., p. 38: "the woman and her chastity are hardly protected in their own right, but only because she is the humble but necessary vehicle for carrying on the *oikos.*"

11. For this distinction between "public" and "domestic," see M. Z. Rosaldo, "Women, Culture, and Society," 17–25. According to her, it is generally true that the most strongly male-dominated societies are also those in which the gap between the public and domestic spheres is the greatest, and certainly this seems to be the case for fifth-century Athens.

12. See Lacey, *The Family,* 167–69. Eteocles (*Septem* 200–1) explicitly contrasts the concerns of men, which are outside the home (*ta exōthen*) with those of women, which are inside (*endon*). Of course this separation would be much less true in lower-class families, where economic necessity would force many women to work along with their husbands.

13. Pickard-Cambridge (*The Dramatic Festivals of Athens,* 264–65) summarizes the conflicting evidence, which favors but does not prove the presence of women in the theater. My own conviction that women must have attended the theater (perhaps in smaller numbers than men)

is based partly on the subjective feeling that Euripides would not have included so many references to the condition of women and their problems in his plays if only men were present to hear them.

14. *Xenia* was a male institution even in Homeric times, since women hardly ever traveled in circumstances that would require them to have *xenoi* ("guest-friends"). Semonides (7.106–107) declares it impossible to entertain a *xenos* when a man's wife is present.

15. In the *Oresteia* the institution of marriage is more highly valued by men than by women and is explicitly praised by Apollo, a clear representative of male values (see *Eu.* 213–18).

16. Note that on the divine level the expedition is favored by Zeus but opposed by the female goddess Artemis, virgin and protector of young things (*Ag.* 140–43), and that, in the omen interpreted by Calchas, a pregnant hare is devoured by male eagles (114–20).

17. I see no need to raise the much discussed question of Agamemnon's free choice here. Winnington-Ingram (*BICS* 21 [1974], 3–6) has a good discussion of the subject, which concludes, "War wins out over the child" (6). As a military commander Agamemnon makes the appropriate decision, and because he is the sort of person who makes such decisions he is a successful military commander. Aeschylus is scarcely interested in deciding between free will and necessity; if Professor Page really were to meet the poet's ghost in Hades and begin asking him questions (see Page's edition of *Agamemnon*, xxvi–xxviii), I suspect that Aeschylus, like Ajax, would turn away in silence, more saddened than angered by the injustice done to his work.

18. We must not, however, excuse Agamemnon's crime as "caused" by circumstance. Under similar circumstances a different man (or woman) might have acted differently.

19. Grossmann (*Promethie und Orestie*, 218) even denies that Clytemnestra's rule in Agamemnon's absence is legal, but there is no evidence to support this. (The figure of Clytemnestra probably resembles what many men today fear will be the ultimate result of women's liberation.)

20. Fraenkel argues that *machēs* (940) refers to combat between Agamemnon and the people, but this is not the issue. What is particularly "unfeminine" is to desire to do battle oneself.

21. It is quite possible that Clytemnestra is on stage during much of the parodos, attending to sacrifices at altars at the rear; see *e.g.*, Page's note on 83 ff.

22. Page believes there is corruption in 327–28, because "it is un-expected that the 'children' should be said to bewail the 'old men' in a context in which (naturally) the old men are usually said to bewail the young." But it is perfectly natural for Clytemnestra to think of children, who would survive and become slaves along with the women, after the men had all been killed.

23. Some editors excise 527. Fraenkel approvingly cites Headlam's view that a "religious herald" would not have made this "proud boast." But these critics fail to see that men such as the herald are "religious" in the context of their military duties—prayers for victory, thanksgiving after battle, etc.—and may quite easily violate other religious considera-tions that are not of such high value according to their male military code.

24. The rather abrupt transition from the troubles of the past (427–28) to those of the present (429 ff.) suggests poetically the unity be-tween the suffering of a man (Menelaus) when his woman is gone and the suffering of the women when the men are gone.

25. It is quite likely true, for instance, that false reports of Agamem-non's death came to Argos, and the chorus have already (456–57) told of popular unrest in the city, which is the reason she gives for sending Orestes to live with Agamemnon's *doryxenos* ("spear-friend") Strophius. Cf. *Ch.* 914–16.

26. Agamemnon has so destroyed their marriage from Clytemnestra's point of view that she even claims she is no longer his wife but instead the old spirit of vengeance, the *alastōr* (1497–1501).

27. Kitto (*Form and Meaning*, 68) finds the picture of Apollo as destroyer of Cassandra in *Agamemnon* inconsistent with the portrayal of him as "god of purity and light" in *Eumenides*, and he suggests that this is an indication of a development in the trilogy. But, if Apollo in *Choephoroi* and *Eumenides* represents the forces of male domination (as we shall see), then it is perhaps not so inconsistent that he should treat Cassandra in this way.

28. The irony of 1277, "instead of my father's altar a chopping block awaits me," brings out this parallel between Cassandra and Iphigeneia, since her recollection of Priam's altar where she used to sacrifice brings to mind immediately that other father's altar described in the parados.

29. It is clear in these verses and in Aegisthus' account of Atreus' crime (1587–1602) that the important factor was not killing the children per se but rather serving them to their father to eat. This would be a

shocking religious crime and would pollute Thyestes forever. The killing of the children in itself does not destroy Thyestes' *oikos*, since at least one male heir, Aegisthus, survived (cf. 1605–6).

30. *Ōdina* in 1418 refers specifically to the labor of childbirth.

31. It was traditional to blame Helen for the Trojan War, but Sappho's poem (16LP) shows that Helen had her defenders and that she could be admired from a woman's point of view. Cf. Stesichorus' palinode (*PMG* 192–93).

32. In her response (1521–29) to the chorus' charge, Clytemnestra seems to defend her use of *dolos*, but the text is too damaged for us to determine precisely what she says. That Orestes also uses deceit in his revenge (*Ch.* 726) seems to be overlooked when he and Apollo criticize Clytemnestra's action, in *Eumenides*.

33. *Choephoroi* also balances *Agamemnon* in that (as Cassandra predicts, *Ag.* 1318–19) a woman dies for a woman and a man for a man.

34. The translation of 629–30 is Sidgwick's; the text of 623–30 is corrupt, but I follow him (and others) in accepting Stanley's *tiō* for *tiōn* in 629 (cf. Douglas Young, *GRBS* 12 [1971], 309–10). Others (*e.g.,* Lloyd-Jones in his translation) see a reference to Aegisthus in 629–30, but such a reference would not be at all clear to the audience (unless it is somehow prepared for in 628, which is corrupt).

35. That serious deliberation is a matter for men only is also maintained in *Choephoroi* by Orestes (665–67) and the chorus (849–50).

36. Clytemnestra's deficiency as a mother may perhaps also be suggested by contrast with the nurse, who had to take over some of the motherly duties when Orestes was a child (750). See Vickers, *Towards Greek Tragedy*, 404.

37. Vickers (ibid., 396–97) points out the heavy emphasis in *Choephoroi* on Agamemnon as a father.

38. For the traditional version see the Homeric *Hymn to Apollo* 277–374; cf. Lloyd-Jones' translation of *Eumenides*, pp. 9–10.

39. Note that for Apollo the violation of marriage is a violation of Aphrodite (215; cf. *Ag.* 419).

40. When Orestes asks Apollo to "judge this blood" (*tod' haima krinon*, 613), there is a nice ambiguity in *haima*, which can normally mean "deed of blood" (*i.e.,* homicide) but here also means "matter of blood" (*i.e.,* question of blood tie).

41. The intervening discussion (640–51) about Zeus binding his

father is not strictly relevant, but it does force Apollo to repeat the point that bloodshed is irrevocable (647–48), which is exactly what the Furies want to hear.

42. According to Aristotle (*De Gen. An.* 763b30–33), Anaxagoras held that "the seed comes to be from the male, but the female provides the place for it." There seems to have been quite an interest among fifth-century thinkers in the problem of the contribution of each sex to the process of reproduction. Parmenides (fr. 17) apparently believed that the female determined the sex of the embryo, and both Empedocles and Democritus wrote on the subject (see *De Gen. An.* 764a1–65a3).

43. Although Aristotle nowhere makes it explicit, there certainly seems to be a close connection between his own biological view of the female as a "natural deformity" (*De Gen. An.* 775a16) and his well-known views on the general superiority of males (see, *e.g., Politics* 1254b13–14: "by nature the male is superior, the female inferior; the one rules, the other is ruled").

44. Euripides' Orestes also affirms the true parentage of the father (*Or.* 552–56).

45. It is uncertain whether the final procession of Athenian citizens is composed of women and children only. The text mentions only these (*Eu.* 1027), but many editors for other reasons (see chapter III, note 74) posit a lacuna after this verse, in which men may have been mentioned. *Astikos leōs* (997) implies men as well as women.

46. A summary of previous views can be found in Podlecki, *The Political Background of Aeschylean Tragedy,* 80–94.

47. E. R. Dodds, *PCPhS* 186 (1960), 19–31. In less than a page (19–20), Dodds discusses *Ag.* 883–84, lists other occurrences of *dēmos* in the play, and concludes, "These things are no more than straws in the wind."

48. On the political tendencies of Stesichorus' *Oresteia* and its connection with Spartan ambitions in the sixth century, see C. M. Bowra, *Greek Lyric Poetry,* 112–15.

49. See *PMG* 216. We are told that Simonides also located the palace of Agamemnon in Sparta (*PMG* 549), and Pindar (*P.* 11.31) says he was killed at Amyclae (near Sparta). That Agamemnon as well as Orestes was considered a Spartan hero is indicated by Herodotus (7.159). The Athenian dramatists, on the other hand, locate Agamemnon's home either in Mycenae (as in Homer) or in Argos, never in Sparta. On Orestes in Athens, see below, note 66.

50. Bowra first put forth the view that Stesichorus' stay in Sparta influenced the versions of myths in his poetry (*CQ* 28 [1934], 115–19; cf. above, note 48). This view has recently received support from another fragment that seems to link Stesichorus with Sparta. See M. L. West, *ZPE* 4 (1969), 142–49.

51. Ibycus has the expedition to Troy leave from Argos, and thus he may have been the first to locate the home of Agamemnon or Menelaus there (*PMG* 282, verses 3, 28, 36).

52. Another small change in the earlier version of the myth is worth noting. Stesichorus had given the nurse who helps Orestes a noble Spartan name, Laodamia (*PMG* 218), whereas Aeschylus gives her the name Cilissa (*Ch.* 732). See Bowra, *Greek Lyric Poetry*, 114.

53. I do not mean to deny another obviously important result of joining the two brothers under one roof, namely that this makes Paris' offense against Menelaus' hospitality an offense against Agamemnon too. See Fraenkel on *Ag.* 400. Of course, for this purpose Aeschylus could have located the brothers' house in any city. On the location in Argos for political reasons, see Daube, *Rechtsproblemen*, 24, note 52.

54. The translation of 532–33 is by Fraenkel, who elaborates in his note the meaning of *syntelēs* as "bound together in a common cause (and for a common destiny)." Cf. Hesiod, *WD* 240: "Often the entire city also suffers for the wrong of one man."

55. The word *stasis* in *Ag.* 1117 may be intentionally ambiguous. The primary meaning here seems to be "band" (*sc.* of Erinyes; cf. 1119), but the sense "internal strife" would also be heard by the audience.

56. There is corruption in the text of *Ch.* 864–65, but the sense of the passage is almost certainly as I have given it.

57. On the poetic connection between the sorrow of Menelaus for Helen and the sorrow of the citizens for the army, see above, note 24.

58. The reference to Odysseus' true loyalty, which follows (*Ag.* 841–42), has often puzzled critics. Fraenkel claims that Agamemnon here "unobtrusively and, as it were, by the way, gives an example of that ripe experience in judging human nature as in political affairs, of which he has just spoken" (note to 841), but this alleged skill in judgment is quite at variance with Agamemnon's actual behavior on stage. Much more plausible, it seems to me, is W. B. Stanford's suggestion that the reference to Odysseus, who was, as far as we can tell, unfavorably portrayed in Aeschylus' other plays, was intended to continue the irony of the preceding lines and thereby underscore Agamemnon's inability to

deal with those around him. See *CR* n.s. 4 (1954), 85, and *The Ulysses Theme* (1963), 102–4.

59. Aegisthus of course, has a claim to the throne (1584–86), but no one except Clytemnestra supports this claim.

60. Fraenkel's interpretation of 883–84 is rightly rejected by Page and others. Clytemnestra's fear of anarchy may have been in part a pretext for removing Orestes, but there was also good reason to worry about the popular unrest and discord described by the chorus in the first stasimon (*dēmothrous* in 883 may recall *dēmokrantou aras* in 458).

61. Agamemnon's killing of Iphigeneia is not regarded by the chorus as requiring his exile (1414–20), perhaps because from a political point of view it is a proper exercise of power for military purposes.

62. As the Furies observe (*Eu.* 653–56), Orestes if polluted would be unable even to participate in public life. See below, note 64.

63. It is generally agreed that the meaningless *phaei* in 522 should be replaced by a word such as *deei* or *phoboi* that continues the idea of *to deinon* in 517.

64. Orestes' matricide is obviously a crime against his family; it is also a political crime in the sense that the resulting pollution necessitates his exile from the city and renders him unfit for participation in public life. See *Eu.* 653–56; *phrateroi* (656), it should be noted, are members of a "brotherhood," an Athenian political organization.

65. The references to Athens in these verses (*Eu.* 10–14) mention several points that an Athenian audience would undoubtedly have been pleased to hear: the "ship-frequented shores," the "road-building children of Hephaestus," and the "tamers of wild land."

66. On the connection of Orestes with Athens, cf. *Odyssey* 3.307, where Orestes is said to have returned from Athens to kill Agamemnon. At the festival of the Anthesteria, a drinking ceremony called "Choes" ("Pots") was traced back to the time Orestes spent in Athens while he was still polluted from the killing of Clytemnestra (see Pickard-Cambridge, *Festivals*, 10), but we know of no tradition before Aeschylus that Orestes stood trial in Athens.

67. See Appendix A, especially note 12.

68. The text supplies all the necessary stage directions. The change of setting here is very easy, as is the later change (at 566) from the Acropolis, where the statue of Athena Polias stood, to the neighboring hill of the Areopagus.

69. Whether Aeschylus favored a restoration of the Areopagus to

precisely its pre-462 position seems to me impossible to determine on the evidence we possess (cf. chapter III, note 67).

70. I have purposely avoided a more detailed discussion of the political situation in Athens and possible allusions to it in the trilogy and also the vast literature on the problem. Both of these areas are covered by Podlecki (*Political Background*, 63–100), though he barely mentions Wilamowitz' view that Aeschylus carefully constructed the play so that partisans of both political parties would understand it as supporting their side, although in fact the poet himself stood above all partisanship and favored reconciliation (*Aristoteles und Athen*, vol. 2, pp. 341–42). My view is in some ways similar to Wilamowitz' and to that of Dodds and others (see Podlecki, *Political Background*, 173, note 44, for references). Recently Lloyd-Jones (in his translation of *The Eumenides*, pp. 75–77) has also maintained that Aeschylus both opposed the reforms of the Areopagus and favored the Argive alliance, though it is not quite accurate to say, as Lloyd-Jones does, that Aeschylus makes only a "polite mention" of the alliance.

NOTES TO CHAPTER V

1. Aeschylus presented two other tragedies and a satyr play together with *Persae*, but there was probably no significant connection among the plays, and *Persae* can thus be considered complete in itself. See Broadhead, lv–lx.

2. It is possible that *Prometheus* formed part of a dilogy rather than a trilogy; see below, note 41.

3. We know that *Septem* was produced in 467. *Supplices* was certainly later than this, probably in 463. We have no clear evidence for the date of *Prometheus*, but there seems to be a growing consensus among scholars that it is more likely to be a late play and may even have been produced after the *Oresteia* in 458. See Herington, *The Author of the "Prometheus Bound"* (1970).

4. Kitto, *Greek Tragedy*, 44.

5. The meager evidence for these two plays is discussed by Mette, *Der verlorene Aischylos*, 34–36.

6. The Greek in 637–38 is rather condensed, but C. M. Dawson's translation, though not word for word, succeeds in bringing out the exact reciprocity of Polyneices' intentions: "to avenge [*teisesthai*] in just the same way [*ton auton tonde tropon*]"—*sc.* as he himself was wronged.

7. Some critics maintain that in Aeschylus' version of the legend Polyneices once gave up all claim to the throne of Thebes. Rosenmeyer, for example, concludes (*Arion* 1 [1962], 68): "Polyneices has no case. The audience knows that his departure from Thebes was voluntary and sanctioned by usage. He is in the wrong." But there is no suggestion of this version in *Septem* (it is found only in Hellanicus); rather as I argue, the presentation of the dispute in *Septem* indicates that Aeschylus followed the more common version of the myth. It is certainly possible that the preceding play, *Oedipus*, mentioned a specific version.

8. Kaufmann-Bühler (*Begriff und Funktion der Dike*, 50–59) maintains that Polyneices had a right to take revenge on Eteocles but not to harm the whole city. He relies, however, on the herald's rejection (1050) of Antigone's claim that Polyneices only avenged the wrong he suffered. The herald argues that Polyneices' wrong was against many, though he was wronged by only one man. Even if this passage is genuine (see below, note 24), the herald is no more an objective voice than Eteocles is, and thus his words cannot be used as evidence against Polyneices.

9. Polyneices prays to the gods of his family and of his fatherland (639–40) and thus must feel he has a claim on their support.

10. It is difficult to determine the precise sense of *dikē homaimōn*, which apparently refers to Melanippus' obligation to fight on behalf of his ancestor, the Theban land (cf. 584, where *dikē* must mean "claim" or "justification"). Karsten Wilkens (*Hermes* 97 [1969], 117–21) suggests that *homaimōn* be understood as the genitive plural of *homaimos* and taken with *prostelletai*, but the supposed meaning of this expression "*dikē* gives him preeminence over his fellow-citizens," seems impossible to extract from the Greek and makes no sense in the context.

11. See, *e.g.*, Dawson (on 672): "Polyneices has no *dikē* of any sort, but Eteocles has a special, complicated *dikē homaimōn* (cf. 415 and 477), a duty to his motherland, which involves family relationships."

12. See Dawson's note on 888.

13. I follow Dawson in accepting as authentic 875–1004 and in attributing these lines to the chorus, though I would not necessarily accept his precise distribution of the lines between semichoruses (see also below, note 24). Even if 1005–78 are genuine, they indicate only that the dispute between the two brothers will continue. Neither Antigone nor the herald has any greater objective claim to be right.

14. In 979 the chorus may perhaps be criticizing Polyneices without

any corresponding mention of Eteocles, but the text is in doubt and Page obelizes *edeixat*'; see Tucker on 968 (= 979).

15. A glance at any bibliography of the play, such as Dawson's, will reveal this concern with Eteocles; some of the major views are discussed more fully in Appendix B.

16. For a more detailed study of the sexual aspect of the conflict between Eteocles and the chorus, see Appendix B.

17. On Eteocles' misogyny, see Caldwell, *Arethusa* 6 (1973), 197–231.

18. Dawe, *PCPhS* 189 (1963), 31.

19. *Aischylos Interpretationen,* 69. The word *teknon* (686) is sometimes adduced in support of the view that the chorus are no longer playing the role of young maidens. But the word is not always applied to those younger in age (see Rose *ad loc.*), and their calling Eteocles *Oidipou tekos* in 677 would prepare for *teknon*.

20. The case for Eteocles' complete change after 653 is most strongly argued by Solmsen (*TAPA* 68 [1937], 197–211). Kirkwood (*Phoenix* 23 [1969], 9) argues against Solmsen that "Eteocles' initial role as defender of Thebes is not abandoned in the latter part of the play and is not at odds with his role as the Erinys-driven fulfiller of the family curse."

21. Dawe, *PCPhS* 189 (1963), 32.

22. R. P. Winnington-Ingram, *BICS* 13 (1966), 88–93; see Appendix B, note 7.

23. The issue of the military's domination of the government has been much discussed in recent American politics. Against the claim that the security of the nation depends on its military strength, we should bear in mind the words of Representative Patricia Schroeder, a member of the House Armed Services Committee: "Defense people say they are protecting women and children. As a woman with children, I want to be able to say there are other things we can do to protect us than build [military] bases."

24. Some or all of 861–1078 is usually rejected as a later addition. The case for the possible authenticity of the present end of *Septem* is well argued by Lloyd-Jones (*CQ* n.s. 9 [1959], 80–115). The counterarguments of Fraenkel (*MH* 21 [1964], 58–64) and Dawe (*CQ* n.s. 17 [1967], 16–28) have weakened but by no means destroyed Lloyd-Jones' case. Dawson, who rejects 861–74 and 1005–78, nonetheless admits (in his translation of *The Seven*, p. 25) that "few spurious passages can claim so authentic a tone."

25. See Herington, *Arion* 4 (1965), 387–403.

26. A. F. Garvie, *Aeschylus' Supplices: Play and Trilogy* (1969), 233. My discussion of the trilogy relies on this admirable survey, which offers abundant references to the views of other scholars.

27. In defense of political interpretation in general, it is worth remembering that "most of the scholars who had assigned the Danaid trilogy to a late date had argued from supposed allusions to contemporary political events; most of those who put it early had argued from an analysis of its style, diction, metre and dramatic technique" (Lloyd-Jones, *L'Antiquité Classique* 33 [1964], 357).

28. See Forrest, *CQ* n.s. 10 (1960), 221–41, and Podlecki, *Political Background*, 52–62. Themistocles fled to Argos in about 470.

29. Pelasgus (and presumably the city, too) makes his decision by evaluating the practical consequences of either course of action: on the one hand pollution (472–73), on the other hand war (474–77). Like Agamemnon and others in the *Oresteia*, he is faced with a choice between two evils (439–40), but in the end he fears the wrath of Zeus, "the highest object of fear for mortals," more than the Aegyptians (478–79).

30. Peter Burian (*WS* 87 [1974], 5–14) rightly stresses the dramatic reasons for Pelasgus to consult the Argive assembly, but in addition to their dramatic relevance Pelasgus' actions may also have had a contemporary political relevance. Indeed it is regrettable that scholars have tended to assume that only those aspects of the play that have no dramatic relevance are politically relevant; the *Oresteia* shows clearly that these two aspects may be closely connected.

31. A "happy ending" to the trilogy is generally assumed (*e.g.*, Garvie, *Aeschylus' Supplices*, 225) but is by no means certain. In fact, for all we know, the trilogy may have ended in Athens as the *Oresteia* does.

32. In this regard it is possible that the complete Danaid trilogy would pose a much stronger challenge to the view of an omnipotent, benevolent Zeus than *Prometheus* does.

33. See R. D. Murray, *The Motif of Io in Aeschylus' Suppliants*, 27–31, for "the imagery of contrast of male and female," and Caldwell, *Arethusa* 7 (1974), 45–70.

34. The question of whether the Danaids reject all marriage or only marriage with their cousins seems to me unanswerable on the basis of the apparently conflicting evidence in *Supplices*. It is quite possible that Aeschylus intended it to be so. See Lesky, *Tragische Dichtung*, 104–6.

35. For the connection between Aphrodite and marriage from a male point of view, see *Eu.* 213–18.

36. Caldwell (*Arethusa* 7 [1974], 48–49) rightly opposes the view that in rejecting marriage the Danaids are engaging in masculine behavior.

37. The Aegyptians may have been less brutish than their herald, but they cannot have represented totally different values.

38. Apollodorus relates (2.1.5) that "Hypermestra spared Lynceus because he had kept her a virgin," and Aeschylus may have used a similar version of the myth.

39. I follow the traditional numbering of the lines of this fragment, although Mette prints them as the end of a recently discovered papyrus fragment.

40. See Lesky, *Tragische Dichtung*, 141–42, and Herington, *The Author of the "Prometheus Bound."*

41. Friedrich Focke (*Hermes* 65 [1930], 263–70) first proposed that *Prometheus* and *Prometheus Unbound* ("being loosed" is a more accurate translation of *luomenos*, but "unbound" is traditional) formed a complete dilogy. Cf. Rose, *Commentary*, vol. 1, pp. 9–10. It is true that the release of Prometheus that is predicted in *Prometheus* was certainly achieved in *Prometheus Unbound*, thus leaving little if any action for the third play. But Aeschylus may have done anything in the third play, introduced *dikē* to mankind, as Lloyd-Jones speculates (*Justice*, 98–103), celebrated a contemporary festival, or perhaps even opened a new quarrel. Thus Focke is wrong to dismiss (269) the possibility of a quite different third play.

42. E. R. Dodds ("The *Prometheus Vinctus*," 26–44) presents a good survey of different views on this question; for more recent views, see the brief survey in Lesky, *Tragische Dichtung*, 142–43 (cf. also above, note 32).

43. Dodds ("The *Prometheus Vinctus*," 41–44) argues plausibly for a development in Zeus, but this is a matter of speculation. Lloyd-Jones' suggestion (above note 41) is interesting, but his claim (*Justice*, 96) that, "though Zeus cannot have developed, his attitude must certainly have altered," seems to me to beg the question. See also Lloyd-Jones, *JHS* 76 (1956), 55–67.

44. George Thomson's edition of *Prometheus*, p. 6.

45. Sympathy for Zeus and hostility to Prometheus were especially common in the nineteenth century, but have almost completely died out

today. See Dodds, "The *Prometheus Vinctus*," 31–33; Lloyd-Jones, *JHS* 76 (1956), 56.

46. See H. S. Long, *Proc. Amer. Philos. Soc.* 102 (1958), 231: "it is Zeus' dignity and self-importance that have been offended, not Justice."

47. Kratos calls Prometheus' act a *hamartia* (9), and the chorus accuse him of erring (*hēmartes*, 260), a charge Prometheus accepts in his famous words, "willingly, willingly I erred" (*hekōn hekōn hēmarton*, 266). Note that Io also admits that she erred (579) and laments only the severity of her punishment.

48. Cf. 507, where the chorus warn Prometheus not to help mortals more than is proper (*kairou pera*); on the connection between *kairos* and *dikē*, see L. R. Palmer, *Trans. Philol. Soc.* (1950), 154–57.

49. *Dikē* in these two cases (9, 614) means specifically "punishment" or "penalty," but by using this word Aeschylus also implies that Prometheus' punishment is a result of *dikē* and was thus caused by a violation of *dikē*.

50. This accusation derives additional force from being Prometheus' last utterance in the play: "behold, what wrongs I suffer" (*ekdika paschō*, 1093).

51. See fr. 333 (Loeb fr. 114), in which Prometheus, "having been saved" (*sōtheis*), addresses Heracles as the son of "a father hateful to me" (*echthrou patros moi*), *i.e.*, Zeus. In *Pr.* 771–72, moreover, it may be implied that Prometheus is released against the will of Zeus (*akontos Dios*). See Herington, *Author of "Prometheus Bound,"* 125.

52. See Mette, *Der verlorene Aischylos*, 21–26.

53. See Podlecki, *Historia* 15 (1966), 129–41; Forrest, *CQ* n.s. 10 (1960), 237, note 4.

54. As J. A. Davison does, *TAPA* 80 (1949), 66–93.

55. F. M. Cornford, *Thucydides Mythistoricus*, viii.

NOTES TO APPENDIX A

1. The "other sacrifice" (150) is that of Iphigeneia, the first sacrifice being the killing of the hare (137). But the expression also suggests the coming sacrifice of Agamemnon, as Lebeck (*The Oresteia*, 34–35) rightly observes.

2. I do not mean to suggest that the chorus' remarks in the hymn to Zeus have only one reference; indeed, as we shall see later, there is certainly an ironic sense in which *pathei mathos* refers to Agamemnon's

return. But the chorus' general observations here and elsewhere usually have one immediate reference, even though they are often applicable to several other characters or situations. The parable of the lion cub, for instance, as B. M. W. Knox has shown (*CP* 47 [1952], 17–25), is applicable to most of the characters in the trilogy, but still has a "local application" to Paris, Helen, and Troy.

3. It is disputed whether *apo* (166) should be taken with *phrontidos* (*e.g.*, Fraenkel) or with *balein* by tmesis (*e.g.*, Page). The difference between these two interpretations is not great, since in either case the burden is one of anxiety and it is cast off from one's (anxious) mind. I have tried to indicate this in my translation, which to some extent incorporates both interpretations. For *phrontis* as "worry, anxiety" see *Ag.* 102; elsewhere in the *Oresteia* (*e.g.*, *Ag.* 912) it is a positive "concern, care."

4. That *achthos* (166) refers to worry bred of ignorance (vain because it is useless) is supported by the context. Fraenkel (p. 103) interprets *to matan achthos* as "the burden of the folly which induces men to believe that Zeus is not the almighty ruler, who directs all that is done among mankind." But if this is so, the chorus are reduced to saying, "there is no one like Zeus to rid one of the burden of not believing in Zeus," which seems a rather empty observation at best.

5. See Page (note to 160 ff): "The chorus has in mind the danger which impends over Agamemnon on his return."

6. Rose (note on 169–72) denies that 167–75 refer to the overthrow of Ouranos and Cronos, but few others agree with this view. Certainly *epinikia* (174) implies that Zeus is the *triaktēr* of 171.

7. In *Eumenides* (641) the Furies make the point that Zeus overthrew his father, but, as Apollo points out, this deed involved no bloodshed.

8. In *Agamemnon*, *klazō* and *apoklazō* are used of prophecy (156, 201; cf. *klangāi*, 1152) and once of the Atreidae (*klazontes Arē*, 48). Thus the expression *epinikia klazōn* (174) would support the view that the primary context of the chorus' remarks is the prophecy of the capture of Troy.

9. The text is uncertain in places. I have followed Fraenkel (and others) as opposed to Page in reading *tōi* (177; see below, note 16), *anth'* (179) and *biaiōs* (182). The first and third of these are the manuscript readings, and *anth'* is read by most modern editors. Recently Maurice Pope (*JHS* 94 [1974], 100–13) has defended the manuscript accentuation, πоῦ (182), by taking 182–83 as an ironic denial that

there is any *charis* of the gods anywhere. Pope's arguments are forceful, and I certainly agree with many of his remarks on the general meaning of the hymn to Zeus, but I am not ultimately persuaded to read interrogative ποῦ in 182. In all ten instances of interrogative ποῦ with no verb expressed (listed by Pope, *JHS* 94 [1974], 101) the context is much clearer and more compelling than it is here, and it is especially clear where the interrogative is ironically equivalent to a denial. Moreover Pope ignores the beginning of the hymn, where the chorus certainly imply that they do find some positive value in Zeus, and he ignores the possibility that *charis* may refer primarily to the capture of Troy. The reference in 182–83 may be ambiguous, but other rhetorical questions with ποῦ in Aeschylus are not. I thus feel it best to follow almost all modern editors and read indefinite που.

10. *Anth' hypnou* recalls the watchman's remark that "instead of sleep fear stands by me" (*phobos gar anth' hypnou parastatei*, 14), and the image of something dripping before the heart recurs in 1121–22, where the chorus do not understand Cassandra's prophecy but sense that she is predicting trouble for the house. Their emotional state is precisely one of fear bred of ignorance.

11. In 180 *ponos* is often translated "pain" (Fraenkel, Page, Lloyd-Jones), but this is a technical medical sense for which there are no parallels in tragedy. It thus seems doubtful that it could be understood here, especially in view of the frequent occurrence in the trilogy of *ponos* as "toil" or "trouble." See below, note 13.

12. The echo is clearly intentional and is reinforced by the repetition of *ankathen* (*Ag.* 3, *Eu.* 80), a word found in only these two places in Greek literature (if we follow most editors in emending *Eu.* 373 for metrical reasons).

13. Other significant occurrences of *ponos* in the trilogy are *Ag.* 354 (emphatically at the end of the verse, referring to the toil of the Greeks before Troy; cf. *Ag.* 330, 567) and *Ch.* 466 (*ō ponos engenēs*). Note, too, the irony of Clytemnestra's welcome to the house that has (besides warm baths) *ponōn thelktēria* (*Ch.* 670).

14. There are two other references to the *charis* of a god in the trilogy: Cassandra says (1206) that Apollo breathed his *charis* (*i.e.,* love) on her, and the Furies (*Eu.* 938) describe the *charis* they will bring to men (no more blights etc.). This final *charis* no longer needs to come by force.

15. Note that immediately after this the chorus begin the first stasimon

(355–66) by thanking Zeus for accomplishing the destruction of Troy.

16. See Fraenkel's note in defense of *tōi* (176). He paraphrases the phrase to bring out the full force of this *tōi*: "through (or by means of) the *pathos* appropriate to any given *mathos*." This indicates that it is a particular suffering that brings learning, not a general condition of suffering, as I too have tried to convey by my translation "*a* suffering."

17. Cf. the similar expression in Hesiod (*WD* 218), *pathōn de te nēpios egnō*. Dörrie, *Leid und Erfahrung*, briefly discusses these and other passages relating to *pathei mathos*, without, however, shedding much light on the meaning of the phrase in *Agamemnon* (pp. 22–25).

18. That the sufferer himself learns is clear also from Croesus' allusion to *pathei mathos* (Herodotus, 1.207.1): "my experiences [*pathēmata*], being unfavorable [*acharita*], have become lessons [*mathēmata*]." No one in the *Oresteia* has an experience similar to that of Croesus, whose miraculous escape from death enables him truly to learn the lessons of his experiences. Croesus could not learn from Solon, however, nor can the advice he gives to Cyrus prevent the king's death. See Hans-Peter Stahl, *YCS* 24 (1975), 1–36.

19. It is better not to follow Fraenkel and Page in inserting *d'* after *mellon* (251), which produces a "slightly smoother text" (Fraenkel). This is not a good reason for emendation in an Aeschylean chorus.

20. I am omitting as trivial *Eu.* 276 where Orestes says that "schooled in troubles I have learned" when to speak and when not to speak in purification ceremonies. This aspect of Orestes' purification is never referred to again, and it seems highly unlikely that these words alone indicate any general learning on the part of Orestes. One other passage may be relevant: in *Ag.* 388–93 the chorus sing of the harm (*sinos*) in a man shining forth like the black spots in bad bronze after it is battered. This may suggest that punishment teaches someone (and others who see him) that he has done wrong, something he did not know until his punishment.

21. For this sense of "learn a lesson," compare also Dionysus' ironic prediction in *Bacchae* (859–60) that Pentheus will soon know Dionysus (*gnōsetai*), as indeed he will.

22. *Sōphronein* is used twice more in the trilogy (in addition to *Ag.* 181, 1425, 1620). In *Eumenides*, the Furies sing of the need to preserve a certain terror in the city, and they continue, "it is beneficial to show discretion under force" (*xympherei / sōphronein hypo stenei*, 520–21). Here the sense of obedience through punishment or the threat of punish-

ment is certainly present. The other example, *sōphronountes en chronōi* (*Eu.* 1000), was discussed above, p. 83. For this sense of obedience, cf. also *Pr.* 982; the passages in Sophocles discussed by Knox, *HSCP* 65 (1961), 17 and 35, note 87; the adjective *sōphrōn* in *Ag.* 1664 and *Eu.* 136; and Pope, *JHS* 94 (1974), 107–8.

23. For Cassandra's suffering see chapter III, note 66.

24. Of the many attempts to find a wider sense of *pathei mathos* in the suffering of various figures two recent ones are typical. Dodds (*PCPhS* 186 [1960], 29–31) has postulated a four-stage progression: Agamemnon learns nothing, Clytemnestra a little, Orestes quite a bit, and finally the Athenians themselves learn—for them *pathei mathos* is "writ large in the destiny of a whole people and ushering in a new age of understanding." For Knox it is the whole human race, but also the chorus in *Agamemnon*, who "do learn, in the end, and from Cassandra, to face reality, bitter though it may be, to see things as they actually are and must and will be" (*AJP* 93 [1972], 123). I do not deny that the Athenians learn from their experience of watching the *Oresteia*; nor is it impossible that the old men in *Agamemnon* learn something, though I see no evidence in the text for this (their opposition to Clytemnestra and Aegisthus is certainly not the result of any particular wisdom). But I resist the conclusion that such learning is a manifestation of *pathei mathos*. It does not come to the one who suffers, as *pathei mathos* requires, but to one who observes the suffering of others.

25. I write as one who learned from more than one convincing teacher that *pathei mathos* was the central doctrine of the *Oresteia*.

26. One recent discussion of "Zeus in Aeschylus" is typical. Grube acknowledges that we must not "make the Zeus of Aeschylus into a Christian God" (*AJP* 91 [1970], 51), but, in his solution to the problem he has set himself, he sees "Aeschylus feeling his way to a kind of monotheism . . . . He is then faced with a problem which every monotheistic thinker has to face, how to reconcile omnipotence with benevolence or at least with justice" (47–48). In fact, divine omnipotence is a Christian doctrine and was of little or no concern to classical Greek thinkers, even those such as Plato and Aristotle, who might more properly be called "monotheistic." On this score Dover's recent advice (*JHS* 93 [1973], 58) bears repeating: "It is normal and salutary practice in discussing Aeschylean morality and theology to issue a warning against the anachronistic importation of Christian ideas into the fifth century B.C. This warning

could profitably be extended, strengthened and made more specific, and in the category 'Christian' we should include not only peculiarly Christian ideas but also some modern ideas which have been widely adopted by Christians, others which may be reflexes of Christianity, and traditional ingredients of Christianity which have roots in the Hellenistic or even the Classical period." In this last category I would certainly include some of the basic moral views of Plato and Aristotle.

NOTES TO APPENDIX B

1. Three of the most eminent proponents of this view are Wilamowitz (*Aischylos Interpretationen*, 56–69), who speaks of the chorus' "Paroxysmus der Angst" (61) and states later that this *Angst* is "das Komplement zu der Besonnenheit des Feldherrn" (68); Snell (*Aischylos und das Handeln im Drama*, 78–90), who contrasts the *sōphrosynē* of Eteocles ("er selbst ist ganz Haltung," 80) not only with the terror of the chorus but also with their barbaric softness, luxury, and general *hybris*; and Lesky (*WS* 74 [1961], 5–17), who sees the second confrontation between Eteocles and the chorus (677–719) as a "Streit von Entschlossenheit und Widerrede" (13). It is difficult not to sense in such words a strong sympathy for Eteocles' male, militaristic values. Notable exceptions to this general approach are the views of Winnington-Ingram (*BICS* 13 [1966], 88–93), J. H. Finley (*Pindar and Aeschylus*, 234–45), and especially Caldwell (*Arethusa* 6 [1973], 197–231), whose psychoanalytic interpretation of the play has certain points in common with my own.

2. It is difficult to know what emotional tone the dochmiac meter conveys in *Septem*, since this is the earliest surviving play to make extended use of the meter, which Aeschylus himself may have created. As C. M. Dawson reminds us, moreover (translation of *The Seven against Thebes*, p. 38), we have no evidence that anapests were the normal opening meter of Aeschylus' parodoi except in the first plays of trilogies or in single plays, such as *Persae*.

3. The parallel with the beginning of *Eumenides* is dubious, and Tucker's contention (note on 78–164) that it would be "dramatically ludicrous" for the women to enter in regular formation begs the question. Paley, Murray, and Rose also favor division of the chorus.

4. Verrall is the extreme proponent of this view. He accepts, for ex-

ample, the imperfect *prosistanto* in 119 (= 126) as indicating that "among the imaginary terrors of this scene this is the only piece of pure fact" (note *ad loc.*).

5. *Stratos* (79), *stratopedon* (79), *hippotas* (80), *konis* (81), *pedia* (83), and *hoploktupa* (84) all echo the same or similar words in 59–61. Cf. also *boan* (84) and *boäi* (64).

6. For the religious concerns of military men, compare the herald in *Agamemnon* (see chapter IV, note 23).

7. Winnington-Ingram (*BICS* 13 [1966], 88–93) sees a possible connection between *kratousa* (189) and *kratētheis* (750), and makes the interesting suggestion that the theme of women conquering men may have been present from the beginning of the trilogy, when Jocasta persuaded Laius to disobey the oracle and have a child.

8. On the relation of Eteocles' misogyny to his family history, see Caldwell, *Arethusa* 6 (1973), 197–231.

9. Commentators generally reject attempts to find a serious meaning in *ho ti tōn metaichmion* (197), rightly I feel. See Tucker, *ad loc.*, for two such attempts.

10. See, *e.g.*, Dawson, "he is just too angry to speak with complete coherence," and Rose, "too furious to be logical."

11. This belief of the chorus' is often belittled by scholars. Verrall (on 208 = 222) refers to "the naive simplicity of their religious feeling," Lesky (*WS* 74 [1961], 13) speaks of their "kindlich fromme Glaube," and Wilamowitz (*Aischylos Interpretationen*, 66) scornfully calls the women's emphasis on prayer "die Gesinnung des Ablasskrämers" ("the mentality of a seller of indulgences").

12. There is some dispute whether *de* in 234 is continuative (Paley, Rose) or adversative (Verrall, who translates *de* as "while," and Dawson, who translates it as "though"). It seems to me unlikely that the chorus could reverse their previous position on the power of the gods (which is what the latter translations imply) without making a clearer contrast between 233 and 234.

13. There is much disagreement about how to understand the first half of 217, which some editors (and all mss. except *M*) attribute to the chorus. In my opinion the best discussion is offered by Verrall, who translates it as a rhetorical question indicating Eteocles' "sceptical irony": "will not that be the act of the gods?"

14. There may be implicit scorn in the expression *daimonōn genos*

(236). Dawson calls it "somewhat derogatory," and Verrall speaks of Eteocles' "contemptuous liberality."

15. Cf. Semonides 7.96–97: "Zeus made this the one greatest evil: women."

16. Eteocles' remark in 258, *palinstomeis au thinganous' agalmatōn*, is usually translated "do you blaspheme with your hands on the statues [of the gods]?" Several commentators point out that *palinstomeō* (a *hapax legomenon*) should mean "contradict," and they then try to explain how "blaspheme" can be derived from this sense (see, *e.g.*, Verrall and Tucker). But perhaps Eteocles does in fact mean "do you contradict me?" in which case he implies that such disregard for his authority is a blasphemy.

17. It is assumed by some (*e.g.*, Verrall, xii–xiii; Dawson on 245–63; Kitto, *Greek Tragedy*, 47) that Eteocles agrees to fight only in order to pacify the chorus, but there is nothing in the text to suggest this. Leaders of armies in the epic tradition always fought, unless, like Adrastus, they were too old (see Rose, p. 192), and the audience probably assumed from the beginning that Eteocles would fight. There is no implication in 283–86 that his fighting along with the other six is a recent decision. He merely announces that it is now time for the defenders (including himself) to get to their stations. Thus, the chorus are in no way the cause of Eteocles' fighting at the seventh gate.

18. The first word of the stasimon, *melei* (287), is correctly explained by the scholiast: μέλει μοι, φησίν, ὧν εἶπεν ὁ Ἐτεοκλῆς. The chorus acknowledge but do not submit to Eteocles' wishes. The common translation of *melei*, "I heed," may thus be misleading, and Dawson's "I obey" is quite wrong.

19. In the phrase *lechaiōn dyseunētoras* (293) one hears *lechos* and *eunē*, both of which commonly refer to the sexual aspect of the bed. See Tucker, *ad loc.*

20. The recurrence of the theme of sexual violation at the end of this ode is part of a loose structural symmetry or "ring-composition" that can be outlined as follows: violation of the dove's bed (291–94) / violation of captured women (363–68); fertility (304–11) / infertility (357–62); evils of slavery for women (321–35) / further evils for women (348–51); men killing each other (338–41) / men killing each other (345–47). In the center (343–44) stands the picture of war polluting piety.

21. "One who dies [*ton phthimenon*], I think, fares better than these [captives]" (336–37). These words mean literally that the dead are better off than the living after defeat in battle; in the context of this ode the chorus also imply that the male soldier (*ton phthimenon*), who is killed rather than taken prisoner, is better off than the captured women.

22. In 343, Page changes *mainomenos* to *mainomenois* (his own conjecture), presumably in order to provide a dative object for *epipnei*. A complement for the verb can easily be assumed, however, from *allos allon* in 340 (as Rose and others do), and I have thus translated the ms. reading.

23. Tucker (*ad loc.*) compares *Su.* 231 (= 225), *miainontōn genos*. He also sees a sexual sense in *epipnei* (cf. *epipnoia*, *Su.* 17).

24. Finley (*Pindar and Aeschylus*, 243) says of the end of the first stasimon, "The lines describe a state of horror which is the obverse of masculine heroism, the violence which heroism does to the settled order of peace." Finley's brief treatment of this theme is excellent, but he errs in following Snell's view (*Aischylos und das Handeln*, 79–81) that the "extremest agitation" (241) of the women is analogous to the violence of the Argives.

25. In their lyrics the chorus tremble to think of the death of their own soldiers (419–21), they are frightened by the thought of defeat (454–56) and by the spy's description of the enemy (563–64), and they pray that the gods will destroy the enemy (*e.g.*, 626–30).

26. It is significant that most critics ignore the chorus' role in this central scene. See, *e.g.*, Fraenkel's important treatment of the scene (*Sitzb. Bayer. Ak.* [1957], 5).

27. I do not wish to add to the lengthy debate concerning Eteocles' decision. I agree generally with Lesky's conclusions (*WS* 74 [1961], 5–17), that "Eteokles hat die Fügung, die ihn am siebenten Tore seinem Bruder entgegenstellt, als sein Schicksal auf sich genommen und in der Form eines persönlichen Entschlusses bejaht" (12), and "Was von aussen über ihn verhängt ist, das wird zu seiner persönlichen Schuld, weil er das Notwendige in seinen eigenen Willen hineinnimmt, weil er das, was er tun muss, schliesslich auch zu tun begehrt" (15).

28. *Theos* in 689 is usually understood as referring to Apollo alone, but it seems to me to be intentionally indefinite and thus to suggest Ares as well as Apollo and others. The audience would probably not think of Apollo until he is mentioned directly in 691.

29. Eteocles never argues that the defense of the city requires his

presence, and he does not deny the chorus' implication in 716 that the city will be victorious even without him (*nikēn ge mentoi kai kakēn timāi theos*). Some have taken *nikēn kakēn* as a suggestion that Eteocles yield to the chorus' wish ("a victory which consists in a defeat," notes Paley on 713), but this interpretation is the result of an erroneous comparison with *Ag.* 942 and makes little sense in the present context.

30. The sense of 703, *charis d' aph' hēmōn olomenōn thaumazetai*, is disputed, but the sense I have given (following Paley, Tucker, and Dawson) is the only appropriate one in this context, since 699–701 presumably contain the ironic implication that the Erinys *will* leave the house after the gods receive a sacrifice (*i.e.*, of the two brothers).

31. On the authenticity of the present end of *Septem*, see chapter V, note 24. No matter how the play ended, it is unlikely that it presented a resolution of the basic conflict.

32. See chapter V, note 20.

33. See above, note 7.

Bibliography

N.B.: This bibliography contains full references for all works cited in the book. It is by no means a complete bibliography for Aeschylus and does not include many works that I have consulted but not cited.

Several of the articles are reprinted (English articles in German translations) in volume 87 of the Wege der Forschung series, *Wege zu Aischylos*, edited by Hildebrecht Hommel, 2 vols. (Darmstadt, 1974). Page references for each reprinted article are given in parentheses.

GREEK AUTHORS (TEXTS, COMMENTARIES, TRANSLATIONS)

Aeschylus
The Tragedies of Aeschylus. Edited, with commentary, by F. A. Paley. 3d ed. London, 1870.
Tragoediae. Edited by U. von Wilamowitz-Moellendorff. Berlin, 1914.
Tragoediae. Edited by Gilbert Murray. 2d ed. Oxford, 1955.
Tragoediae. Edited by D. Page. Oxford, 1972.
A Commentary on the Surviving Plays of Aeschylus. By H. J. Rose. 2 vols. Amsterdam, 1957–58.
Agamemnon. Edited, with translation and commentary, by Eduard Fraenkel. 3 vols. Oxford, 1950.
Agamemnon. Edited, with commentary, by J. D. Denniston and D. Page. Oxford, 1957.

Agamemnon. Translated, with commentary, by H. Lloyd–Jones. Englewood Cliffs, N.J., 1970.

Choephoroi. Edited, with commentary, by A. Sidgwick. 2d ed. Oxford, 1902.

The Libation Bearers. Translated, with commentary, by H. Lloyd-Jones. Englewood Cliffs, N.J., 1970.

Eumenides. Edited, with commentary, by A. Sidgwick. 2d ed. Oxford, 1895.

Eumenides. Edited, with translation and commentary, by A. W. Verrall. London, 1908.

Eumenides. Edited, with commentary, by P. Groeneboom. Groningen, 1952.

The Eumenides. Translated, with commentary, by H. Lloyd-Jones. Englewood Cliffs, N.J., 1970.

Oresteia. Translated by R. Lattimore. Chicago, 1953.

The Oresteia. Edited, with commentary, by George Thomson. 2 vols. 2d ed. Prague, 1966.

The Oresteia. Translated, with notes, by Douglas Young. Norman, Okla., 1974.

Persae. Edited, with commentary, by A. Sidgwick. Oxford, 1903.

Persae. Edited, with commentary, by P. Groeneboom. Groningen, 1930.

The Persians. Translated by Gilbert Murray. London, 1939.

Persae. Edited, with commentary, by H. D. Broadhead. Cambridge, 1960.

The Prometheus Bound. Edited, with translation and commentary, by George Thomson. Cambridge, 1932.

The Seven against Thebes. Edited, with translation and commentary, by A. W. Verrall. London, 1887.

The Seven against Thebes. Edited, with translation and commentary, by T. G. Tucker. Cambridge, 1908.

The Seven against Thebes. Translated, with commentary, by C. M. Dawson. Englewood Cliffs, N.J., 1970.

Die Fragmente der Tragödien des Aischylos. Edited by H. J. Mette. Berlin, 1959.

Agamemnon, Libation Bearers, Eumenides, Fragments. Loeb Classi-

cal Library. Edited and translated by H. W. Smyth with appendix by H. Lloyd-Jones. Cambridge, Mass., 1957.
Scholia Graeca. Edited by G. Dindorf. Oxford, 1851.

Other Greek Authors
Aristotle, *Poetics.* Commentary by D. W. Lucas. Oxford, 1968.
Euripides. *Andromache.* Commentary by P. T. Stevens. Oxford, 1971.
Homer. *The Odyssey.* Translated by R. Lattimore. New York, 1967.
Plato. *The Republic.* Translated by F. M. Cornford. Oxford, 1941.

Fragments
Anthologia Lyrica Graeca. Edited by Ernst Diehl. 3d ed. vols. 1 and 3. Leipzig, 1949, 1952.
Iambi et Elegi Graeci. Edited by M. L. West. 2 vols. Oxford, 1971–72.
Poetae Melici Graeci. Edited by D. Page. Oxford, 1962.
Poetarum Lesbiorum Fragmenta. Edited by E. Lobel and D. Page. Oxford, 1955.
Supplementum Lyricis Graecis. Edited by D. Page. Oxford, 1974.
Tragicorum Graecorum Fragmenta. Edited by B. Snell. vol. 1. Göttingen, 1971.
Die Fragmente der Vorsokratiker. Edited by H. Diels and W. Kranz. 3 vols. 6th ed. Berlin, 1951–52.

MODERN AUTHORS

Adkins, A. W. H. *Merit and Responsibility.* Oxford, 1960.
———. "Aristotle and the Best Kind of Tragedy." *CQ* n.s. 16 (1966), 78–102.
———. "Homeric Values and Homeric Society." *JHS* 91 (1971), 1–14.
Arrowsmith, William. "The Criticism of Greek Tragedy." *Tulane Drama Review* 3, no. 3 (1959), 31–57.
Avery, Harry C. "Dramatic Devices in Aeschylus' *Persians.*" *AJP* 85 (1964), 173–84.
Bachofen, J. J. *Das Mutterrecht.* Stuttgart, 1861.
Bamberger, Joan. "The Myth of Matriarchy: Why Men Rule in Primi-

tive Society." In *Women, Culture, and Society*, edited by M. Z. Rosaldo and L. Lamphere, pp. 263–80. Stanford, 1974.

Barron, J. P. "Ibycus: *To Polycrates.*" *BICS* 16 (1969), 119–49.

Beauvoir, Simone de. *The Second Sex.* New York, 1953.

Bowra, C. M. "Stesichorus in the Peloponnese." *CQ* 28 (1934), 115–19.

———. *Greek Lyric Poetry.* 2d ed. Oxford, 1961.

Bremer, J. M. *Hamartia.* Amsterdam, 1969.

Burian, Peter. "Pelasgus and Politics in Aeschylus' Danaid Trilogy." *WS* 87 (1974), 5–14.

Caldwell, R. S. "The Misogyny of Eteocles." *Arethusa* 6 (1973), 197–231.

———. "The Psychology of Aeschylus' *Supplices.*" *Arethusa* 7 (1974), 45–70.

Calhoun, G. M. *The Growth of Criminal Law in Ancient Greece.* Berkeley, 1927.

Cherniss, Harold. *Aristotle's Criticism of Presocratic Philosophy.* Baltimore, 1935.

Claus, David. "Phaedra and the Socratic Paradox." *YCS* 22 (1972), 223–38.

Cornford, F. M. *Thucydides Mythistoricus.* London, 1907.

Daube, Benjamin. *Zu den Rechtsproblemen in Aischylos' Agamemnon.* Zurich and Leipzig, 1939.

Davison, J. A. "The Date of the *Prometheia.*" *TAPA* 80 (1949), 66–93.

Dawe, R. D. "Inconsistency of Plot and Character in Aeschylus." *PCPhS* 189 (1963), 21–62. (*Wege zu Aischylos* vol. 1, 175–250.)

———. "The End of *Seven Against Thebes.*" *CQ* n.s. 17 (1967), 16–28.

Dirksen, H. J. *Die aischyleische Gestalt des Orest.* Nuremberg, 1965.

Dodds, E. R. *The Greeks and the Irrational.* Berkeley, 1951.

———. "Morals and Politics in the 'Oresteia,'" *PCPhS* 186 (1960), 19–31. Reprinted in *The Ancient Concept of Progress*, 45–63. Oxford, 1973. (*Wege zu Aischylos* vol. 2, 149–72.)

———. "The *Prometheus Vinctus* and the Progress of Scholarship." In *The Ancient Concept of Progress*, 26–44. Oxford, 1973.

Dörrie, Heinrich. *Leid und Erfahrung. Abh. Akad. Mainz, geistes- u. sozialwiss. Kl.*, 1956, no. 5.

Dover, K. J. "The Political Aspect of Aeschylus's *Eumenides*." *JHS* 77 (1957), 230–37.

————. "The Poetry of Archilochos." *Archiloque*, 181–212. Fondation Hardt vol. 10, Geneva, 1964.

————. "Some Neglected Aspects of Agamemnon's Dilemma." *JHS* 93 (1973), 58–69.

Easterling, P. E. "Presentation of Character in Aeschylus." *G&R* 20 (1973), 3–19.

Engels, Friedrich. *The Origin of the Family, Private Property and the State.* 4th ed. Moscow, 1891.

Finley, J. H., Jr. *Pindar and Aeschylus.* Cambridge, Mass. 1955.

Focke, Friedrich. "Aischylos' Prometheus." *Hermes* 65 (1930), 259–304.

Forrest, W. G. "Themistokles and Argos." *CQ* n.s. 10 (1960), 221–41.

Fraenkel, Eduard. "Die sieben Redepaare im Thebanerdrama des Aeschylus." *Sitzb. Bayer. Akad.*, Ph.-Hist. Kl. (1957), Heft 3.

————. "Zum Schluss der Sieben gegen Theben." *MH* 21 (1964), 58–64. (*Wege zu Aischylos* vol. 2, 38–47.)

Fritz, Kurt von. "Tragische Schuld und poetische Gerechtigkeit in der griechischen Tragödie." In *Antike und moderne Tragödie*, pp. 1–112. Berlin, 1962.

Gagarin, Michael. "*Dikē* in the *Works and Days*." *CP* 68 (1973), 81–94.

————. "*Dikē* in Archaic Greek Thought." *CP* 69 (1974), 186–97.

————. "The Vote of Athena." *AJP* 96 (1975), 121–27.

Garvie, A. F. *Aeschylus' Supplices: Play and Trilogy.* Cambridge, 1969.

Gould, Thomas. "The Innocence of Oedipus: The Philosophers on *Oedipus the King*." *Arion* 4 (1965), 363–86, 582–611, and *Arion* 5 (1966), 478–525.

Grossmann, Gustav. *Promethie und Orestie.* Heidelberg, 1970.

Grube, G. M. A. *How Did the Greeks Look at Literature?* Cincinnati, 1967. Lectures in Memory of Louise Taft Semple (Second Series).

————. "Zeus in Aeschylus." *AJP* 91 (1970), 43–51. (*Wege zu Aischylos* vol. 1, 301–11.)

Hare, R. M. *The Language of Morals.* Oxford, 1952.

————. *Essays on the Moral Concepts.* Berkeley, 1972.

Harrison, A. R. W. *The Law of Athens.* 2 vols. Oxford, 1968–71.

Hart, H. L. A. *Punishment and Responsibility.* Oxford, 1968.

Havelock, E. A. *Preface to Plato.* Cambridge, Mass., 1963.

————. *Prologue to Greek Literacy.* Cincinnati, 1971. Lectures in Memory of Louise Taft Semple (Second Series).

————. "The Socratic Self as It Is Parodied in Aristophanes' *Clouds.*" *YCS* 22 (1972), 1–18.

Herington, C. J. "Aeschylus: The Last Phase." *Arion* 4 (1965), 387–403.

————. *The Author of the "Prometheus Bound."* Austin, 1970.

Huxley, Elspeth. *The Flame Trees of Thika.* New York, 1959.

Jones, John. *On Aristotle and Greek Tragedy.* Oxford, 1962.

Kaufmann-Bühler, Dieter. *Begriff und Funktion der Dike in den Tragödien des Aischylos.* Heidelberg, 1951.

Kirkwood, G. M. "Eteocles Oiakostrophos." *Phoenix* 23 (1969), 9–25.

Kitto, H. D. F. *Form and Meaning in Drama.* London, 1956.

————. *Greek Tragedy.* 3d ed. London, 1961.

Knox, B. M. W. "The Lion in the House (*Agamemnon* 717–36 [Murray])." *CP* 47 (1952), 17–25. (*Wege zu Aischylos* vol. 2, 202–18.)

————. "The *Ajax* of Sophocles." *HSCP* 65 (1961), 1–37.

————. "Aeschylus and the Third Actor." *AJP* 93 (1972), 104–24.

Kovesi, Julius. *Moral Notions.* London, 1967.

Lacey, W. K. *The Family in Classical Greece.* London, 1968.

Lattimore, Richmond. "Aeschylus on the Defeat of Xerxes," in *Classical Studies in Honor of W. A. Oldfather*, pp. 82–93. Urbana, 1943.

————. *Story Patterns in Greek Tragedy.* Ann Arbor, 1964.

Lebeck, Anne. *The Oresteia: A Study in Language and Structure.* Cambridge, Mass., 1971.

Lesky, Albin. *Göttliche und menschliche Motivation im homerischen Epos. Sitzb. Heidelb. Akad.*, Ph.-Hist. Kl. (1961), 4 Abh.

―――. "Eteokles in den Sieben gegen Theben." *WS* 74 (1961), 5–17. (*Wege zu Aischylos* vol. 2, 23–37.)

―――. *Die tragische Dichtung der Hellenen.* 3d ed. Göttingen, 1972.

Lloyd-Jones, Hugh. "Zeus in Aeschylus." *JHS* 76 (1956), 55–67. (*Wege zu Aischylos* vol. 1, 265–300.)

―――. "The End of the *Seven Against Thebes.*" *CQ* n.s. 9 (1959), 80–115.

―――. "The Guilt of Agamemnon." *CQ* n.s. 12 (1962), 187–99.

―――. "The 'Supplices' of Aeschylus: The New Date and Old Problems." *L'Antiquité Classique* 33 (1964), 356–74. (*Wege zu Aischylos* vol. 2, 101–24.)

―――. "Problems of Early Greek Tragedy: Pratinas, Phrynichus, the Gyges Fragment." *Estudios sobre la tragedia griega*, 9–33. Fundacion Pastor, vol. 13, Madrid, 1966.

―――. "The Cologne Fragment of Alcaeus." *GRBS* 9 (1968), 125–39.

―――. *The Justice of Zeus.* Berkeley, 1971.

―――. *Females of the Species.* London, 1975.

―――. "The Morals of the Majority" (review of Dover, *Greek Popular Morality in the Time of Plato and Aristotle*). *TLS* for 14 March 1975, 273.

Long, A. A. "Morals and Values in Homer." *JHS* 90 (1970), 121–39.

Long, H. S., "Notes on Aeschylus' *Prometheus Bound.*" *Proc. Amer. Philos. Soc.* 102 (1958), 229–80.

MacDowell, D. M. *Athenian Homicide Law in the Age of the Orators.* Manchester, 1963.

McLuhan, Marshall. *Understanding Media.* New York, 1964.

Meiggs, Russell. *The Athenian Empire.* Oxford, 1972.

Mette, H. J. *Der verlorene Aischylos.* Berlin, 1963.

Millett, Kate. *Sexual Politics.* New York, 1970.

Montmollin, D. de. "Le sense du term *philanthrōpon* dans la *Poétique* d'Aristote." *Phoenix* 19 (1965), 15–23.

Mourelatos, A. P. D. "Heraclitus, Parmenides, and the Naive Metaphysics of Things." In *Exegesis and Argument*: Studies in Greek Philosophy Presented to Gregory Vlastos, pp. 16–48. *Phronesis* Supplement, vol. I. Assen, 1973.

Müller, K. O. *Dissertations on the Eumenides of Aeschylus*. Cambridge, 1835.

Murray, Gilbert. *Aeschylus, the Creator of Tragedy*. Oxford, 1940.

Murray, R. D. *The Motif of Io in Aeschylus' Suppliants*. Princeton, 1958.

O'Neill, E. G., Jr. "The Prologue of the *Troades* of Euripides." *TAPA* 72 (1941), 288–320.

Palmer, L. R. "The Indo-European Origins of Greek Justice." *Trans. Philol. Soc.* (Oxford), (1950), 149–68.

Parry, Adam. "The Language of Achilles." *TAPA* 87 (1956), 1–7.

Parry, Milman. *The Making of Homeric Verse*, edited by Adam Parry. Oxford, 1971.

Pembroke, Simon. "Women in Charge: The Function of Alternatives in Early Greek Tradition and the Ancient Idea of Matriarchy." *Journ. Warb. & Court. Inst.* 30 (1967), 1–35.

Pickard-Cambridge, A. W. *Dithyramb, Tragedy and Comedy*. 2d ed. by T. B. L. Webster. Oxford, 1962.

———. *The Dramatic Festivals of Athens*. 2d ed. by J. Gould and D. M. Lewis. Oxford, 1968.

Podlecki, A. J. *The Political Background of Aeschylean Tragedy*. Ann Arbor, 1966.

———. "The Political Significance of the Athenian 'Tyrannicide'-Cult." *Historia* 15 (1966), 129–41.

Pomeroy, Sarah B. *Goddesses, Whores, Wives, and Slaves*. New York, 1975.

Pope, Maurice. "Merciful Heavens? A Question in Aeschylus' *Agamemnon*." *JHS* 94 (1974), 100–13.

Pritchett, W. K. "The Transfer of the Delian Treasury." *Historia* 18 (1969), 17–21.

Reinhardt, Karl. *Aischylos als Regisseur und Theologe*. Bern, 1949.

Robinson, Richard. Review of Adkins, *Merit and Responsibility*. *Philosophy* 37 (1962), 277–79.

Rosaldo, M. Z., "Women, Culture, and Society: A Theoretical Overview." In *Women, Culture, and Society,* edited by M. Z. Rosaldo and L. Lamphere, pp. 17–42. Stanford, 1974.

Rosenmeyer, Thomas. "Seven against Thebes: The Tragedy of War." *Arion* 1 (1962), 48–78.

Russo, Joseph. "Reading the Greek Lyric Poets (Monodists)" (review of Kirkwood, *Early Greek Monody*). *Arion* n.s. 1 (1973/74), 707–30.

Russo, Joseph, and Simon, Bennett. "Homeric Psychology and the Oral Epic Tradition." *JHI* 29 (1968), 483–98.

Scott, W. C. "The Mesode at *Persae* 93–100." *GRBS* 9 (1968), 259–66.

Skinner, B. F. *Beyond Freedom and Dignity.* New York, 1971.

Slater, P. E. *The Glory of Hera.* Boston, 1968.

Smyth, H. W. *Aeschylean Tragedy.* Berkeley, 1924.

Snell, Bruno. *Aischylos und das Handeln im Drama. Philologus* Supplementband 20.1. Leipzig, 1928.

———. *The Discovery of the Mind.* Cambridge, Mass. 1953.

———. "Gyges und Kroisos als Tragödien-Figuren." *ZPE* 12 (1973), 197–205.

Solmsen, Friedrich. "The Erinys in Aischylos' *Septem.*" *TAPA* 68 (1937), 197–211.

———. *Hesiod and Aeschylus.* Ithaca, 1949.

Stahl, Hans-Peter. "Learning through Suffering? Croesus' Conversations in the History of Herodotus." *YCS* 24 (1975), 1–36.

Stanford, W. B. " 'The Looking-Glass of Society' in Aeschylus, *Agamemnon* 838–40." *CR* n.s. 4 (1954), 82–85.

———. *The Ulysses Theme.* 2d ed. Oxford, 1963.

Taylor, Richard. "Determinism." In *The Encyclopedia of Philosophy,* vol. 2 pp. 359–73. New York, 1967.

Thomson, George. *Aeschylus and Athens.* London, 1941.

Vickers, Brian. *Towards Greek Tragedy.* London, 1973.

Vogt, Joseph. *Von der Gleichwertigkeit der Geschlechter in der bürgerlichen Gesellschaft der Griechen. Abh. Akad. Mainz, geistes- u. sozialwiss. Kl.* 1960, no. 2.

Wardman, A. E. "Tactics and the Tradition of the Persian Wars." *Historia* 8 (1959), 49–60.

West, M. L. "Stesichorus Redivivus." *ZPE* 4 (1969), 135–49.

Whitman, C. H. *Sophocles: A Study of Heroic Humanism.* Cambridge, Mass., 1951.

Wilamowitz-Moellendorff, U. von. *Aristoteles und Athen.* Berlin, 1893.

——. *Aischylos Interpretationen.* Berlin, 1914.

Wilkens, Karsten. "*DIKE HOMAIMON?* Zu Aischylos Sieben 415." *Hermes* 97 (1969), 117–21.

Will, Edouard. *Le Monde Grec et l'Orient.* Paris, 1972.

Winnington-Ingram, R. P. "Aeschylus. *Eumenides,* 674–680." CR 49 (1935), 7–8.

——. "Clytemnestra and the Vote of Athena." *JHS* 68 (1948), 130–47.

——. Review of Broadhead, *The Persae of Aeschylus.* CR n.s. 12 (1962), 122–25.

——. "Aeschylus, *Septem* 187–190; 750–757." BICS 13 (1966), 88–93.

——. "Zeus in the *Persae.*" JHS 93 (1973), 210–19.

——. "Notes on the *Agamemnon* of Aeschylus." BICS 21 (1974), 3–19.

Young, Douglas. "Readings in Aeschylus' *Choephoroe* and *Eumenides.*" GRBS 12 (1971), 303–30.

——. "Readings in Aeschylus' Byzantine Triad." GRBS 13 (1972), 5–38.

Zeitlin, F. I. "The Motif of the Corrupted Sacrifice in Aeschylus' *Oresteia.*" TAPA 96 (1965), 463–508.

——. "Postscript to Sacrificial Imagery in the *Oresteia* (*Ag.* 1235–37)." TAPA 97 (1966), 645–53.

Index to Aeschylean Passages

General Index

(The plays of Aeschylus are abbreviated as follows: *Ag.* = *Agamemnon*; *Ch.* = *Choephoroi*; *Eu.* = *Eumenides*; *Or.* = the *Oresteia*; *Pe.* = *Persae*; *Pr.* = *Prometheus*; *Se.* = *Septem*; *Su.* = *Supplices*.)